H.L. MENCKEN
ON RELIGION

H.L. MENCKEN
ON RELIGION

EDITED BY S.T. JOSHI

Prometheus Books
59 John Glenn Drive
Amherst, New York 14228-2119

Published 2002 by Prometheus Books

Inquiries should be addressed to
Prometheus Books
59 John Glenn Drive
Amherst, New York 14228–2119
VOICE: 716–691–0133, ext. 210
FAX: 716–691–0137
WWW.PROMETHEUSBOOKS.COM

12 11 10 09   5 4 3

Library of Congress Cataloging-in-Publication Data

Mencken, H. L. (Henry Louis), 1880–1956.
    H. L. Mencken on religion / edited by S.T. Joshi.
        p. cm.
    Includes bibliographical references and index.
    ISBN 1–57392–982–4 (alk. paper)
        1. Religion—Controversial literature. 2. Christianity—Controversial literature.
I. Title: On religion. II. Joshi, S. T., 1958–ΙΙΙ. Title.

BL2775.3 .M46 2002
200—dc21
                                                                        2002072443

Printed in Canada on acid-free paper

CONTENTS

V. SPIRITUALISM, THEOSOPHY, AND CHRISTIAN SCIENCE 139

VI. THE SCOPES TRIAL 161

VII. RELIGION AND SCIENCE   225

VIII. RELIGION AND POLITICS   249

IX. RELIGION AND SOCIETY   269

EPILOGUE: MEMORIAL SERVICE   293

NOTES   299

GLOSSARY OF NAMES   307

INDEX   321

INTRODUCTION

Henry Louis Mencken (1880–1956) was one of the last American intellectuals to speak out forcefully, pungently, and satirically against the follies of religion. In the course of a long career as journalist, essayist, and social commentator, Mencken relentlessly—but always with a liberal dose of wit, persiflage, and dry humor—exposed the multitudinous absurdities presented to his gaze by a country in which Fundamentalists, Christian Scientists, theosophists, and religionists of every other creed and sect cavorted before a populace too foolish and credulous to detect the logical fallacies and contradictions to known fact that every religion offers in such abundance. Himself a "theological moron"—one who was "absolutely devoid of what is called religious feeling"—he could gaze with insouciance and bland objectivity at the circus-show offered by American religion.

Mencken speaks of his own religious upbringing in "The Schooling of a Theologian" (1939), testifying that his father, an avowed unbeliever, enrolled Mencken and his brother Charlie in a Methodist Sunday school for the sole purpose of having his own afternoons free for a nap. After all, the two hours a week spent in this school could be easily counteracted by the influence of the infidel Papa Mencken the rest of the time. Mencken claimed to be relatively impartial on the subject of religion—"I am anything but a militant atheist and haven't the slightest objection to church-going, so long as it is honest," he wrote in "Confessions of a Theological Moron" (1920)—but the course of his literary work makes it plain that he sided with heretics on the great majority of issues where religion came into conflict with science, politics, and the advance of civilization.

The fundamental tenet of Mencken's thought is libertarianism, in the purest sense of the term: "I am, in brief, a libertarian of the most extreme variety, and know of no human right that is one-tenth as valuable as the simple right to utter what seems (at the moment) to be the truth. Take away this right, and none other is worth a hoot; nor, indeed, can any other long exist."[1] This remark was made in the context of literature and literary criticism, but its implication is clearly broader than that. What Mencken most strongly objected to in religion was not the expression of nonsensical views—these could easily be combated by rebuttal from the other side—but the inveterate tendency of religion to seek the enforcement of its views by the power of the government. As he wrote of the antievolutionist Fundamentalists he saw during the Scopes trial, "They believe . . . that men who know too much should be seized by the secular arm and put down by force. They dream . . . of a world unanimously sure of Heaven and unanimously idiotic on this earth."

Mencken found abundant opportunities in his long literary career for lampooning religion. Although some antireligious diatribes appear in his early newspaper work for the *Baltimore Evening Sun* (whose staff he joined in 1906 as an editorial writer), Mencken's accession to the coeditorship of the *Smart Set* in 1914 provided a broader forum for his opinions on a wide variety of issues. He had been the magazine's book reviewer since November 1908, writing a monthly column of nearly 5,000 words with mechanical regularity; but the bulk of this column was devoted to reviews of new fiction, mostly novels, and it was only occasionally—as when he reviewed Willard Huntington Wright's *What Nietzsche Taught* (1915) or a new biography of Billy Sunday—that he allowed himself to expatiate on religious issues in the course of reviewing a book. But in April 1919 Mencken and his coeditor George Jean Nathan initiated a column entitled "Répétition Générale," which lasted to the end of his editorship of the magazine in December 1923. In this column Mencken and Nathan felt at liberty to pontificate on the widest array of subjects, and Mencken himself frequently chose to lambaste religion with the flamboyant wit that he was developing as his trademark. (The various segments of the "Répétition Générale" column are unsigned, but Mencken's contributions—especially on religious subjects—are easy to identify by internal evidence.) The *Smart*

Set, a self-styled "magazine of cleverness," was the ideal organ for writing that stretched the limits of polite discourse in matters of religion, politics, society, and sexuality. It is no surprise that Mencken's uncannily prescient article "Venture into Therapeutics" (1923)—in which he urged African Americans to convert en masse to Islam for the purpose of battling the Ku Klux Klan and, perhaps, of initiating a general race war in the South—appeared in the final year of his editorship of the *Smart Set.*

Meanwhile, the *Baltimore Evening Sun* was proving to be a useful venue for Mencken's jeering at religion. His editorial column generally appeared on Mondays, and often provoked controversy not only in Baltimore but throughout the nation. By the early 1920s, after all, Mencken had become one of the leading cultural commentators in the nation. His early treatises on Shaw (1905) and Nietzsche (1908) had not attracted much attention, but his *Smart Set* reviews had gained him notoriety, and such works as *A Book of Prefaces* (1917), *In Defense of Women* (1918), and, especially, the first of his six volumes of *Prejudices* (1919–27) had catapulted him into celebrity as an iconoclast and gadfly. In his *Baltimore Evening Sun* columns he felt the need to be topical, but he would frequently use some relatively transient event—the appearance of a new and critical biography of Mary Baker Eddy, for example—as the stepping-stone to a broader discussion of religious issues.

In 1924 Mencken and Nathan, having resigned from the *Smart Set* because the owners of that magazine wished to make it a popular organ for the masses rather than a highbrow periodical for the elite, established the *American Mercury,* quickly making it one of the leading intellectual forums of the day. In the ten years of his editorship, Mencken systematically published some of the keenest political and social commentators of his time. His own contributions were largely restricted to tart editorials, chiefly of a political nature (and chiefly lampooning the Republican presidents Calvin Coolidge and Herbert Hoover), and a book review column. In 1924–25 Mencken, in collaboration with Nathan, revived the "Répétition Générale" column under the title "Clinical Notes," but thereafter Mencken allowed Nathan to write the column by himself. In accordance with the overall emphasis of the magazine, Mencken reviewed far fewer works of fiction and many more works on politics, society, and especially religion. He rarely passed up the opportunity to skewer some particularly foolish venture into Christian apologetics—as in Howard A. Kelly's *A*

Scientific Man and the Bible (1925)—or to praise an astute dissection of religious fraud, as in Joseph Wheless's *Is It God's Word?* (1926) or Robert Briffaut's *Sin and Sex* (1931).

It might seem that Mencken's views on religion were codified in his substantial *Treatise on the Gods* (1930), but this monograph, lengthy as it is, proves to be a rather dry anthropological account of the evolution of religion—specifically the Christian religion—and its role in ethics (a subject more exhaustively discussed in the later *Treatise on Right and Wrong* [1934]), politics, and other areas. Mencken seems to have made a tactical mistake in attempting to write a sober and pseudoscholarly tome on the subject, especially as he decided to eschew the piquant humor that makes his newspaper and magazine work so distinctive. His anthropology is now a bit antiquated, and the work as a whole cannot stand up to intellectual scrutiny. Accordingly, I have not included any of it in the present compilation.

In the final fifteen or so years of his career—prior to the stroke that incapacitated him in 1949—Mencken wrote chiefly, and almost exclusively, on politics. Although taking rich satisfaction in the repeal of Prohibition in 1933 (he had, all along, rightly considered it an intolerable infringement of civil liberties and a virtual repudiation of the Bill of Rights), he developed an almost fanatical loathing of Franklin Delano Roosevelt, believing him to be a fascist and a dictator little different from the "uplifters" and "right-thinkers" who had inflicted Prohibition upon a recalcitrant nation. Mencken, cynical as he was about the ability of politicians to do anything but preserve their own jobs, was entirely unaware that the depth and severity of the depression required extraordinary measures from the government, and his inveterate hatred of governmental intrusion into the social and economic sphere turned him into a reactionary and a crank. Little that he wrote during this time—except his always lively and perspicacious reports of the quadrennial Democratic and Republican national conventions—is of any lasting importance. In any event, Mencken wrote little on religion at this time, evidently believing that he had said all he had to say on the subject.

Mencken's views on religion are intimately related to his political philosophy. Throughout his career—and most vigorously in the treatise *Notes on Democracy* (1926)—he reiterated the opinion that ordinary people are incapable of grasping the complexities of the world around them. To be blunt, they are too stupid to have an intelligent opinion on religion, science, society, or even politics, so that the very principle of democracy (by which Mencken really meant universal suffrage) is a farce and a tragedy. It is difficult to deny the force of Mencken's criticism, even though universal suffrage has become the chief shibboleth of American political thought. What this means as far as religion is concerned is (as he writes in "The Black Art") that the great majority of people are credulous and superstitious to a degree almost impossible for the "very, very small" number of genuinely intelligent persons to grasp. And it is not merely that people are ignorant; the problem is worse than that. "*Homo boobiens* is a fundamentalist for the precise reason that he is uneducable." This statement from "Fundamentalism: Divine and Secular" (written a few months after the conclusion of the Scopes trial) gets to the heart of the matter: if people are, in the mass, uneducable, then any attempt to convince them of the erroneousness of their views is doomed from the start. It is for this reason that Mencken found evangelical atheism futile and preposterous. The matter is not one of intellect but of psychology: people are so psychologically dependent upon the comfort their religion provides that no amount of proof of the falsity of their beliefs will have the slightest influence upon them. There seems little denying Mencken's assertion that "freedom from such superstitions, like the capacity for truth and honor, is the exclusive possession of a very small minority of the human race—even in America, a country where education is free and universal, probably not more than one-tenth of one per cent."

In Mencken's view, "religion belongs to a very early stage of human development, and . . . its rapid decay in the world since the Reformation is evidence of genuine progress" ("The Ascent of Man"). The ideas of progress and civilization were important to Mencken. As he wrote in the late essay "What I Believe" (1930), ". . . men become civilized, not in proportion to their willingness to believe, but in proportion to their readiness to doubt." It is a sentiment exactly echoed by Bertrand Russell: "William James used to preach the 'will to believe.' For my part, I should wish to preach the 'will to doubt.' "[2] And yet, Mencken believed that the "genuine progress" he sought affected only a tiny proportion of the human race; as he wrote in "Homo Neandertalensis," one of his opening salvos in the Scopes trial:

It is common to assume that human progress affects everyone—that even the dullest man, in these bright days, knows more than any man of, say, the Eighteenth Century, and is far more civilized. This assumption is quite erroneous. The men of the educated minority, no doubt, know more than their predecessors, and of some of them, perhaps, it may be said that they are more civilized—though I should not like to be put to giving names—but the great masses of men, even in this inspired republic, are precisely where the mob was at the dawn of history. They are ignorant, they are dishonest, they are cowardly, they are ignoble. They know little if anything that is worth knowing, and there is not the slightest sign of a natural desire among them to increase their knowledge.

But if this is the case, what is to be done? Is there any use even in speaking out against religion, given that it is not likely to affect the ignorant masses in any way? There is, because it is that "educated minority" who will carry on the banner of civilization, and whose opinions are therefore worth influencing. Mencken was relentless in asserting his and others' freedom to speak boldly and forthrightly on religion and in denying that religious views in themselves are somehow immune from criticism. This latter point is of particular importance. Religionists have long claimed that their opinions, merely because they are religious, are sacrosanct; in prior ages they were able to enforce this view by the notably effective means of burning heretics and infidels at the stake, but the notion persists today. The feeble apologist Stephen L. Carter is constantly demanding "respect" for religious views without establishing that those views are deserving of respect. His stance was refuted more than seventy years ago by Mencken: "There is, in fact, nothing about religious opinions that entitles them to any more respect than other opinions get. On the contrary, they tend to be noticeably silly. . . . No; there is nothing notably dignified about religious ideas. They run, rather, to a peculiarly puerile and tedious kind of nonsense."

This point is of particular relevance in the matter of the conflict between religion and science. In his earliest essay on the Scopes trial, "The Tennesee Circus," Mencken resolutely maintained that "there can be no honest compromise" between the theory of evolution and Fundamentalist religion: "Either Genesis embodies a mathematically accurate statement of what took place during the week of June 3, 4004 B. C. or Genesis is not actually the Word of God. If the former alternative be accepted, then all of modern science is nonsense: if the latter, then evangelical Christianity is nonsense." It is a truth that many "reconcilers" of religion and science are reluctant to acknowledge, for the conflict goes well beyond that between science and Fundamentalism: all religion is really at stake. In sympathizing with J. Gresham Machen, who tellingly rebutted the Modernists who were seeking to paper over the numerous erroneous or embarrassing utterances in the Bible in order to make them more palatable to modern sensibilities, Mencken asserts: "The instant they [the Modernists] admit that only part of the Bible may be rejected, if it be only the most trifling fly-speck in the Pauline Epistles, they admit that any other part may be rejected. Thus the divine authority of the whole disappears and there is no more evidence that Christianity is a revealed religion than there is that Mohammedanism is."

Mencken gained the greatest celebrity for his religious views during the Scopes trial of 1925, which he witnessed almost in its entirety. (Regrettably, he had left Dayton, Tennessee, just before Clarence Darrow dramatically placed William Jennings Bryan on the stand for his celebrated cross-examination.) His role as an acerbic commentator on the trial gained him both notoriety and infamy; in thinly disguised form, he is the original of the character E. K. Hornbeck in Jerome Lawrence and Robert E. Lee's play *Inherit the Wind* (1955). And yet, Mencken's complete writings on the Scopes trial—which began with "The Tennessee Circus" and other articles written weeks before the actual trial got underway, and ended with several follow-up essays after the trial's conclusion, including two outrageous obituaries of the late William Jennings Bryan—have never been reprinted in their entirety until now.

Although Mencken was nominally in Dayton not in his usual role as editorialist but as an actual reporter (his essays almost invariably appeared on the front page of the *Baltimore Evening Sun* rather than on the editorial page), he makes little effort at any objective or exhaustive account of the actual proceedings of the trial.[3] (The *Evening Sun* had, in any case, sent another reporter to cover the bare events, and his articles also appeared on the front page.) Accordingly, we do not gain any clear impression of the salient features of the two-week trial; even its three most dramatic events—Darrow's great speech for the dismissal of the case; the judge's decision to exclude expert testimony by scientists on the truth of evolution; and Darrow's cross-examination of Bryan—are alluded to only in passing in Mencken's screeds. Instead, he uses the trial as a springboard for broader discussions—the conflict of science and religion, the role of the government in enforcing religious views, the ignorance of the common people, and, most emphatically, the need to combat religious obscurantism by vigorous rebuttal and refutation. It is no surprise that, a year after the trial's conclusion, Mencken is speaking strongly about an active campaign against religion: "A defensive war is not enough; there must be a forthright onslaught upon the theological citadel, and every effort must be made to knock it down. For so long as it remains a stronghold, there will be no security for sound sense among us, and little for common decency." It is unfortunate that so few public commentators—with the solitary but distinguished exception of Gore Vidal—have taken up Mencken's call to arms.

Mencken has taken the greatest heat for his merciless skewering of William Jennings Bryan both during the trial and immediately after his sudden death a few days after the end of the trial. To be sure, Mencken was not liberally endowed with any reverence for the adage *de mortuis nil nisi bonum,* and some of his statements ("Bryan was a vulgar and common man, a cad undiluted. He was ignorant, bigoted, self-seeking, blatant and dishonest") might seem to justify L. Sprague de Camp's assessment: "Mencken succeeded in being even more unjust to Bryan than Bryan had been to Darrow in his post-trial statement. He also succeeded in shocking Bryan's admirers as severely as if he had literally scalped Bryan's corpse and done a war dance around it, waving his bloody trophy."[4] But was Mencken "unjust" to Bryan? Was Mencken not justified in writing the following prior to Bryan's death?

> This old buzzard, having failed to raise the mob against its rulers, now prepares to raise it against its teachers. He can never be the peasants' President, but there is still a chance to be the peasants' Pope. He leads a new crusade, his bald head glistening, his face streaming with sweat, his chest heaving beneath his rumpled alpaca coat. . . . But let no one, laughing at him, underestimate the magic that lies in his black, malignant eye, his frayed but still eloquent voice. He can shake and inflame these poor ignoramuses as no other man among us can shake and inflame them, and he is desperately eager to order the charge. In Tennessee he is drilling his army. The big battles, he believes, will be fought elsewhere.

The mere fact that Bryan happened to die before he could continue carrying the banner of ignorant Fundamentalism should not require Mencken to pull his punches. If Bryan had been only a fool, he would have been deserving only of pity; but Bryan was a dangerous and powerful fool, and that combination justifiably required the most vigorous possible combat.

For Mencken, the most ominous feature of the whole antievolution movement in Tennessee was the intrusion of the government into areas in which it had no legitimate place. He had already expressed repeated outrage over Prohibition, and the Tennessee statute offered further cause for alarm that the Bill of Rights—and specifically the First Amendment—was in jeopardy. Is it then a paradox that, in the essay "In Tennessee," Mencken actually defends the role of the Tennessee legislature in passing the law? It was this essay that initially led Bryan to think of Mencken as an ally—an impression that was quickly scotched as he read Mencken's subsequent reports of the trial. But "In Tennessee" must be read in the context of Mencken's long-standing disdain of "pedagogues," both in the high schools and in the colleges; he saw them merely as the mindless pawns of a national educational system that not merely failed to educate the great mass of its citizens (who, in any case, were incapable of being properly educated), but which actively sought not to educate but to indoctrinate its subjects into socially and politically acceptable points of view. For Mencken, "A pedagogue, properly so called—and a high-school teacher in a country town is properly so called—is surely not a searcher for knowledge. His job in the world is simply to pass on what has been chosen and approved by his superiors." And yet, the half-bantering tone of "In Tennessee" should not deceive us. Two years after the end of the Scopes trial, Mencken in "Another Inquisition Fails" (1927) is gleefully trumpeting the failure of Fundamentalists to pass antievolution statutes in other states.

One of Mencken's most controversial stances in the issue of religion and politics is his assertion that religions—specifically the Methodist and Baptist churches—were behind the movement to pass the Prohibition amendment and, even more notoriously, were behind the reemergence of the Ku Klux Klan in 1915. The matter is too complex for detailed treatment here, but the historical evidence suggests that Mencken was pretty much on target in the first claim but somewhat off the mark in the second. The central role of the Anti-Saloon League in advocating Prohibition, from as early as the 1890s, is not in doubt; nor is there any doubt of its fundamentally religious character and basis. F. Scott McBride, general superintendent of the league, stated: "The Anti-Saloon League was born of God.

It has been led by Him, and will fight on while He leads." Herbert Asbury, author of the tart autobiography *Up from Methodism* (1926), shows how intimately certain churches were behind the temperance movement, particularly in regard to its exercise of political influence:

> The Anti-Saloon League always called itself "the church in action against the saloon," and claimed to have brought the Protestant denominations into the fight and into politics.... In a declaration published in 1892 the Methodist Church, afterward the principal supporter of the Anti-Saloon League, said under the heading of *Political Action,* "We recommend all members ... who enjoy the elective franchise to use that solemn trust so as to promote the rescue of our country from the guilt and dishonor which have been brought upon it by a criminal complicity with the liquor traffic.... we record our deliberate judgment that no political party has a right to expect, nor ought it to receive, the support of Christian men so long as it stands committed to the license policy, or refuses to put itself on record in an attitude of open hostility to the saloon." The Convention of the Southern Baptist Church said in 1890 that "no Christian citizen should ever cast a ballot for any man, measure, or platform that is opposed to the annihilation of the liquor traffic." That same year the Christian Church, or Disciples of Christ, urged "a political party committed to the policy of state and national prohibition and to the enforcement of the law." Similar positions were taken by other Protestant churches.[5]

It was clearly the Baptist and Methodist churches as a whole, and not merely individual members of them acting independently, who formed the core of the Anti-Saloon League and engaged in political pressure upon politicians to pass the Prohibition amendment. While it is true that Prohibition was in part a reaction by Anglo-Saxon Americans against what they perceived to be the excessive imbibing of recent European immigrants, there was always a subtle anti-Catholic bias mixed with this xenophobic prejudice—a bias that emerged openly with the nomination in 1928 of the "wet" Democratic presidential candidate Al Smith, the first Catholic nominated by any major American party for the presidency.

As for the Ku Klux Klan, Mencken is on somewhat shakier ground. For the first decade or two of the Klan's existence after its reconstitution in 1915, its chief foes were not African Americans or Jews but Catholics, who were seen as symbols of the perceived immorality, influx of foreigners, and social changes that were affecting the United States in the early decades of the twentieth century. Individual Klansmen, and even some Klan leaders, were indeed associated with the Baptist or Methodist churches, but there was no concerted support of the Klan by any church. As Kenneth T. Jackson, historian of the Klan, writes:

> Although there was no formal connection between the Invisible Empire and any religious denomination, Fundamentalism was the central thread of the Klan program. Declaring that "America is Protestant and so it must remain," the KKK glorified the "old-time religion," rejected evolution and higher criticism, and admonished its members to attend church regularity. Protestant clergymen were reminded that Klansmen accepted the Bible as the literal and unalterable word of God. As proof of their devotion, masked Knights frequently appeared unannounced before quiescent congregations for the purpose of making a well-publicized donation.[6]

Jackson goes on to point to the Klan's role in supporting Prohibition and other conservative moral and social causes.

With the election of Herbert Hoover in 1928, Mencken saw another figure as representative of the unwarranted influence of religion in the political sphere—Monsignor James Cannon, the leading Methodist clergyman of his time. Cannon had been instrumental both in the Prohibition movement and in the effort to woo several normally Democratic states away from Al Smith to Herbert Hoover in the election of 1928. Mencken therefore feared that Cannon would in effect establish a state religion based upon dogmatic Methodism. But his concerns were much exaggerated. Cannon's electioneering efforts had engendered hostility both in and out of his church, and in the next several years he was dogged by accusations ranging from misuse of church funds to adultery. Opponents in the Methodist church dissolved the church's Board of Temperance and Social Service, which had served as a major platform for Cannon's temperance battles, and his influence waned thereafter.

What distinguishes H. L. Mencken's writing on religion is not merely its cogency and force as logical argument, but its piquancy, vibrancy, and satirical wit. Mencken knew that satire and ridicule are important weapons in the battle against religious obscurantism; the ignorant masses, of course, are not likely to be affected by them (as they are still less likely to be affected by logical argument), but the tiny residue of the intelligent might perhaps be shamed into abandoning or modifying their sheepish adherence to outmoded religious creeds by a shower of abuse. The proper response to religious folly is not outrage but amused contempt. Mencken could rarely avoid the temptation to lampoon: consider "The Anthropomorphic Delusion" (1919), in which he asserts that "man is botched and ridiculous," and thereby hardly the work of an omnipotent deity (he follows up this argument in "Hints to Theologians" by maintaining that, because human beings are so imperfect, they must have been the creation not of a single god, but of an incompetent committee of gods); consider further "Services for the Damned," which urges the creation of nonreligious marriage and death ceremonies "for the admittedly damned"; or "Religious Prejudice" (1924), in which Mencken claims that the spectacle of various religious sects battling each other provides a good show for the rest of us; or his imperishable accounts of attending revival meetings by Billy Sunday and Aimée Semple McPherson; or, perhaps best of all, "The Spirit World" (1922), in which he sensibly asks why the spirits of human beings should exhibit any greater intelligence after death than the human beings themselves did in life. Madame Blavatsky's theosophist "hooey" comes in for merciless ridicule, as does Christian Science, of which Mencken asserted: "the idea behind it is one of the few human ideas in which I can find no sense or logic whatever." As for Fundamentalists, his scorn was unrelenting. Did they reject the notion that their grandfathers had been gorillas? They certainly did, and for a very good reason: "most of them had seen their grandfather—and so the plausibility of the notion made them shiver."

And yet, Mencken could also be remarkably prescient. I have already pointed out his whimsical suggestion that African Americans convert to Islam. In "The Decline of Protestantism" (1925) he accurately predicts the decline of mainline Protestant churches and the resurgence of Fundamentalism, as a wider and wider dichotomy emerges between a secular intelligentsia and an increasingly backward general populace. Mencken's call, in "What Is to Be Done about Divorce?" (1930), that the clergy with their primitive dogmas get out of the business of dictating divorce laws has been fulfilled by the passage of sensible divorce legislation in most states in this country; and in "Democracy and Theocracy" (1928), his observation that the United States has "always diluted democracy with theocracy" in defiance of the First Amendment is as true now as it was in his time.

Will another commentator, with a prominence analogous to what Mencken achieved in the period from around 1915 to 1930, ever duplicate his boldness, his forthrightness, his pungency in battling orthodox religion? The prospects do not seem favorable. In contrast to Mencken's own strictures, religions have even more forcefully asserted the bad taste of criticizing their tenets, as if it were a sign of religious bigotry to point out the manifest errors and implausibilities that are fossilized in every sacred scripture ever devised by human beings. The various religious sects in this country have merely become a succession of political parties, each striving to gain a numerical majority of adherents without any regard to the truth or falsity of their dogmas; or worse, they have become hawkers of their wares, advertising their faith exactly as if it were just another commodity in our consumeristic culture. An H. L. Mencken of the twenty-first century would be a refreshing tonic against the buffooneries of American religion, but the chances of his emergence do not seem at the moment to be good.

—S. T. Joshi

A NOTE ON THIS EDITION

I have reprinted the articles in this volume directly from the magazines and newspapers in which they originally appeared. I have made no alteration in the texts save for the correction of a few obvious typographical errors and (especially in the book review columns) a replacement of Mencken's quotation marks for book titles with italics. Even in the few instances in which these articles were later reprinted (usually with revisions) in various of Mencken's books, I have chosen to use the original versions as more accurately reflecting his views on the date they were written.

The titles of some of the selections are of my own invention. These include: "Immortality," "Nietzsche on Religion" (originally a book review column in the *Smart Set,* titled "The Bugaboo of the Sunday Schools"), "The Need for an Ingersoll," "Services for the Damned," "The Decline of Protestantism," "A Day with Billy Sunday" (originally a book review column in the *Smart Set,* titled "Savonarolas A-Sweat"), "Evangelical Ignoramuses," "What's the Matter with the Churches?" and "The Churches and the Depression." Several items are titled subsections in the "Répétition Générale" column in the *Smart Set*: "Confession of a Theological Moron," "The Anthropomorphic Delusion," "The Ascent of Man," "The Spirit World," "Venture into Therapeutics," and "Vox Populi, Vox Dei." (The item I have placed as an epilogue, "Memorial Service," was originally a section titled "Threnody" in "Répétition Générale.") Three items—"Hint to Theologians," "The Ghostly Fraternity," and "Religious Prejudice"—are titled subsections in the "Clinical Notes" column in the *American Mercury*. All book reviews from the *American Mercury* bear titles created by Mencken.

In order to minimize the number of footnotes, I have prepared a glossary of names mentioned in the text. Mencken was fond of dropping names, most of whom were known to his readers but many of whom have now fallen into obscurity. In a few cases I have found it easier to elucidate these names in a footnote.

I am grateful to Douglas A. Anderson and Scott Connors for supplying some of the texts included in this book. My colleagues Ray Stevens, Richard J. Schrader, S. L. Harrison, and Vincent Fitzpatrick have been supportive of my work on Mencken and have lent valuable advice. Leslie G. Boba has lent support in other and still more valuable ways.

I

THE BELIEFS
OF AN ICONOCLAST

THE SCHOOLING OF A THEOLOGIAN

In the days of my earliest memories my father had an acquaintance named Mr. Garrigues, a highly respectable gentleman of French origin who operated a men's hat store in West Baltimore, not far from our home on Hollins Street. This hat store of his, though it drove an excellent trade, occupied him only on weekdays; on Sundays he threw himself, rather curiously for a man of his race, into superintending the Sunday school of a little Methodist chapel on nearby Wilkins Avenue. Early one winter evening he dropped in while my brother Charlie and I were playing Indians up and down the front staircase, and proposed to my father that we be articled to his Sunday school. I recall, of course, nothing of his argument, though my brother and I naturally eavesdropped; I remember only that it lasted but a few minutes, and that the very next Sunday afternoon Mr. Garrigues called at the house in a high silk hat and conducted us to his seminary.

It was not until years afterward that I learned why my father had succumbed so quickly, or indeed at all. I understood by that time that he was what Christendom abhors as an infidel, and I took the liberty of expressing some wonder that he had been willing, in that character, to expose his two innocent sons to the snares of the Wesleyan divinity. He hemmed and hawed a little, but finally let go the truth. What moved him, he confessed, was simply his overmastering impulse to give over the Sunday afternoons of winter to quiet snoozing. This had been feasible so long as my brother and I were puling infants and could be packed off for naps ourselves, but as we increased in years and malicious animal magnetism[1] and began to prefer leaping and howling up and downstairs, it became impossible for him to get any sleep. So he was a setup for Mr. Garrigues and succumbed without firing a shot. "The risk," he went on to explain, "was much less than you seem to think. Garrigues and his Methodists had you less than two hours a week, and I had you all the rest of the time. I'd have been a hell of a theologian to let them fetch you."

I recall very little of his counter-revolutionary propaganda save that it took the form of a sort of satirical cross-examination, deliberately contrived to be idiotic. "Have they got you to Jonah yet? Have you heard about him swallowing the whale?"[2] And so on. I recall even less of the teaching in the Sunday school itself, though I apparently picked up from it some knowledge of the dramatis personae of the Old Testament. At all events, I can't remember the time when I did not know that Moses wrote the Ten Commandments and wore a long beard; that Noah built an ark like the one we had in our Christmas garden and filled it with animals which, to this day, I always think of as wooden, with a leg or two missing; that Lot's wife was turned into a pillar of salt; that the Tower of Babel was twice as high as the Baltimore shot tower; that Abraham greatly pleased Jahveh by the strange device of offering to butcher and roast his own son; and that Leviticus was the father of Deuteronomy. But all this learning must have been imparted by a process resembling osmosis, for I have no recollection of any formal teaching, or even of any teacher.

The one thing I really remember about that Sunday school is the agreeable heartiness of the singing. It is, of course, the thing that all children enjoy most in Sunday schools, for there they are urged to whoop their loudest in praise of God, and that license is an immense relief from the shushing they are always hearing at home. Years later I lived for a while beside a Christian Science establishment in which the larval scientificos were taught, presumably, that their occasional bellyaches were only mortal error, but all I ever heard of this teaching was their frequent antiphon of cheerful song, with each singer shrilling along in a different key. If the Bach Choir could work up so much pressure in its pipes, the Mass in B minor would become as popular as "Sweet Adeline." So far as I can make out, I attended Mr. Garrigues' hive of hymnody but two winters, and yet I carried away from it a repertoire of Methodist shouts and glees that sticks to me to this day and is turned loose every time I let three-bottle men take me for a ride.

My favorite then, as now, was "Are You Ready for the Judgment Day?," a gay and even rollicking tune with a saving hint of brimstone in the words. I am told by Paul Patterson, of the Baltimore *Sunpapers,* who got his vocal training in the Abraham Lincoln Belt of Inner Illinois, that the No. 1 hymn there in the eighties was "Shower of Blessing," but in Baltimore, though we sang it, it was far down the list. We grouped it, in fact, with such *dolce* but unexhilarating things as "The Sweet By-and-By" and "God Be with You Till We Meet Again"—pretty stuff, to be sure, but sadly lacking in bite and zowie. The runner-up to "Are You Ready?" was "I Went Down the Rock to Hide My Face," another hymn with a very lively swing to it, and after it came "Stand Up! Stand Up for Jesus!," "Draw Me Nearer, Nearer, Blessed Lord," "What a Friend We Have in Jesus" and "Revive Us Again," which last was cabbaged by the I.W.W.'s[3] years later and converted into proletarian ribaldry. We also learned the more sombre classics— "Nearer, My God, to Thee," "Onward, Christian Soldiers," "From Greenland's Icy Mountains," "Rock of Ages," "There Is a Green Hill Far Away," and so on—but they were not sung often and my brother and I had little fancy for them. It was not until I transferred to another Sunday school that I came to know such lugubrious horrors as "There Is a Fountain Filled with Blood." The Methodists avoided everything of that kind. They surely did not neglect Hell in their preaching, but when they lifted up their voices in song they liked to pretend that they were booked to escape it.

My early preference for "Are You Ready?" was no doubt supported by the fact that it was also a favorite among the Aframerican evangelists who practiced in the alley behind Hollins Street, alarming and shaking down the resident sinners. These evangelists did not confine themselves to Sundays but worked seven days a week, and it seemed to me as a boy that there was always one of them in operation. They were both male and female. I recall clearly a female who wore a semi-ecclesiastical robe of violent purple and had a voice so raucous that the white neighbors often begged the cops to chase her away. Whenever she was hustled out, she kept on shouting warnings over her shoulder, always to the effect that the Day of Judgment was just round the corner. Her chief target was a low-down white man who lived in the alley with a colored woman and had a large family of mulattoes. When he retreated into his house, she howled at him through the window. So far as I know, she never made any impression on him or on his children, though his lady sometimes gave her a penny. This sinful white man, who never did any work, eventually disappeared, and the colored people reported that he had been killed in a brawl and his body hauled to the University of Maryland dissecting room. Of his children, one son was later hanged.

The evangelists always began their proceedings by lining out a hymn, and usually it was "Are You Ready?" It brought out all the colored people who happened to be at home, and in a few minutes white boys began to leap over the Hollins Street back fences to join the congregation. (In those days no self-respecting boy ever went through a gate. It was a point of honor to climb over the fence.) After the opening hymn had reached its tenth and last stanza, the evangelist would pray at length, mentioning salient sinners by name. Then there would be another hymn, and after that he would launch into his discourse. Its subject was always the same: the dreadful state of Aframerican morals in West Baltimore. It was delivered in a terrifying manner—in fact, it ran mainly to shrieks and howls—but it was seldom long, for the colored people preferred their theology in small and powerful doses. Then there would be another hymn, and the reverend would begin to show signs that a collection was impending. The moment those signs were detected, nine-tenths of his audience vanished. Not infrequently, in fact, ten-tenths of it vanished, and all he could do, after mopping his brow and stuffing his handkerchief into his hat, was to shuffle on to some other alley.

We white boys always joined in the hymns and listened to the sermons. From the latter we picked up a great deal of useful information about the geography, dimensions, temperature, social life and public works of Hell. To this day I probably know more about the matter than most ordained clergymen. The Hell we heard about was chiefly peopled, of course, by the colored damned; it was some time later before I began to understand clearly that there was also accommodation for Caucasians. We seldom attempted to roughhouse these services, though once in a while a boy whose people had family prayers and who thus hated religion would heave a dead cat over the fence or run down the alley yelling "Fire!" The colored communicants commonly gave ear to the evangelist with perfect gravity. Indeed, the only one who ever ventured to dispute the theology on tap was Old Wesley, the alley metaphysician, and he reserved his caveats for the preaching of his brother, a divine who pastored a tar-paper tabernacle down in Calvert County and showed up only to rowel and bedevil Wesley for living in adultery with our next-door neighbor's colored cook.

It was the dream of every alley evangelist to be called to a regular church, and sometimes that dream was realized. The call consisted in renting a room in a tumbledown house, putting in a couple of rows of benches, and finding two or three pious colored women to feed the pastor and pay the rent. There was always a sign outside giving the name of the establishment, the name of the pastor (invariably followed by D.D.), and the order of services. These signs followed an invariable pattern, with all of the "s"s backward, and plenty of small "a"s, "e"s and "r"s scattered through the capitals. Such signs are still plentiful in the poorer colored neighborhoods of Baltimore, and the old church names survive—the Watch Your Step Baptist Temple, the Sweet Violet Church of God, the No More Booze Pentecostal Tabernacle, and so on. One such basilica that I recall stood in the middle of a lot down near the Baltimore & Ohio tracks, surrounded by Jimson weeds and piles of rusting tin cans. The sistren of the Ladies' Aid roved the vicinity, cadging contributions from white passers-by. Whenever my father and his brother passed of a Sunday morning on their way to George Zipprian's beer garden across the tracks, they gave up ten cents apiece to the first collector who flagged them.

We were not permitted to enter any of these tabernacles, for they were supposed to swarm with ticks, fleas, spiders, lice, thousand legs and other Arthropoda. But we were free to attend the street-corner hullabaloos of the Salvation Army, which was a novelty in the United States at the end of the eighties and almost as good as a circus. Here our training in Wesleyan hymnody stood us in good stead, for the hymns the Army howled were the same that we had howled ourselves in Mr. Garrigues' chapel. We let go with all brakes off, and greatly enjoyed the ensuing confessions of the saved. There was one old man who admitted such revolting crimes that we never got enough of him, and it was a sad day when he failed to appear and the cop on the beat intimated that he had been hauled off to a lunatic asylum. When the beautiful Amazons of God began circulating in the crowd with their tambourines, we took to our heels, for we believed in conscience that salvation should be free.

As I have said, my brother and I sat under Mr. Garrigues and his acolytes in winter only, for in summer we were in the country. When he died suddenly in 1888, my father shifted us to another and much larger Sunday school, run by the English Lutherans in Lombard Street. It met, unfortunately, on Sunday mornings, so he had to suffer some interruption of his afternoon nap, but as we grew older and more decorous that objection faded out. We liked this Lutheran basilica very much during the first few years, for the superintendent, Mr. Harman, was a Methodist at heart and often lined out the rousing hymns that we knew and esteemed. We also greatly enjoyed the cornet-playing of the treasurer, whose name I recall as Mr. Mentzer. He was an elegant fellow in a silky mustache, a white choker collar and an immaculate cutaway, and when he lifted his cornet to his lips it was with a very graceful flourish—at all events, it seemed so to us. When he let go *fortissimo*, the whole Sunday school heaved and the stained glass rattled in the church upstairs. In the singing that went with his blasts of tone, ordinary yelling was not enough; a boy of any spirit had to scream. More than once I came home hoarse and was put to gargling with painkiller.

The pastor of the church in those days was the Reverend Dr. Sylvanus Stall, a tall, gaunt Pennsylvanian with a sandy beard. I find on investigation that he was precisely forty years old in 1887, but he seemed to my brother and to me to be as ancient as Abraham. He looked at first glance like a standard-model Class B Protestant ecclesiastic, but there was much more to him than met the eye. One Sunday morning in 1889 or thereabout, he showed up in Sunday school with a strange contraption under his arm. Rapping for order, he announced that it was a newly invented machine that could talk like a human being, and not only talk but even sing. Then he instructed us to sing his favorite hymn, which was "God Be with You Till We Meet Again." We bawled it dutifully, and he explained that the machine would now bawl it back. "But not," he went on, "as loudly as you did. Listen carefully and you will hear it clearly enough. The sound of the machine is very faint, but it is also very penetrating." Then he turned it on, and we heard a phonograph for the first time. Ah, that it had been the last!

A little while later, the good Doctor quit pastoring to take the editorship of a church paper, with dashes into book-writing on the side. His first books had such depressing titles as *Methods of Church Work, Five-Minute Object Sermons to Children* and *Bible Selections for Daily Devotion*, and appear to have scored only spiritual successes. But in 1897, long after I had escaped his Sunday school and almost forgotten him, he brought out a little volume called *What a Young Boy Ought to Know,* and thereafter he began rolling up money with such velocity that when he died in 1915 he was probably the richest Lutheran pastor, at least in the earned brackets, that this great Republic has ever seen. For that little volume founded the science of sex hygiene, which eventually developed into a major American industry, with thousands of practitioners and a technique become as complicated as that of polo or astrophysics.

He wrote all its official texts for male seekers—*What a Young Man Ought to Know, What a Man of Forty-five Ought to Know,* and so on—and he inspired, copyread, and published all its texts for females, beginning with *What a Young Girl Ought to Know* and ending, I suppose, with *What a Decent Grandmother Ought to Forget.* Indeed, he held the field unchallenged until the explosion of the Freud ammunition dump of horrors, and by that time he was so well heeled that he could afford to laugh ha-ha. He left his money, I believe, to a college for training missionaries to the sexually misinformed and underprivileged, but where it is located I don't know and don't care.

Of the theology he radiated in his Baltimore days, I retain precisely nothing. There was, in fact, little expounding of doctrine in his Sunday school; the instruction, in so far as there was any at all, was predominantly ethical and had as its chief apparent aim the discouragement of murder, robbery, counterfeiting, embezzlement and other such serious crimes, none of which occurred in the student body in my time. Those were the candle days of religious pedagogy, and the teachers confined themselves mainly to expounding the week's International Sunday-School Lesson and trying to induce their pupils to memorize the Golden Text. Inasmuch as I could never memorize anything, I failed regularly. But there was no penalty for failure, and my own was hardly remarked, for virtually all the other boys in my class failed too.

Tiring of this puerile futility, I began at the age of ten to agitate for my release and finally escaped when I went into long pants. My father, it turned out, had not underestimated the potency of his evil influence; it left me an infidel, as he was, and as his father had been before him.

[*New Yorker,* July 8, 1939]

CONFESSION OF A
THEOLOGICAL MORON

One of my heaviest handicaps in this world is the fact that I am absolutely devoid of what is called religious feeling. That is to say, I have no sense whatever of the divine presence or of a divine personality; neither ever enters into my thinking. I have faced, in my time, all the great disasters that man must suffer—professional failure, financial catastrophe, social ignominy, the treachery of friends, the loss of a best girl, intolerable physical pain, even the threat of death itself. Yet I cannot remember that even in the blackest moments of long and ghastly nights have I ever had the slightest impulse to pray to God for help. Twice I have been shot at, deliberately and at short range. Both times I was scared stiff, and yet neither time did it occur to me to ask any aid of the celestial hierarchy. As for the impulse to worship, it is as foreign to my nature as the impulse to run for Congress.

I am anything but a militant atheist and haven't the slightest objection to church-going, so long as it is honest. I have gone to church myself many times, honestly seeking to experience the great inward exaltation that religious persons speak of. Not even at St. Peter's in Rome have I sensed the least trace of it. The most I ever feel at the most solemn moment of the most pretentious religious ceremonial is a sensuous delight in the beauty of it—a delight exactly like that which comes over me when I hear, say, *Tristan and Isolde* or Brahms' stupendous fourth symphony. The effect of such music, in fact, is much keener than the effect of the liturgy. Brahms moves me far more powerfully than the holy saints.

As I say, this deficiency is a handicap in a world peopled, in the overwhelming main, by men who are inherently religious. It sets me apart from my fellows and makes it difficult for me to understand many of their ideas and not a few of their acts. I see them responding constantly and robustly to impulses that to me are quite inexplicable. Worse, it causes these folks to misunderstand me, and often to do me serious injustice. They cannot rid themselves of the notion that, because I am anaesthetic to the ideas which move them most profoundly, I am, in some vague but nevertheless certain way, a man of aberrant morals, and hence one to be kept at a distance. I have never met a religious man who did not reveal this suspicion. No matter how earnestly he tried to grasp my point of view, he always ended by making an alarmed sort of retreat. All religions, in fact, teach that dissent is a sin; most of them make it the blackest of all sins, and all of them punish it severely whenever they have the power. It is impossible for a religious man to rid himself of the notion that such punishments are just. He simply cannot imagine a civilized rule of conduct that is not based upon the fear of God.

Let me add that my failing is in the fundamental religious impulse, not in mere theological credulity. I am not kept out of church by an inability to believe the current dogmas. In point of fact, a good many of them seem to be reasonable enough, and I probably dissent from most of them a good deal less violently than many men who are assiduous devotees. Among my curious experiences, years ago, was that of convincing an ardent Catholic who balked at the dogma of papal infallibility. He was a very faithful son of the church and his inability to accept it greatly distressed him. I proved to him, at least to his satisfaction, that there was nothing intrinsically absurd in it—that if the dogmas that he already accepted were true then this one was probably true also. Some time later, when this man was on his deathbed, I visited him and he thanked me simply and with apparent sincerity for resolving his old doubt. But even he was unable to comprehend my own lack of religion. His last words to me were a pious hope that I would give over my lamentable contumacy to God and lead a better life. He died firmly convinced that I was headed for hell, and, what is more, that I deserved it.

[*Smart Set,* January 1920]

ON HAPPINESS

I

The following letter, apparently quite genuine, comes to me from a young man who says that he was born a Jew, and into an orthodox family:

> I am 25 years old. Not an old man, as old men are considered; not a wise man, as wisdom is counted. But life has changed for me. I am almost an atheist. Almost, because I cannot discard the fear of the Unknown that was drilled into my young heart. I still faintly fear that Something. Yet I cannot believe the Bible; I cannot accept it as God-given. My simple

reason tells me that death is the end of all; that the force that propels life is Nature, a Nature that does not perform miracles. And with this new idea has come misery, unhappiness, the desire to forsake this life. Does enlightenment mean misery? Does non-belief mean unhappiness?

Why this young man sends his problem to me instead of to a clergyman I don't know, save that he recognizes my colossal theological gift. My advice to him does not differ appreciably from that he would receive from a regular practitioner of the ghostly art. (When I say a regular practitioner, of course, I mean a true believer, not one of the shameless frauds who try to conceal their agnosticism by calling themselves Modernists.[4]) I advise him to give his new skepticism six months' trial. If, at the end of that time, he finds that its effects upon him are still indistinguishable from those of a bad case of cholera morbus, I advise him to go the nearest orthodox rabbi, tell his troubles, pay his fine (if fines are levied in such cases) and reconcile himself to the faith of his fathers.

Why not, indeed? What ails him is simply pride, which Holy Church long ago put among the seven deadly sins. Unfitted by training, and perhaps also by nature, for a life of doubt, and seduced into it at twenty-five by the rhetoric of men of a quite different kidney, he now finds himself ashamed to admit that he longs to go back whence he came. But why should he be ashamed? Some men are born religious as others are born with long legs or outstanding ears. If that is the bent of their nature, they should follow it. More, I believe that they are inevitably bound to do so. The moment they step outside the borders of faith they are unhappy. And if they try desperately and against their inner inclination to remain there, their unhappiness becomes unendurable. The colleges of the land turn out thousands of such sad cases every year. A few of the victims hang themselves. But the vast majority, at thirty, are again comfortably within the fold, as they were in early youth, and as their fathers were before them.

II

Now and then, desiring to be unpleasant to persons who dislike me, I propose that a vast campaign of so-called education be launched in the late Confederate States, to acquaint the youth of the region with the elements of the physical sciences, and so rescue them from the naïve and negroid theology of their elders. But that proposal is never taken seriously by anyone who actually knows me, for every such person knows that I never do anything to execute it. More, they know that I'd protest if it were executed by others.

Why, indeed, should it be executed? Why should I (or anyone else) get into a sweat about what is believed by the boys and girls of Georgia, or Mississippi, or Tennessee? Above all, why should anyone want to change what they believe into something else? Is their religion idiotic? Then their science would also be idiotic. If they are actually mainly numskulls, as appears to be probable, then there is no known way to cure their numskullery. Every attempt to do so, by the devices of the logician, can have only the result of making them unhappy. And why make them unhappy?

I am, indeed, against all proselyters, whether they be on my side or on some other side. What moves nine-tenths of them, I believe, is simply the certainty of the result that I have just mentioned. Their lofty pretensions are all tosh. The thing they yearn for is the satisfaction of making someone unhappy: that yearning is almost as universal among them as thirst is in dry Congressmen. Sometimes they deceive themselves, but probably not often. The wowser is a wowser the whole world over, no matter what banner he flies. What he craves above all is resistance. He wants to break it down, to force his ideas upon his victims, to watch them writhe and suffer. If the Chinese asked for missionaries, it would be hard to find recruits for the dreadful trade. But the Chinese resist them and are made unhappy by them, and so every Y.M.C.A. tank in the land is gorged with candidates.

III

In this department, by God's grace, my own conscience is perfectly clear—perhaps my own plausible boast as a moral agent. I have never consciously tried to convert anyone to anything. Like any other man bawling from a public stump I have occasionally made a convert; in fact, in seasons when my embouchure has been good I have made a great many. But not deliberately, not with any satisfaction. Next to a missionary, a convert is the most abhorrent shape I can imagine. I dislike persons who change their basic ideas, and I dislike them when they change them for good reasons quite as much as when they change them for bad ones. A convert to a good idea is simply a man who confesses that he was formerly an ass—and is probably one still. When such a man favors me with a certificate that my eloquence has shaken him I feel about him precisely as I'd feel if he told me that he had started (or stopped) beating his wife on my recommendation.

No; it is not pleasant to come into contact with such flabby souls, so lacking in character and self-respect. Their existence embitters the life of every man who deals in ideas. The hard-boiled fellows are far more agreeable, no matter what their concrete notions. Some of those who appear to depart the farthest from the elements of sense are the most charming, for example, certain varieties of evangelical pastors. I have known many such pastors, and esteemed not a few of them. But only, I should add, the relatively unsuccessful, who seldom if ever achieved the public nuisance known as saving a soul. They believed their depressing rubbish firmly, but they did not press it upon either their inferiors or their superiors. They were not wowsers.

Unluckily, there are very few such pastors in the average Christian community, especially in the United States. The great majority, forgetting their office of conducting worship, devote themselves mainly to harassing persons who do not care to join them. This harassing is bad enough when it fails of its purpose; when it succeeds its consequence is simply an increase in the sum of human degradation, publicly displayed. It is well known that natural believers are always suspicious of converts. No wonder. For precisely the same reason sober automobilists are suspicious of drunken drivers, and Prohibition agents of Prohibitionists.

IV

My correspondent raises a question that cannot be answered here at any length: it would take five or six columns. It has to do with the emotional effects of skepticism. Is the skeptic ever happy, in the sense that a man who believes that God is watching over him is happy? Privately, I often doubt it. Here the pious seem to have a certain bulge on the doubters. Immersed in their faith, they enjoy a quiet contentment that is certainly never apparent in a man of restless, inquisitive, questioning mind. The happiest people in the world, accepting this definition of happiness, are probably Christian Scientists—that is, until they come down with appendicitis or gallstones.

But there is a kind of satisfaction that is quite as attractive, to certain rugged types of men, as this somewhat cowlike form of contentment. It is related to the latter just as the satisfaction of a soldier on active duty is related to the satisfaction of a man securely at home. The man at home is quite safe, and the soldier runs a considerable risk of being killed or wounded. But who will argue that the man at home, on the whole, is happier than the soldier—that is, assuming that the soldier is a volunteer? The one is tightly comfortable, and hence happy. But the other, though in grave peril, is happy too—and I am inclined to think that his happiness is often of a palpably superior variety.

So with the skeptic. His doubts, if they are real, undoubtedly tend to make him uneasy, and hence unhappy, for they play upon themselves quite as much as upon the certainties of the other fellow. What comforts him, in the long run, I suppose, is his pride in his capacity to face them. He is not wobbled and alarmed, like my correspondent; he gets a positive thrill out of being uneasy, as the soldier gets a thrill out of being in danger. Is this thrill equal, as a maker of anything rationally describable as happiness, to the comfort and security of the man of faith? Ask me an easier question! Is a blonde lovelier than a brunette? Is *Dunkles* better than *Helles*?[5] Is Los Angeles the worst town in America, or only next to the worst? The skeptic, asked the original question, will say yes; the believer will say no. There you have it.

[*Baltimore Evening Sun*, May 9, 1927]

WHAT I BELIEVE

I

"Faith," said the unknown author of the Epistle to the Hebrews, "is the substance of things hoped for, the evidence of things not seen."[6]

The definition, in these later days, seems to be pretty well forgotten, especially by those master forgetters, the Christian theologians, for it is common to hear them discussing (and denouncing) the beliefs of men of science as if they were mere articles of faith. The two things, of course, are quite distinct. Belief is faith in something that is known; faith is belief in something that is not known. In my own credo there are few articles of faith; in fact, I have been quite unable, in ten days and nights of prayer and self-examination, to discover a single one.

What I believe is mainly what has been established by plausible and impartial evidence, *e.g.,* that the square on the hypotenuse of a right triangle is equal to the squares of the other two sides, that water is composed of oxygen and hydrogen, and that man is a close cousin to the ape. Further than that I do not care to go. Is there a life after death, as so many allege, wherein the corruptible puts on incorruption and the mortal immortality? I can only answer that I do not know. My private inclination is to hope that it is not so, but that hope is only a hope, and hopes and beliefs, it seems to me, can have nothing in common. If, while the taxidermists are stuffing my integument for some fortunate museum of anatomy, a celestial catchpole summons my psyche to Heaven, I shall be very gravely disappointed, but (unless my habits of mind change radically at death) I shall accept the command as calmly as possible, and face eternity without repining.

Most of the sorrows of man, I incline to think, are caused by just such repining. Alone among the animals, he is dowered with the capacity to invent imaginary worlds, and he is always making himself unhappy by trying to move into them. Thus he underrates the world in which he actually lives, and so misses most of the fun that is in it. That world, I am convinced, could be materially improved, but even as it stands it is good enough to keep any reasonable man entertained for a lifetime.

As for me, I roll out of my couch every morning with the most agreeable expectations. In the morning paper there is always massive and exhilarating evidence that the human race, despite its ages-long effort to imitate the seraphim, is still doomed to be irrevocably human, and in my morning mail I always get soothing proof that there are men left who are even worse asses than I am.

It may be urged that such satisfactions are lowly; nevertheless, the fact remains that they are satisfactions. Would the tinsel world that idealists pant for be better? Would it be really habitable at all? I am ready to doubt it formally. It would be swept, at best, by chill winds; there would be no warming glow of human folly. There would be no Lindberghs in it, to risk their necks preposterously and charmingly; there would be no Comstocks and Wayne B. Wheelers, no Hoovers and Coolidges; there would be no poets with their pretty bellyaches; above all, there would be no theologians. And maybe no Americans.

II

One hears complaint that the existing world is being Americanized, and hence ruined. It may be that my steadfast refusal to join in that complaint is patriotism; if so, make the most of it. Here in these States, if we have accomplished nothing else, we have at least brought down all the more impossible varieties of human aspiration to absurdity, and so made life the more endurable. Alone among the great nations of history we have got rid of religion as a serious scourge—and by the simple process of reducing it to a petty nuisance. Alone again, we have rid ourselves of the worst curses that lie in politics—and by the easy and obvious device of making politics comic.

The Fathers of the Republic, I believe, were far cleverer fellows than they are commonly represented to be, even in the schoolbooks. If it was not divine inspiration that moved them, then they must have drunk better liquor than is now obtainable on earth. For when they made religion a free-for-all, they prepared the way for making it ridiculous; and when they opened the doors of office to the mob, they disposed forever of the delusion that government is a solemn and noble thing, by wisdom out of altruism. The bald facts stand before every eye to-day; it is a joyous and instructive business to contemplate them. And it is even more joyous and instructive to contemplate the sad heavings of those who still refuse to face them, but try to get rid of them by the arts of the prestidigitator and the rhetorician.

When I travel abroad, which is no oftener than I can help it, I am always depressed by the gloom of the so-called intellectuals. My acquaintance among them, in most of the countries of Europe, is somewhat large, and so I can't escape their agonies. Everywhere they fret themselves to death over the problem of government. Everywhere they plan to bring in Utopia by turning this gang out and putting that gang in. Everywhere they believe in wizards and messiahs. It seems to me that we in America—that is, those of us who have become immune to rhetoric—have got beyond that naïveté, and that we are the sounder and happier for it. Reconciling ourselves to the incurable swinishness of government, and to the inevitable stupidity and roguery of its agents, we discover that both stupidity and roguery are bearable—nay, that there is in them a certain assurance against something worse.

The principle is surely not new in the world: everyone ought to know by this time that a mountebank, thinking only of to-morrow's cakes, is far safer with power in his hands than a prophet and martyr, his eyes fixed frantically upon the rewards beyond the grave. So a prudent man prefers Hoover to Stalin or Mussolini, or even to Ramsay MacDonald, a Scotsman and hence a fanatic. No doubt Al Smith would have been better, if only on Burke's theory that politics is at its best when it is most closely adjusted, not to reason, but to human nature. But Hoover is natural enough for all everyday purposes; and where his timidity makes him fall short, his failure is concealed by the glorious labors of such corn-doctors as Borah, Jim Watson, Charlie Curtis, Andy Mellon and Old Joe Grundy.

Here I do not argue that mountebanks are more admirable than honest men; I merely argue that, in such fields as those of politics and religion— to which, of course, the master-quackery of pedagogy ought to be added— they are socially safer and more useful. The question before us is a practical one: how are we to get through life with a maximum of entertainment and a minimum of pain? I believe that the answer lies, at least in part, in ridding solemn ponderosities of their solemn ponderosity, in putting red noses on all the traditional fee-faw-fo-fums.

That enterprise, by the cunning of the Fathers, we have been able to carry further in the United States than it is carried anywhere else. Do strong men blubber against the outrage of prohibition? Then smell their breaths to see how real their grievance is. Are there protests against the clubs of the police? Then compare a few amiable bumps on head to a quart of Mussolini's castor oil. Do jobholders consume the substance of the people? Then ask the next Englishman you meet to show you his income tax bill. And are the high places of the land held by trashy and ignoble fellows, bent only upon their own benefit? Then take a look at the scoundrels who constitute the state in France.

III

I have said that the Fathers, by making religion a free-for-all, reduced it to innocuous absurdity. No doubt many a saddened patriot will enter a caveat to that, thinking of Cardinal O'Connell and his effort to make Boston a Dublin slum, and Bishop Cannon and his bold attempt to run the whole United States. But these rev. gentlemen really prove my case. For after all, Monsignor Cannon, even with both White House and Capitol quaking every time he looks up from the stock ticker, has *not* succeeded in forcing prohibition upon the country: all he has succeeded in doing is to make his whole moral system odious and the theology behind it infamous. Nor has His Eminence of South Boston achieved anything better. When he came into his princely dignity, the church he serves was plainly making progress in America, and there was a steady infiltration of intellectuals into it. But now it is headed in the other direction, and every time he arises to denounce Einstein or to launch his janissaries against a new book, its momentum is accelerated.

In this department I have myself been an eyewitness of a large and salubrious change—and it is a pleasure, from the opposition bench, to offer it as a set-off to all the public skullduggery that the tender-minded complain of. That change has to do with the general American attitude toward ecclesiastical organizations, and especially toward the one that Dr. Cannon adorns. I well remember the uproar that followed a polite allegation I chanced to make, now nearly twenty years ago, that the Methodist Church, at least in the South, was operated by charlatans and manned by ignoramuses. The editor of the paper in which it appeared—his dark, innocent eyes wet with tears—stared at me as if I had denounced female chastity or advocated cannibalism. His office was overrun for weeks by prancing pastors, threatening him with disaster. They met in conclave and passed resolutions against him and me; some of them, with their fingers carefully crossed, prayed publicly for my salvation.

Fortunately, they also challenged my facts, and under the pretense of meeting that challenge it was possible for me to renew and reiterate my allegation. But it went down very badly, and for a long while I was under the displeasure of so-called fair men for raising a religious rumpus, and for failing in that respect which, so it appeared, was due to all bodies of believers. Even when, five or six years later, the Anti-Saloon League began running its trails of corruption across the country, and I ventured to point out the patent fact that it was the offspring of Methodism and as anti-social as its parent—even then such charges were generally felt to be somewhat advanced. So again when the Ku Klux emerged from the swamps and began trying to put down civilization. The first article in which I spoke of it as no more than the secular arm of the Methodist-Baptist Inquisition was badly received, and I was widely advised to confine myself to constructive criticism.

This advice made some impression on me: I became, in fact, more or less constructive. But meanwhile Bishop Cannon and his friends went into politics full tilt, brandishing clubs and howling for blood, and before long what had once seemed scandalous became only too self-evident. The Southern editors, for a time, had very hard sledding; they had to discuss politics without mentioning the principal current politicians. But that was soon a sheer impossibility, even to publicists so subtle, and presently they were ventilating the facts with candor, and politics in their dismal section became realistic again, and very lively. To-day they all belabor the Methodist Crokers and Charlie Murphys[7] in a hearty and open manner, and have their say about the whole evangelical camorra in precisely the same terms they use against the Italian Black Hand, the Vice Trust and the American Civil Liberties Union.

Nor is this new frankness confined to the South. The last presidential campaign brought the subject of evangelical theology into open discussion everywhere, and the result, as I see it, is a great increase in public pleasure, and, to some extent at least, in public enlightenment. With all the old taboos got rid of, that theology is being revealed as what it actually is—a decadent form of Puritanism, preposterous in its ideology and brutal and dishonest in its practices. If the hinds of the farms and villages still cling to it, then certainly it is fast losing its hold upon all the ranks above them. To confess to a belief in it to-day is to confess not only to stupidity, but also to a kind of malignancy—a delight in opposing decent ideas and harrowing honest men.

For that change, so swift and so sanitary, we have to thank Bishop Cannon and his colleagues of the Anti-Saloon League, the Ku Klux Klan and the Methodist Board of Temperance, Prohibition and Public Morals. They have gained (at least transiently) a formidable power over politicians even worse than they are, but they have wrecked their church. They have won a battle and lost a war.

The wrecking of such churches as these, whether they be spiritual or secular, seems to me to be an excellent gauge of the progress of civilization. For men become civilized, not in proportion to their willingness to believe, but in proportion to their readiness to doubt. The more stupid the man, the larger his stock of adamantine assurances, the heavier his load of faith.

IV

There is a darky living in the alley behind my house who knows a great deal more than I do, and is far more positive and confident in his kind of knowledge than I am in mine. He knows that he will be snow-white in the life beyond the grave, and that the Twelve Apostles will be very polite to him. He knows that a rabbit-foot carried in his pocket will protect him against thieves, warts, and the police. He knows that the fall of the die may be conditioned by verbal formulas, mainly theological in character. He knows that meeting a black cat on a dark night is comparable, practically speaking, to meeting a locomotive head-on. He knows precisely why the stars were hung in the sky, and how they are kept there, and what their influence is upon the destiny of man. He knows what Moses said to Abraham, and what Abraham said to Pontius Pilate. He is the proprietor of a perfect epistemology, and his cosmogony, pathology and political science are neat, well-rounded and completely sufficient for his standards of judgment. To find his match as a wiseacre one must resort to the Rev. Billy Sunday, to Arthur Brisbane, or to the Pope.[8]

Nevertheless, I am iconoclast enough to doubt his whole stock of wisdom, as I doubt, indeed, that of his three colleagues in omniscience. His certainty that cancer is caused by incantations seems to me to be somehow dubious. I prefer to believe that no one knows what causes it, and to reckon that belief a kind of knowledge.

The common view of science is that it is a sort of machine for increasing the race's store of dependable facts. It is that only in part; in even larger part it is a machine for forgetting *un*dependable facts. When Copernicus proved that the earth revolved around the sun, he did not simply prove that the earth revolved around the sun; he also proved that the so-called revelation of God, as contained in the Old Testament, was rubbish. The first fact was relatively trivial: it made no difference to the average man then, as it makes no difference to him to-day. But the second fact was of stupendous importance, for it disposed at one stroke of a mass of bogus facts that had been choking the intelligence and retarding the progress of humanity for a millennium and a half.

So with every other great discovery in the physical world: it had immediate repercussions in the world of ideas, and often they were far more important than its immediate effect. The long line of glorious workers in medicine are not to be regarded merely as cheaters of the grave, for the grave, in the long run, has cheated every one of them in turn; their service to man was that they dissuaded him from laying vain blames for his ills and making vain and ignominious appeals for and against them, and set him to examining them, and himself with them, in a rational and self-respecting manner. That medicine saves to-day thousands who must have died yesterday is a fact of small significance, for most of them will leave no more marks upon the history of the race than so many June bugs; but that all of us have been persuaded thereby to turn from priests and magicians when we are ill to doctors and nurses—that is a fact of massive and permanent importance. It benefits everybody worthy of being called human at all. It rids the thinking of mankind of immense accumulations of intellectual garbage. It increases the dignity of every honest man and it diminishes the puissance of every fraud.

To believe in frauds, it seems to me, is incompatible with any sort of dignity. It may be held, by the sorry standards which prevail in certain quarters, to be virtuous, but it is plainly not dignified. Is it a fact that the authors of the New Testament were inspired by God, and compiled a record that is innocent of error? It is not a fact. They were ignorant and credulous men, and they put together a narrative that is as discordant and preposterous, at least in material parts, as the testimony of six darkies in a police court. Is it a fact that believing that narrative is an act of merit, and that its reward is deliverance from Hell and entrance upon an eternity of bliss? It is not a fact. More, it is not even an innocent fiction. For its necessary implication is that the test of a proposition is something unrelated to its truth—that lying is virtuous so long as it brings a reward.

There, it seems to me, pragmatism is run to earth at last and turns out to be, not a lion, but only a fox. I can imagine no self-respecting man haggling for advantage on any such terms. It involves not only a repudiation of every rational criterion of truth; it also involves a repudiation of every sort of decency. Whenever such an idea is unhorsed in the world, the integrity of man increases.

The supply, unluckily, still remains very large. Its reservoir is the mob, uneducable and irrational, and along the banks of that reservoir many enterprising frauds—theological, political and philosophical—find profitable fishing. There are impatient men who long to heave the whole company overboard at one swoop: they are the fashioners of Utopias. But human progress, of course, can never be so facile. It must be carried on, not with the cosmic engines of gods, but with the puny machinery at hand; and that machinery, as everyone knows, is always breaking down.

The Fathers of the Republic, despite the sagacity that I have been praising, were a bit too confident and impatient. I suppose they believed that by setting religion adrift they had got rid of it, but all they had really done was to make it ready for self-wrecking years after their day was done. Again and even worse, they bent their hardest endeavors to setting up a government of the most sagacious, the most honorable, the most fit—but all they actually achieved was to let in the least fit, and a century and a half afterward we are still struggling to get rid of the Hardings, Coolidges and Hoovers.

V

Things would move faster if there were a general agreement as to the goal, but that is too much to hope for. There are men in the world, and some of them not unintelligent men, who have a natural appetite for the untrue, just as there are others who have a natural appetite for the ugly. A bald fact somehow affrights them: they long to swathe it in comforting illusions. Thus one hears from them that it is somehow immoral for an artist to depict human life as it actually is: the spectacle of the real must be ameliorated by an evocation of the ideal, which is to say, of the *un*real. So Thomas Hardy becomes a bad artist, and the author of *Pollyanna* a good one.[9]

One hears again, and from the same men, that religious faith is a valuable thing *per se,* even if it be faith in propositions revolting to the most elementary intelligence. And one hears that it is an evil business to dwell upon the gross and intolerable failures of democracy, lest the general belief in democracy itself be converted into doubt. The facts, it appears, are nothing; the important thing is to retain a hopeful and pleasant frame of mind. The most valuable philosopher is that one who conjures up glittering universes in which two and two make five, six or even ten; the most despicable is the fellow who keeps on insisting that they make only four.

Of such sort are the reconcilers of science and religion, the more naïve variety of Liberals in politics, and the various disciples of Hamilton Wright Mabie and Edward W. Bok in the arts. I daresay the first-named were an active and expectant party in the day of Copernicus; if so, they must have given a great deal less comfort to Copernicus than to Pope Paul III. They continue energetically to-day, proving that Genesis and the Darwinian hypothesis are not in conflict, that curved space is still reconcilable with the Book of Revelation, and that, in any case, it is better to go to church on Sunday than to stay away.

The tragedy of such men is that, in the long run, they are bound to find that they are holding empty bags. The Popes, soon or late, always go over to Copernicus, as Dr. Andrew D. White once proved in two noble tomes. The truth, battered and torn, yet survives all the pretty nothings that beset it. Out of the welter of hopes and fears, of cautions and evasions, there always arises in the end the gaunt, immovable figure of a solid fact.

Certainly the Liberals in our midst should have learned long ago how dangerous it is to tackle such facts with no better weapons than hosannas. Is it so soon forgotten that they once believed in Roosevelt? And then in Wilson? And then in the War to End War? And then in a long series of other impostures, ranging from the initiative and referendum to the direct primary, and from woman suffrage to prohibition? There is more here than mere innocence; there is also, it seems to me, a downright libido for the improbable, a thirst to believe what can scarcely be imagined as true.

Certainly something of the sort must be sought in the current Liberal crush upon Holmes, J., an upright judge but no more fit to be a hero of Liberals than his predecessor in their adoration, the limber Borah. I have been vastly diverted of late by reading the volume of Dr. Holmes's dissenting opinions, so conveniently arranged by Mr. Alfred Lief. It shows that his juridic theory, taking it by and large, is hardly to be distinguished from that of the late Mr. Chief Justice Taft, and that not a few of his dissenting opinions have been launched against a more liberal majority![10] Yet the Liberals, with their craving for unrealities, continue to hail him as one of them, and when disillusionment overtakes them at last, as overtake them it must, they will no doubt turn to some even more impossible hero—maybe even to Mr. Chief Justice Hughes or Old Joe Grundy.

Such is the will to believe. Holding it to be a great nuisance in the world, and worse even than the will to power, I try to keep myself as free of it as I can. On gloomy days I speculate as to the probable state of modern man if it had ever been universal. We'd still be following Pope Paul; nay, not the Pope of that name but the Saint, with his cocksure ignorance and his Little Bethel moral scheme. Perhaps we'd be even further back than that—among the sheiks of the Palestine plateau and the primitive shamans of the Central Asian wilderness. It seems to me that such prophets as Dr. Robert A. Millikan, when they flirt gravely with the rev. clergy, ask us to go back almost that far.

Are the clergy true teachers or false? Is the body of ideas that they merchant true or not true? If it is not true, then I can imagine no prudent and profitable traffic with them. They have a right, of course, to be heard, but they have no more right to be attended to than the astrologers and necromancers who were once their colleagues and rivals.

There is only one man who has a right to be attended to, and that is the man who is trying, patiently, fairly, earnestly, diligently, to find out the truth. I am willing to give him my ear at any time of the day or night, year in and year out. But I am not willing to listen to the man who argues that what might be or ought to be true is somehow superior to what *is* true. Copernicus, it seems to me, is worth all the Popes who ever lived, and all the bishops and archbishops, and all save a baker's dozen of holy saints.

VI

The title of this article is far too wide. No man, within the bounds of a magazine, could make anything approaching a complete or even a fair statement of his credo. I must content myself, after the foregoing prolegomenon, with a few random notes.

I believe that religion, generally speaking, has been a curse to mankind—that its modest and greatly overestimated services on the ethical side have been more than overborne by the damage it has done to clear and honest thinking.

I believe that no discovery of fact, however trivial, can be wholly useless to the race, and that no trumpeting of falsehood, however virtuous in intent, can be anything but vicious.

I believe that all government is evil, in that all government must necessarily make war upon liberty; and that the democratic form is at least as bad as any of the other forms.

I believe that an artist, fashioning his imaginary worlds out of his own agony and ecstasy, is a benefactor to all of us, but that the worst error we can commit is to mistake his imaginary worlds for the real one.

I believe that the evidence for immortality is no better than the evidence for witches, and deserves no more respect.

I believe in complete freedom of thought and speech, alike for the humblest man and the mightiest, and in the utmost freedom of conduct that is consistent with living in organized society.

I believe in the capacity of man to conquer his world, and to find out what it is made of, and how it is run.

I believe in the reality of progress.

I—

But the whole thing, after all, may be put very simply. I believe that it is better to tell the truth than to lie. I believe that it is better to be free than to be a slave. And I believe that it is better to know than to be ignorant.

[*Forum,* September 1930]

IMMORTALITY

Immortality without consciousness would obviously be absurd, and I can imagine no consciousness without the integrity of the physical organism. The evidences of survival amassed by spiritualists seem to me to be almost as preposterous as the evidences and arguments put forward by theologians. I have been examining them carefully for many years; they leave me more convinced that death is the end than I was when I began. The only plausible argument for survival that I have ever encountered was put forward by the late Cardinal Gibbons. It was to the general effect that a belief in immortality is universal in man, that it is instinctive rather than logical, and that its instinctive character offers ground for believing that there must be some foundation of fact under it. But even that argument is full of holes. It is going beyond the facts, in the first place, to say that all men believe in immortality. I do not, and I know hundreds of other men who do not. In the second place, a universal belief is by no means evidence, for if it were, then the existence of dragons and phoenixes, not to say demons and witches, might have been established in the Middle Ages. Finally, I doubt that instinct is always, or even generally sound. It may be false and absurd, and even fatal, as every zoölogist knows.

The other arguments for survival seem to me to be palpably fallacious. The spiritualists offer evidence that should shock any intelligent schoolboy, and the theologians lay down dogmas that scarcely deserve to be discussed. In all such men there is an obviously eager desire to survive. But that desire is by no means universal. I lack it, and so do many other men. It is my hope, as it is my belief, that death is the end. Life is pleasant and I have enjoyed it, but I have no yearning to clutter up the Universe, a shape without a habitation or a name, after it is over.

[Contribution to Jacob Helder, *Greatest Thoughts on Immortality*
(New York: Smith, 1930), pp. 112–14]

II

SOME OVERVIEWS

NIETZSCHE ON RELIGION

Of the late Professor Friedrich Wilhelm Nietzsche, Ph.D., of the University of Basel, one hears a lot of startling gabble in these days of war, chiefly from the larynxes of freshwater college professors, prima donna preachers, English novelists, newspaper editorial writers, Chautauqua yapyankers and other such hawkers of piffle. He is depicted as an intellectual pestilence, a universal fee-faw-fum, a high priest of diabolism. All bowels of compassion are denied him. It is solemnly and indignantly argued, not only that he plotted and hatched the burning of Louvain (as if a special devil were needed to account for so commonplace an act of war!), but also that he left behind him detailed plans and specifications for the blowing up of all the churches of Christendom, the butchery of all their rectors and curates and the sale into levantine bondage of all their communicants, without regard to age, virtue or sex. It is more than hinted that the Turks have adopted him as their god, vice Allah, resigned in disgust. His hand is seen in the last forty or fifty massacres of Armenians, the *pogrom* of Kishinev, the *Titanic* disaster, the cruise of the *Emden,* the eruption of Mont Pelée, the Claflin failure, the assassination of King Carlos, the defeat of the Prohibition amendment, the torpedoing of the *Audacious,* the shelling of Rheims and the Italian earthquake. He is credited with advocating a war of extermination upon all right-thinking and forward-looking men, especially his fellow Germans. He is hailed as the patron and apologist of all crimes of violence and chicane, from mayhem to simony, and from piracy on the high seas to seduction under promise of marriage. And his critics and expositors, as if to prove their easy familiarity with him, spell his name variously Nietshe, Neitzsky, Nittzske, Neitzschi, Nietschke, Neatsche, Nietzkei, Niztzsche, Nzeitsche, Neitzschy, Nieztskie and Nistskie.

I dare say you have got enough of this windy nonsense, this imbecile Nietzsche legend, and so thirst for no more of it. But an accurate and intelligent account of Nietzsche's ideas by one who has studied them and understands them, is, as Mawruss Perlmutter would say, yet another thing again.[1] Seek in *What Nietzsche Taught,* by Willard H. Wright, and you will find it. Here, in the midst of the current obfuscation, are the plain facts, set down by one who knows them. Wright has simply taken the eighteen volumes of the Nietzsche canon[2] and reduced each of them to a chapter. All of the steps in Nietzsche's arguments are jumped; there is no report of his frequent disputing with himself; one gets only his conclusions. But Wright has arranged these conclusions so artfully and with so keen a comprehension of all that stands behind them that they fall into logical and ordered chains, and are thus easily intelligible, not only in themselves, but also in their interrelations. The book is incomparably more useful than any other Nietzsche summary that I know. It does not, of course, exhaust Nietzsche, for some of the philosopher's most interesting work appears in his arguments rather than in his conclusions, but it at least gives a straightforward and coherent account of his principal ideas, and the reader who has gone through it carefully will be quite ready for the Nietzsche books themselves.

These principal ideas all go back to two, the which may be stated as follows:

1. Every system of morality has its origin in an experience of utility. A race, finding that a certain action works for its security and betterment, calls that action good; and finding that a certain other action works to its peril, it calls that other action bad. Once it has arrived at these valuations it seeks to make them permanent and inviolable by crediting them to its gods.

2. The menace of every moral system lies in the fact that, by reason of the supernatural authority thus put behind it, it tends to remain substantially unchanged long after the conditions which gave rise to it have been supplanted by different, and often diametrically antagonistic conditions.

In other words, systems of morality almost always outlive their usefulness, simply because the gods upon whose authority they are grounded are hard to get rid of. Among gods, as among office-holders, few die and none resign. Thus it happens that the Jews of today, if they remain true to the faith of their fathers, are oppressed by a code of dietary and other sumptuary laws—*i.e.,* a system of domestic morality—which has long since ceased to be of any appreciable value, or even of any appreciable meaning, to them. It was, perhaps, an actual as well as a statutory immorality for a Jew of ancient Palestine to eat shell-fish, for the shell-fish of the region he lived in were scarcely fit for human food, and so he endangered his own life, and worked damage to the community of which he was a part when he ate them. But these considerations do not appear in the United States of today. It is no more imprudent for an American Jew to eat shell-fish than it is for him to eat *süss-und-sauer.* His law, however, remains unchanged, and his immemorial God of Hosts stands beind it, and so, if he would be counted a faithful Jew, he must obey it. It is not until he definitely abandons his old god for some more modern and intelligible god that he ventures upon disobedience. Find me a Jew eating oyster fritters and I will show you a Jew who has begun to doubt very seriously that the Creator actually held the conversation with Moses described in the nineteenth and subsequent chapters of the Book of Exodus.

It is Nietzsche's chief thesis that most of the so-called Christian morality of today is an inheritance from the Jews, and that it is quite as much out of harmony with the needs of our race and time as the Mosaic law which prohibits the eating of oysters, clams, swine, hares, swans, terrapin and snails, but allows the eating of locusts, beetles and grasshoppers (Leviticus 11:4–30). Christianity, true enough, did not take over the Mosaic code *en bloc.* It rejected all these dietary laws, and it also rejected all the laws regarding sacrifices and most of those dealing with the family relations. But it absorbed unchanged the ethical theory that had grown up among the Jews during the period of their decline—the theory, to wit, of humility, of forbearance, of non-resistance. This theory, as Nietzsche shows, was the fruit of that decline. The Jews of David's day were not gentle. On the contrary, they were pugnacious and strong, and the bold assertiveness that seemed their best protection against the relatively weak peoples surrounding them was visualized in a mighty and thunderous Jehovah, a god of wrath and destruction, a divine Kaiser. But as their strength decreased and their enemies grew in power they were gradually forced into a more conciliatory policy. What they couldn't get by force they had to get by a show of complaisance and gentleness—and the result was the renunciatory morality of the century or two preceding the birth of Christ, the turn-the-other-cheek morality which Christ erected into a definite system, the "slave-morality" against which Nietzsche whooped and raged nearly two thousand years afterward.

The whole of Nietzsche's protest may be thus reduced to a single question: Why should a strong nation of to-day continue to give lip service to a system of morality which was devised by a weak race—in his own words, a race of slaves—to conciliate and mollify its masters, and so protect it from wrath and destruction? The cause of that survival is plain enough: it lies in the fact that the supernatural authority behind the system is still accepted. The necessities of life impose upon all healthy peoples and upon all healthy individuals an incessant compromise in morality, but Christianity still remains the general ideal, and every violation of it, however unescapable, is felt to be a wrong. The result is an almost universal hypocrisy. The Germans, on the one hand, argue with a great show of plausibility that their invasion of Belgium was absolutely necessary for their own security, and yet, on the other hand, they admit in so many words that it was wrong. The English, in the same way, argue that they could not avoid taking sides with the Mongolian races against the integrity of the white race, and yet they are plainly full of doubts about the morality of it, and devote all their traditional casuistry to the business of apologizing for it. And here at home we Americans go to church and call upon the Most High to stop the war forthwith—and then proceed to wring a bloody profit from the necessities of the contending nations. The best Christian among us is inevitably the most shameless hypocrite. There is probably no man in America who harbors a more genuine belief in the Christian doctrine of brotherhood and good will than the Hon. William Jennings Bryan, and yet it would be difficult to find a man who has devoted a larger part of his life to furious and merciless combat, or who seeks with greater ardor to rout, cripple and destroy his enemies. The whole uplift is Christian in theory, and yet the whole uplift is inordinately savage and vindictive in practise.

Keep all this in mind, and nine-tenths of Nietzsche becomes crystal clear. His objection to Christianity is simply that it is mushy, preposterous, unhealthy, insincere, enervating. It lays its chief stress, not upon the qualities of vigorous and efficient men, but upon the qualities of the weak and parasitical. True enough, the vast majority of men belong to the latter class: they have very little enterprise and very little courage. For these Christianity is good enough. It soothes them and heartens them; it apologizes for their vegetable existence; it fills them with an agreeable sense of virtue. But it holds out nothing to the men of the ruling minority; it is always in direct conflict with their vigor and enterprise; it seeks incessantly to weaken and destroy them. In consequence, Nietzsche urged them to abandon it. For such men he proposed a new morality—in his own phrase, a "transvaluation of values"—with strength as its highest good and renunciation as its chiefest evil. They waste themselves to-day by pulling against the ethical stream. How much faster they would go if the current were with them! But as I have said—and it cannot be repeated too often—Nietzsche by no means proposed a general repeal of the Christian ordinances. He saw that they met the needs of the majority of men, that only a small minority could hope to survive without them. In the theories and faiths of this majority he had little interest. He was content to have them believe whatever was most agreeable to them. His attention was fixed upon the minority. He was a prophet of aristocracy. He planned to strike the shackles from the masters of the world. . . .

[*Smart Set,* March 1915]

THE ANTHROPOMORPHIC DELUSION

Religion, as religion, gradually dies out in the world, but the anthropocentric delusion at the bottom of it still flourishes. What else is behind charity, philanthropy, pacifism, the uplift, all the rest of the current pishposh? One and all, these sentimentalities are based upon the notion that man is a noble animal, and that his continued existence and multiplication ought to be facilitated and made safe. Nothing could be more gratuitous and absurd. As animals go, even in so limited a space as our world, man is botched and ridiculous. Few other brutes are so stupid, so docile or so cowardly. The commonest yellow dog has far sharper senses and is infinitely more courageous, not to say more honest and dependable. The ants and the bees are more intelligent and ingenious; they manage their government with vastly less quarrelling, wastefulness and imbecility; the worship of cads and poltroons is unknown among them. The lion is more beautiful, more dignified, more majestic. The antelope is swifter and more graceful. The ordinary house-cat is cleaner. The horse, foamed by labor, has a better smell. The gorilla is kinder to his children and more faithful to his wife. The ox and the ass are more industrious and patient. But most of all, man is deficient in courage, perhaps the noblest quality of them all. He is not only mortally afraid of all other animals of his own weight, or half his weight—save a few that he has debased by inbreeding—he is even mortally afraid of his own kind—and not only of their fists and hooves, but even of their snickers.

Moreover, man is also a physical weakling—the most fragile and ridiculous creature in all creation. No other animal is so defectively adapted to its environment. The human infant, as it comes into the world, is so puny that if it were neglected for two days running it would infallibly perish, and this congenital infirmity, though more or less concealed later on, persists until death. Man is ill far more than any other animal, both in his savage state and under civilization. He has more different diseases and he suffers from them oftener. He is more easily exhausted and injured. He dies more horribly, and sooner. Practically all the other higher vertebrates, at least in their wild state, live longer and retain their faculties to a greater age. Here even the anthropoid apes are far beyond their human cousins. An orang-outang marries at the age of seven or eight, raises a family of seventy or eighty children, and is still as hale and hearty at eighty-five as a Seventh Day Adventist at forty-five.

All the amazing errors and incompetencies of the Creator reach their climax in man. As a piece of mechanism he is the worst of them all; put beside him, even a mullet or a staphylococcus is a sound and efficient machine. He has the worst kidneys known to comparative zoölogy, and the worst lungs, and the worst heart. His eye, considering the work it is called upon to do, is less efficient than the eye of an earth-worm; an optical instrument maker who made an instrument so intolerably unfit for its work would starve to death. Alone of all animals, terrestrial, celestial or marine, man is unfit to go abroad in the world he inhabits. He must clothe himself, protect himself, swathe himself, armor himself. He is eternally in the position of a turtle born without a shell, a hog without a snout, a fish without scales or fins. Deprived of his heavy and cumbersome trappings, he is defenseless against even flies. In a state of nature he hasn't even a tail to switch them off.

We now come to man's one point of superiority: he has a soul. This is what sets him off from all other animals, and makes him, in a way, their master. The exact nature of this soul has been in dispute for thousands of years, but regarding its function it is possible to speak with some accuracy. That function is to bring man into direct contact with God, to make him aware of God, above all, to make him resemble God. Well, consider the colossal failure of the device! If we assume that man actually does resemble God, then we are forced into the impossible theory that God is a coward, an idiot and a bounder. And if we assume that man, after all these years, does *not* resemble God, then it appears at once that the human soul is as inefficient a machine as the human liver or tonsil, and that man would probably be better off, as the chimpanzee undoubtedly *is* better off, without it.

Such, indeed, is the case. The only practical effect of having a soul is that it fills man with anthropomorphic and anthropocentric vanities—in brief, with the cocky superstitions that make him disgusting. He struts and plumes himself because he has this soul—and overlooks the fact that it doesn't work. Thus he is the supreme imbecile of creation, the *reductio ad absurdum* of animated nature. He is like a cow who believed that she could jump over the moon, and ordered her whole life upon that theory. He is like a bullfrog boasting eternally of fighting lions, and flying over the Matterhorn, and swimming the Hellespont. And yet this is the poor brute we are asked to venerate as a gem in the forehead of the cosmos! This is the worm we are asked to defend as liege lord of the earth—with all its millions of braver, nobler, decenter quadrupeds—its superb lions, its lithe and gallant leopards, its imperial elephants, its honest dogs, its courageous rats! This is the insect we are besought, at infinite trouble, labor and expense, to reproduce!

[*Smart Set,* August 1919]

THE BLACK ART

I

Who was amazed a week or so ago when the local *Polizei,* stumped in their efforts to find the murderer of little Clare Stone, turned to a lady sorcerer to aid them, and promptly jugged an innocent man at her suggestion? Certainly not any one who is familiar with the normal workings of the constabulary mind. A cop believes in spells, witches and ghosts just as every other member of the American booboisie believes in them, and it would be idle to deny it. When I was a police reporter, twenty years or more ago, I knew all of the police captains of Baltimore pretty well, and had the confidence of most of them. There were eight of them in those days, and five of the eight, in my personal knowledge, carried rabbits' feet, and two of them wore strings around their waists to keep off rheumatism.

The most ardent spiritualist I ever knew was a police sergeant of that era, now dead. He visited all the professional mediums of the town, and believed in the powers of nearly all of them. But he did not usually consult them about police business, he was far more interested in playing the lotteries that then flourished, especially the Danish and Cuban lotteries. Every time a new issue of tickets was on sale in the barber shops he would go to see a medium and ask her advice. Once a medium on North Pace street gave him a number which he managed to obtain by paying a premium to a police lieutenant who had bought it, and it won him $100. The news got all over the Police Department, and thereafter only a few cynics kept up any show of skepticism. When, some time later, a new Police Board ordered a round-up of fortunetellers it was hard to get cops to arrest them. Nine-tenths of the gendarmes, in fact, believed fully that a practitioner thus molested had the power to put a spell on them, and I was told seriously that several who had let duty override self-interest actually came down with mysterious illnesses.

II

I hope I may not be mistaken for one who derides the faculties of the constabulary. The truth is that policemen, as a class, are probably appreciably more intelligent than any other group of men of the same general education and environment. The examination that they have to undergo before they join the force is not of such a character that it would strain the cerebrum of a Leibnitz, but it presents very considerable difficulties to simple-minded men, and so the more stupid of them are plucked. Thus they stand above any like group which does not have to face such a test, for example, those of union leaders, City Councilmen, Congressmen, jail guards, Young

Men's Christian Association secretaries, shop-keepers, actors and ordinary workingmen. If they are to be grouped at all, it is not with such morons, but with the generality of lawyers, saloonkeepers, authors, clergymen, osteopaths, hand-books and public officials. Moreover, their everyday duties, after they get into uniform, tend to polish their intellects. It is dull plodding a beat, but it is certainly not as deadening as sitting in an engine house, writing editorials, drawing up deeds, teaching school or adding up figures. Very few policemen ever go crazy.

But, as I say, they are normal 100 per cent. Americanos, obeying the laws and loving the flag, and so it follows necessarily that they believe in the supernatural. The wonders of God enchant and puzzle them, and they turn for light and leading, like all other simple men, at all times and everywhere, to the facile revelations of sorcerers. A few, mainly products of the late Billy Sunday revival, mellow their belief in witchcraft with various modern theological conceptions, but all the same they stick to the elementary demonology that flourished among their remote forebears of the Mediterranean coasts and the Teutonic forests. This demonology is still almost universal in America. It includes a belief in the return of the spirits of the departed, a belief in the efficacy of various ancient spells, a belief in dreams, and a belief in the abnormal talents of professional necromancers, whether spiritualists, seventh sons of seventh sons, crystal gazers, palm-readers, authors of dream books or diviners by cards and tea leaves. There goes therewith an unshakable faith in baleful signs and portents. Observe the report of marriage licenses issued in Baltimore on any Friday. Only a few heretics take the chance. And try to figure out how many bank presidents would show up if the Honorary Pallbearers held their next annual banquet on Friday the 13th.

III

The truth is that freedom from such superstitions, like the capacity for truth and honor, is the exclusive possession of a very small minority of the human race—even in America, a country where education is free and universal, probably not more than one-tenth of one per cent. The whole tendency of human knowledge—I had almost said the whole purpose—is to rid mankind of its primitive fear of the unknown—to push the borders of the known further and further into the darkness—to liberate the human spirit from its helplessness and its dreads. The best definition of civilization that I can think of is one which simply says that it is a state of society in which men have lost their congenital fears—of the dark, of spirits, of death, of wild beasts, of other men. It is to this end that all the greatest men of the race have labored unceasingly. It to this emancipation from unreasoned fear—this substitution of exact knowledge for childish credulity and alarm—that separates the civilized man from the savage.

But how large a part of the human race, under civilization, has a full share in this emancipation? Obviously, it must be a very, very small part. The average man, even the average educated man, is a long way behind the most enlightened minority of men. He has got rid, perhaps, of most of the superstitions that afflicted his grandfather, and of many of those that harassed his father, but he still retains enough out of the original store of the race to make him act, on occasion, not as a rational creature but as an alarmed animal. He may tell you that he doesn't believe in ghosts, but the next moment he will be defending spiritualism on the ground that, in the face of so much testimony, there must be something in it. He may laugh at Christian Science, and yet go to a chiropractor. He may wait under ladders, kiss red-haired girls, kill black cats and boast that he has thirteen letters in his name, and yet refuse to sign a contract on a Friday.

I know very few men, even among those devoted professionally to the acquirement and increase of exact knowledge, who are absolutely free from such lingering weaknesses. I hasten to add that I am certainly not free from them myself. Nothing, save it be spiritualism, seems to me to be more idiotic than palmistry. Yet once a palmist told me that I would be engaged during such-and-such a month, and all through that month I was off my feed, and had nightmares, and could scarcely work.

IV

What we always forget is that civilization is something very new under the sun—that it is no more to the whole of human history than the epidermis is to the whole man. It is nowhere thick enough to stand much strain; it is constantly being abraded. We have sound evidence that man has existed on the earth in much his present state, organized into societies, building houses, making war and keeping records, for nearly 10,000 years—but it is not more than 500 years since even the most enlightened men abandoned their belief in witches, and not more than 200 years since the abandonment become general. When I say general, I mean among the educated class. The ignorant still believe in them. Go into southern Maryland and you will find that practically every darky orders his whole life upon his belief in them, and that fully two-thirds of his white neighbors, though they may deny it, share his ideas.

The belief that it is possible to communicate with the dead goes back to the infancy of man; it was probably one of the first general ideas that engaged the emerging anthropoid; there is reasonable ground for regarding it as the foundation of all religion. If anything should be plain in the world to-day it is the fact that this belief is erroneous. The most overwhelming sort of evidence against it has been accumulated, and this evidence is open to any inquirer. Yet only a year or two ago an eminent British physicist made a tour of the United States retailing a puerile account of his adventures with spooks, and everywhere he went huge crowds flocked to hear him, and all of the crowd were made up of the "best people" of the towns he visited!

[*Baltimore Evening Sun,* March 6, 1922]

THE ASCENT OF MAN

Long ago I proposed the application of Haeckel's biogenetic law—to wit, that the history of the individual rehearses the history of the species—to the domain of human ideas.[3] So applied, it leads to some superficially startling but probably quite sound conclusions . . .

As I say, my suggestion has not been adopted by psychologists, who, in the main, are a very conservative and unimaginative body of men. If they applied the biogenetic law in the field of religion they might make some interesting observations. The chances are, indeed, that religion belongs exclusively to a very early stage of human development, and that its rapid decay in the world since the Reformation is evidence of genuine progress. Reduced to its essence, every religion is simply the doctrine that there are higher powers which take an interest in the affairs of men, and not infrequently intervene in them. This doctrine is not purely romantic and *a priori;* it is based upon what is regarded by its subscribers as objective evidence. But it must be plain that that evidence tends to go to pieces as human knowledge widens—that it appears massive and impressive in direct proportion as the individual impressed is ignorant. A few hundred years ago practically every phenomenon of nature was ascribed to superhuman intervention. The plague, for example, was caused by God's anger. So was war. So was lightning. To-day no enlightened man believes anything of the kind. All these phenomena are seen to be but links in an endless chain of causation, and it is understood that, given a certain quite intelligible and usually inevitable combination of causes, they will appear infallibly as effects. Thus religion gradually loses its old authority, and becomes no more than a sentimentality. An enlightened man's view of it is almost indistinguishable from his view of the Spirit of 1776, the Henty books and the rosewood casket containing his grandmother's false teeth.

Such a man is not "dead" to religion. He was not born with a congenital inaptitude for it. He has simply outgrown it, as he has outgrown poetry, Socialism and love. At adolescence practically all individuals have attacks of piety, but that is only saying that their powers of perception, at that age, outrun their knowledge. They observe the phenomenon, but cannot account for it. Later on, unless their development is arrested, they gradually emerge from that romantic and spookish fog, just as they emerge from the hallucinations of poetry and love. I speak here, of course, as individuals capable of education—always a small minority. If, as the Army tests of conscripts showed, nearly 50 per cent of American adult males never get beyond the mental development of a twelve-year-old child, then it must be obvious that a much smaller number get beyond the mental development of a youth at the end of his teens. I put that number, at a venture, at 5 per cent. The remaining 95 per cent never quite free themselves from religious ideas. They may no longer believe that it is an act of God every time an individual catches a cold, or sprains his ankle, or cuts himself shaving, but they are pretty sure to see some trace of divine intervention in it if he is struck by lightning, or hanged, or afflicted with leprosy or syphilis. That God causes wars has been believed by all the Presidents of the United States, save Grover Cleveland, since Jefferson's time. During the late war the then President actually set aside a day for praying to God to stop what He had started as soon as possible and on favorable terms. This was not done, remember, by a voodoo man in the Congo forest, but by a sound Presbyterian, a Ph.D. of Johns Hopkins University, and the best-dressed professor ever seen at Princeton.

I have said that all religions are based on this notion that there are higher powers which observe all the doings of man, and often take a hand in them. It should be added that a corollary is almost always appended, to the effect that these higher powers pronounce ethical judgments upon human acts, and are themselves animated by a lofty and impeccable morality. Most religions, of course, also embrace the concept of higher powers that are not benign, but malignant—that is, they posit the existence of demons as well as of gods. But there are very few in which the demons are regarded as superior to the gods, or even as their full equals. The great majority of creeds, East and West, savage and so-called civilized, put the gods far above the demons, and teach that the gods always wish the good of man, and that man's virtues run in direct ratio to his obedience to their desires. That is, they are all based upon the doctrine of what is called the goodness of God. This is true preeminently of the chief oriental faiths: Buddhism, Brahmanism and Confucianism. It is true even of Christianity, despite its luxuriant demonology. No genuine Christian can believe that God ever deliberately and wantonly injures him, or could conceivably wish him ill. The slings and arrows of God, he believes, are brought down upon him by his own ignorance and viciousness. He thinks that if he could be like God he would be perfect.

This doctrine of the goodness of God, it seems to me, is no more, at bottom, than an evidence of arrested intellectual development. It does not fit into what we know of the nature and operations of the cosmos today; it is a survival from a day of universal ignorance. That it is still given credit in the Far East is not surprising, for the intellectual development of the Far East, despite all the nonsense that is talked about Indian and Chinese "philosophy," is really no further advanced than that of Europe was in the time of St. Louis. The most profound Hindoo or Chinese "philosopher" believes, as objective facts, things that would make even the Hon. Cal Coolidge snicker, and so his "philosophy" is chiefly worthless, as was that of the Greeks. The Greeks sometimes guessed right, just as the swamis and yoghis of Los Angeles sometimes guess right today, but in the main their speculations, being based upon false observations, were valueless, and no one would pay any attention to them today if it were not for the advertising they get from theologians, who find them to their taste, and professional "philosophers," who make a living trying to teach them to sophomores. But if the belief in the goodness of God is natural to misinformed orientals, as it was natural to the singularly ignorant Greeks, it is certainly *not* natural to the enlightened races of the West today, for all their science is simply a great massing of proofs that God, if He exists, is neither good nor bad, but simply indifferent—an infinite Force carrying on the operation of infinite processes without the slightest regard, either one way or the other, for the comfort, safety and happiness of man.

Why, then, does this belief survive? Largely, I am convinced, because it is supported by another hoary relic from the adolescence of the race, to wit, the weakness for poetry. The Jews fastened their religion upon the western world, not because it was more reasonable than the religions of their contemporaries—as a matter of fact, it was vastly less reasonable than many of them—but because it was far more poetical. The poetry in it was what fetched the decaying Romans, and after them the barbarians of the North; not the so-called Christian evidences. For the Jews were poets of a truly colossal eloquence, and they put their fundamental superstitions into dithyrambs of such compelling loveliness that they disarmed the common sense even of skeptical Romans, and so knocked out all other contemporary religions, many of which were in far closer accord with what was then known of the true operations of the universe. To this day no better poetry has ever been written. It is so powerful in its effects that even men who reject its content in toto are more or less susceptible to it. One hesitates, on purely æsthetic grounds, to flout it; however dubious it may be in doctrine, it is nevertheless almost perfect in form, and so even the most violent atheist tends to respect it, just as he respects a beautiful but deadly toadstool. For no man, of course, ever quite gets over poetry. He may seem to have recovered from it, just as he may seem to have recovered from the measles of his school-days, but exact observation teaches us that no such recovery is ever quite perfect: there always remains a scar, a weakness and a memory.

Now, there is reason for maintaining that the taste in poetry, in the process of human development, marks a stage measurably later than the stage of religion. Savages so little cultured that they know no more of poetry than a cow have elaborate and often very ingenious theologies. If this be true, then it follows that the individual, as he rehearses the life of the species, is apt to carry his taste for poetry further along than he carries his religion—that if his development is arrested at any stage before complete intellectual maturity that arrest is far more likely to leave him with poetical hallucinations than it is to leave him with religious hallucinations. Thus, taking men in the mass, there are many more natural victims of the former than of the latter—and here is where the talent of the ancient Jews does its execution. That is to say, it holds countless thousands to the faith who are actually against the faith: what hamstrings and halters them is their weakness for poetry. Put into plain words, the articles of the faith would revolt them, but intoned as poetry they still work their old magic. This fact, no doubt, explains the great growth of ritualism in an age of skepticism. Almost every day theology gets another blow from science; so badly has it been battered, indeed, that educated men now give it little more credit than they give to witchcraft. But the poetry remains, and it is still powerful enough to hold the allegiance of millions. More, I incline to think that it will be powerful enough forevermore. Soon or late the last surviving theological superstition will be laid by science. But while that business is going on religion will be growing more and more ritualistic, and so, when the final catastrophe comes, it will survive as poetry, as the history of Greece has survived.

In view of all this, I am convinced that the Christian church, as a practical organization, is quite safe from any danger of extinction, despite the rapid growth of agnosticism. The religion it merchants is full of palpable absurdities; many other religions are far more plausible and scientific. But all of these religions contain the fatal defect that they appeal primarily to the reason. Christianity will survive because it appeals to the sense of poetry—to what, in men of arrested development, which is to say, average men, passes for the instinct to seek and know beauty.

[*Smart Set,* May 1923]

HINT TO THEOLOGIANS

The argument by design, once the bulwark of Christian apologetics, is so full of holes that it is no wonder that it has been abandoned. The more, indeed, the theologian seeks to prove the acumen and omnipotence of God by His works, the more he is dashed by evidences of divine incompetence and irresolution. The world is not actually well run; it is very badly run, and no Huxley was needed to point out the obvious fact. The human body, magnificently designed in some details, is a frightful botch in other details;

every first-year student of anatomy sees a hundred ways to improve it. How are we to reconcile this mixture of infinite finesse and clumsy blundering with the concept of a single omnipotent Designer, to whom all problems are equally easy? If He could contrive so efficient and durable a machine as the human hand, then how did He come to make such dreadful botches as the tonsils, the gall-bladder, the uterus and the prostate gland? If He could perfect the hip joint and the ear, then why did He boggle the teeth?

Having never encountered a satisfactory—or even a remotely plausible—answer to such questions, I have had to go to the labor of devising one myself. It is, at all events, quite simple, and in strict accord with all the known facts. In brief, it is this: that the theory that the universe is run by a single God must be abandoned, and that in place of it we must set up the theory that it is actually run by a board of gods, all of equal puissance and authority. Once this concept is grasped all the difficulties that have vexed theologians vanish. Human experience instantly lights up the whole dark scene. We observe in everyday life what happens when authority is divided, and great decisions are reached by consultation and compromise. We know that the effects, at times, particularly when one of the consultants runs away with the others, are very good, but we also know that they are usually extremely bad. Such a mixture of good and bad is on display in the cosmos. It presents a series of brilliant successes in the midst of an infinity of bungling failures.

I contend that my theory is the only one ever put forward that completely accounts for the clinical picture. Every other theory, facing such facts as sin, disease and disaster, is forced to admit the supposition that Omnipotence, after all, may not be omnipotent—a plain absurdity. I need toy with no such nonsense. I may assume that every god belonging to the council which rules the universe is infinitely wise and infinitely powerful, and yet not evade the plain fact that most of the acts of that council are ignorant and foolish. In truth, my assumption that a council exists is tantamount to an a priori assumption that its joint acts are ignorant and foolish, for no act of any conceivable council can be otherwise. Is the human hand perfect, or, at all events, practicable and praiseworthy? Then I account for it on the ground that it was designed by some single member of the council—that the business was handed over to him by inadvertence or as a result of an irreconcilable difference of opinion. Had more than one member participated actively in its design it would have been measurably less meritorious than it is, for the sketch offered by the original designer would have been forced to run a gauntlet of criticisms and suggestions from all the other councillors, and human experience teaches us that most of these criticisms and suggestions would have been inferior to the original idea—that many of them, in fact, would have had nothing in them save a petty desire to maul and spoil the original idea.

But do I here accuse the high gods of harboring discreditable human weaknesses? If I do, then my excuse is that it is impossible to imagine them doing the work universally ascribed to them without admitting their possession of such weaknesses. One cannot imagine a god spending weeks and months, and maybe whole geological epochs, laboring over the design of the human kidney without assuming him to be moved by a powerful impulse to express himself vividly, to marshal and publish his ideas, to win public credit among his fellows—in brief, without assuming him to be egoistic. And one cannot assume him to be egoistic without assuming him to prefer the adoption of his own ideas to the adoption of any other god's. I defy anyone to make the contrary assumption without plunging instantly into clouds of mysticism. Ruling it out, one comes inevitably to the conclusion that the inept management of the universe must be ascribed to clashes of egos, *i.e.,* petty revenges and back-bitings among the gods, for any one of them alone, since we must assume him to be infinitely wise and infinitely powerful, could run it perfectly. We suffer from bad stomachs simply because the god who first proposed making a stomach aroused thereby the ill-nature of those who had not thought of it, and because they proceeded instantly to wreak that ill-nature upon him by improving, *i.e.,* botching, his work. Every right-thinking man admires his own heart, at least until it begins to break down; it seems an admirable machine. But think how much better it would be if the original design had not been butchered by a board of rival designers!

[*American Mercury,* January 1924]

THE GHOSTLY FRATERNITY

Around no class of men do more false assumptions cluster than around the rev. clergy, our lawful commissioners at the Throne of Grace. I proceed at once to a crass example: the assumption that clergymen are necessarily religious. Obviously, it is widely cherished, even by clergymen themselves; the most ribald of us, in the presence of a holy clerk, is a bit self-conscious, reticent and awed. I am myself given to criticizing Divine Providence somewhat freely, but in the company of the rector of my parish, even at the *Biertisch,* I tone down my animadversions to a level of feeble and polite remonstrance. I know the fellow too well, of course, to have any actual belief in his piety. He is, in fact, rather less pious than the average right-thinking Americano, and I doubt gravely that the sorceries he engages in professionally every day awaken in him any emotion more lofty than boredom. I have heard him pray for Coolidge, for the heathen and for rain, but I have never heard him pray for himself. Nevertheless, the public assumption that he is highly devout, though I dispute it, colors all my intercourse with him, and deprives him of hearing some of my most searching and intelligent observations.

All that is needed to expose the hollowness of this ancient delusion is to consider the chain of causes which brings a young man to taking holy orders. Is it, in point of fact, an irresistible religious impulse that sets him to studying exegetics, homiletics and the dog-Greek of the New Testament, and an irresistible religious impulse only, or is it something quite different? I believe that it is something quite different, and that that something may be described briefly as a desire to shine in the world without too much effort. The young theologue, in brief, is commonly an ambitious but somewhat lazy and incompetent fellow, and he studies theology instead of medicine or law because it offers a quicker and easier route to an assured job and public respect. The sacred sciences may be nonsensical bores, but they at least have the vast virtue of short-circuiting, so to speak, the climb up the ladder of security. The young doctor, for a number of years after he graduates, either has to work for nothing or to content himself with the dregs of practise, and the young lawyer, unless he has unusual influence or complete atrophy of the conscience, often teeters on the edge of actual starvation. But the young divine is a safe and distinguished man the moment he is ordained; indeed, his popularity, especially among the faithful who are fair, is often greater at that moment than it ever is afterward. His livelihood is assured instantly. At one stroke, he becomes a person of dignity and importance, eminent in his community, deferred to even by those who question his magic, and vaguely and pleasantly feared by those who credit it.

These facts, you may be sure, are not concealed from ambitious young men of the sort I have mentioned. Such young men have eyes, and even a certain capacity for ratiocination. They observe the four sons of the police sergeant: one a priest at twenty-five, with a fine house to live in, invitations to all christenings and birthday parties for miles around, and plenty of time to go to the ball game on Summer afternoons; the other three struggling desperately to make their livings as piano-movers, tin roofers, motormen or bootleggers. They observe the young Methodist dominie in his Ford sedan, flitting about among the women while their husbands labor down in the yards district, a clean collar around his neck, a solid meal of fried chicken in his gizzard, and his name in the local paper every day. They observe the Baptist dervish in his white necktie, raiding saloons, touring the bawdy houses and raising hell generally, his tabernacle packed every Sunday night, a noble clink of silver in his collection-plates, and a fat purse for him now and then from the Ladies' Aid or the Ku Klux Klan. Only crazy women ever fall in love with young doctors or lawyers, but every young clergyman, if he is so inclined, may have a whole harem, and with infinitely less danger than a struggling lawyer, a bootlegger or a bank clerk runs every day. Even if he is celibate, the sweet ones bathe him in their smiles; in truth, the more celibate he is, the more attention he gets from them. No wonder his high privileges and immunities propagate the sin of envy! No wonder there are still candidates for the pastoral shroud, despite the vast growth of atheism among us!

It seems to me that the majority of the young men who are thus sucked into holy orders are not actually pious at all, but rather somewhat excessively realistic—that genuine piety is far more apt to keep a youth out of the pulpit than to take him into it. The true *dévoté*, frequenting the sacred edifice constantly, becomes too familiar with the daily duties of a clergyman to see any religious satisfaction in them. In the main, they have nothing to do with religion at all, but are basically social or commercial. In so far as a clergyman works at all, he works as the general manager of a corporation, and only too often it is in financial difficulties and rent by factions among the stockholders. His specifically religious duties are of a routine and monotonous nature, and must needs depress him mightily, as a surgeon is depressed by the endless snaring of tonsils and excision of appendices. He debases spiritual exaltation by reducing it to a hollow and meaningless formality, as a politician debases patriotism and a lady of joy debases love. He becomes, in the end, quite anaesthetic to religion, and even hostile to it. The fact is made distressingly visible by the right rev. the bench of bishops. For a bishop to fall on his knees spontaneously and begin to pray to God would make almost as great a scandal as if he mounted his throne in a bathing suit. The piety of the ecclesiastic, on such high levels, becomes chiefly formal and theoretical. The servant of God has been lifted so near to the saints and become so familiar with the inner workings of the divine machinery that the sense of awe and wonder has oozed out of him. He can no more undergo a genuine religious experience than a veteran scene-shifter can laugh at the wheezes of the First Gravedigger. It is, perhaps, well that this is so. If the higher clergy were actually religious some of their own sermons would scare them to death.

True piety survives, not in the pulpit, but in the pew. The young man who is genuinely devout does not risk spiritual suicide by undertaking the study of such subjects as sermon structure, extemporaneous speaking, Bible class management, canon law, elementary Hebrew and the archeology of Asia Minor; he remains on his knees, his soul yearning for kinship with God.

[*American Mercury,* June 1924]

PREACHERS OF THE WORD

I

Misericordia superexaltatur judicio, which is to say, mercy is superior to justice. The saying is credited by the learned to Pope Innocent III, one of the truly great occupants of Peter's chair—in fact, a veritable Harding or even Coolidge among popes.[4] He said it in the first days of the thirteenth century. Since then there have been great improvements in Christian doctrine. In Chicago, the other day, a Catholic parish priest rose in his pulpit, bawled for the blood of the Judean youths, Leopold and Loeb, and delivered a dreadful denunciation of Judge Caverly for sparing their necks.[5]

This Latin brother was singular, considering his rite, but in plenty of company, considering merely his sacred office. On the same day a multitude of Protestant clergymen in Chicago relieved themselves of sentiments to the same general effect. Judging by the press dispatches, indeed, the whole service of God in the town on that day consisted of barbaric yells for the Lord High Executioner. No other subject seems to have been mentioned in the churches. One and all, the anointed of God served Him by heating up the faithful to hatred and revenge, and by reviling a judge who had been guilty of mercy. One and all, they screamed for the lives of two fellow-creatures.

Alas, not a rare spectacle, in this great moral age! A day or two earlier—or was it later?—a gang of clerics from Annapolis, accompanied by pious laymen, appeared before the Hon. Edward M. Parrish, parole commissioner, and protested bitterly against the parole of a man lying in Annapolis jail. Their argument, as reported in the *Sunpaper,* seems to have been very simple. This gentleman, it appeared, had deliberately violated the law. *Ergo,* it was the first duty of the State to keep him in jail—not to dissuade him from his evil ways, but to get revenge upon him!

II

As I say, such episodes are not rare. I could fill columns with them. The sacred office, of late, becomes indistinguishable from that of the policeman and hangman. The Beatitudes are repealed, and re-enacted with jokers. Divine worship becomes a sort of pursuit of villains, with rope and tar-pot. It is the prime duty of the clerk in holy orders, not to combat sin, but to chase, nab and butcher the concrete sinner. The congregation in which the True Faith runs highest is that one in which there is the steadiest and most raucous demand for blood.

Four or five years ago, when the Ku Klux Klan first got on its legs, I made certain inquiries into its origin and nature, and came to the conclusion that it was no more than the Anti-Saloon League in a fresh bib and tucker, and that, in consequence, its head men were mainly Baptist and Methodist clergymen. That conclusion, printed in this place, caused protests, and one amiable Baptist clergyman had at me to the extent of two columns. But who denies the fact today? Surely no one of any intelligence. The Klan, studied at length, turns out to be exactly what the Anti-Saloon League is: a device for organizing the hatreds of evangelical Christians. The Anti-Saloon League is devoted to pursuing those they hate on ethical grounds and the Klan to pursuing those they hate for reasons of dogma. Neither has any other purpose.

Both are run by Baptist and Methodist clergymen, some retired from the sacerdotal office but all full of evangelical zeal and all extraordinarily savage and bloodthirsty. One hears nothing from these holy men save endless demands that this man be deported, that one tarred and feathered, and the other one jailed. The Methodists, a year or so ago, were actually advocating murder. East, West, North and South, the malevolent carnival goes on. Everywhere the faithful are urged to animosity, brutality, hatred, revenge. Everywhere neighbor is aroused against neighbor, and every sign of Christian charity is denounced as criminal. And everywhere this devil's brew is stirred vigorously by men sworn to preach the gospel of Christ.

III

In view of such phenomena, it surely becomes ridiculous to ask, as certain Christians of an elder school do, what is the matter with the churches? What would be the matter with the theaters, if they took off all their plays and put on funerals and surgical operations? What would be the matter with the bootleggers if they swindled their clients with ginger-pop and coca-cola? What ails the churches is that large numbers of them have abandoned Christianity, lock, stock and barrel. What ails them is that some of them, and by no means the least in wealth and influence, are now among the bitterest and most diligent enemies of Christianity ever heard of in this Republic.

Personally, I have little need for the basic consolations of the Christian faith. I am not naturally religious, and seldom seek peace beyond the realm of demonstrable facts. Even my virtues, such as they are, are not properly describable as Christian. If I let an enemy go, it is because I disdain him, not because I pity him. If I do not steal, it is not because I fear hell but because I am too vain. But I am not blind, nevertheless, to the comfort that Christianity gives to other men. It is, for them, an escape from realities too harsh to be borne. It is a way of life that offers them sanctuary from the pains of everyday living, and gives them rest when they are weary and heavy-laden. When they are errant, it offers them mercy. When they faint, it speaks to them of love.

True or not, this faith is beautiful. More, it is useful—more useful, perhaps, than any imaginable truth. Its effect is to slow down and ameliorate the struggle for existence. It urges men to forget themselves now and then, and to think of others. It succors the weak and protects the friendless. It preaches charity, pity, mercy. Let philosophers dispute its premises if they will, but let no fool sneer at its magnificent conclusions. As a body of scientific fact it may be dubious, but it remains the most beautiful poetry that man has yet produced on this earth.

IV

Well, try to imagine a man full of a yearning for the consolations of that poetry. He is tired of the cannibalistic combat that life is; he longs for peace, comfort, consolation. He goes to church. A few hymns are sung, and there arises in the pulpit a gentleman told off to preach. This gentleman, it quickly appears, is not currently merchanting peace. The Beatitudes are not his text. He turns to the Old Testament. There he finds a text to his taste. And, leaping from it as from a springboard, he gives over an hour to damning his fellow-men. He wants them to be sent to jail, to be deported, to be hanged. He demands that the business be dispatched forthwith. He denounces mercy as a weakness and forgiveness as base.

Our Christian friend, with a yell of despair, rushes from the basilica and seeks another. There he hears the pastor call upon the agents of Prohibition to shoot bootleggers. He seeks a third. The pastor denounces girls who kiss their beaux as harlots, and demands that they be taken by the *Polizei* and cast into jail. He seeks a fourth. The pastor praises a Federal judge for refusing a jury trial to a victim of the Anti-Saloon League. He turns to a fifth. The rev. rector calls upon God to singe and palsy the pope. A sixth. The shepherd urges his sheep to watch their neighbors, and report every suspicious whiff. A seventh. The Bolsheviki are on the grill. An eighth. Demands that more prisoners be hanged. A ninth. . . .

But by this time another atheist is on his way to the public library, at 18 knots an hour, to read Darwin, Huxley, Spencer and Nietzsche . . . or maybe Tolstoi. The Christians are being driven out of the churches; their places are being filled by hunters and trappers, *i.e.,* by brutes. A few old-fashioned pastors survive, but they diminish. As they pass, their flocks will have to resort once more to catacombs. There will be, eventually, a Twentieth Amendment. It will proscribe the Beatitudes, as the Eighteenth already proscribes the Eucharist.

[*Baltimore Evening Sun,* September 29, 1924]

THE NEED FOR AN INGERSOLL

What the country lacks is obviously an Ingersoll. It is, indeed, a wonder that the chautauquas have never spewed one forth. Certainly there must be many a jitney Demosthenes on those lonely circuits who tires mightily of the standard balderdash, and longs with a great longing to throw off the white chemise of Service and give the rustics a genuinely hot show. The old game, I suspect, is beginning to play out, even in the Bible Belt. What made the rural Methodists breathe hard and fast at the dawn of the century now only makes them shuffle their feet and cough behind their hands. I have spies in such lugubrious regions, and their reports all agree. The yokelry no longer turn out to the last valetudinarian to gape at colored pictures of the Holy Sepulchre and the Mount of Olives, or to hear a sweating rhetorician on "The Future of America." They sicken of Service, Idealism and Vision. What ails them is that the village movie, the radio and the Ku Klux Klan have spoiled their old taste for simple, wholesome fare. They must have it hot now, or they don't want it at all. The master-minds of chautauqua try to meet the new demand, but cannot go all the way. They experiment gingerly with lectures on eugenics, the divorce evil, women in politics and other such pornographic subjects, but that is not enough. The horticulturists and their wives and issue pant for something more dreadful and shocking—something comparable, on the plane of ideas, to the tarring and feathering of the village fancy woman on the plane of manly sports. Their ears lie back and they hearken expectantly, and even somewhat impatiently. What they long for is a bomb.

My guess is that the one that would blow them highest, and that would shake the most money out of them going up and coming down, is the big black bomb of Atheism. It has not been set off in the Federal Union, formally and with dramatic effect, since July 21, 1899, when Bob Ingersoll was snatched to bliss eternal. Now it is loaded again, and ready to be fired, and the chautauquan who discovers it and fires it will be the luckiest mountebank heard of in these latitudes since George Harvey thrust the halo on Woodrow's brow. For this favorite of fortune, unlike his fellows of the rustic big tops, will not have to drudge out all his days on the lonesome steppes, racking his stomach with fried beefsteak and saleratus biscuit and his limbs with travel on slow and bumpy trains. He will be able almost at once, like

Ingersoll before him and the Rev. Billy Sunday in the lost Golden Age, to horn into the big towns, or, at all events, into the towns, and there he will snore at ease of nights upon clean sheets, with his roll in his pantaloons pocket and a *Schluck* of genuine Scotch under his belt. The yokels, if they want to hear him, will have to come to Babylon in their Fords; he will be too busy and too prosperous to waste himself upon the cow-stable miasmas of the open spaces. Ingersoll, in one month, sometimes took in $50,000. It can be done again; it can be ˼ˍˍˍered. I believe that Dr. Jennings Bryan, if he sold out God tomorrow and went over to Darwin and *Pongo pygmæus,* could fill the largest hall in Nashville or Little Rock a month on end: he would make the most profound sensation the country has known since the Breckenridge-Pollard case, nay, since Hannah and her amazing glands.[6] And what Bryan could do, any other chautauquan could do, if not exactly in the same grand manner, then at least in a grand manner.

But this is a Christian country! Is it, indeed? Then it was doubly a Christian country in the days of Bob the Hell-Cat. Bob faced a Babbittry that still went to church on Sunday as automatically as a Prohibition enforcement agent holds out his hand. No machinery for distracting it from that ancient practise had yet been invented. There were no Sunday movies and vaudeville shows. There were no automobiles to take the whole family to green fields and wet road-houses: the roads were too bad even for buggy-riding. There was no radio. There was no jazz. There were no Sunday comic supplements. There was no home-brewing. Moreover, a high tide of evangelistic passion was running: it was the day of Dwight L. Moody, of the Salvation Army, of prayer-meetings in the White House, of eager chapel-building on every suburban dump. Nevertheless, Bob hurled his challenge at the whole hierarchy of heaven, and within a few short years he had the Babbitts all agog, and after them the city proletariat, and then finally the yokels on the farms. He drew immense crowds; he became eminent; he planted seeds of infidelity that still sprout in Harvard and Yale. Thousands abandoned their accustomed places of worship to listen to his appalling heresies, and great numbers of them never went back. The evangelical churches, fifty years ago, were all prosperous and full of pious enterprise; the soul-snatching business was booming. Since then it has been declining steadily, in prosperity and repute. The typical American ecclesiastic of 1870 was Henry Ward Beecher, a pet of Presidents and merchant princes. The typical American ecclesiastic of 1914 is the Rev. Dr. John

Roach Straton, a pet of yellow journals.

In brief, the United States, despite its gallant resistance, has been swept along, to some extent at least, in the general current of human progress and increasing enlightenment. The proofs that it resists are only too often mistaken for proofs that it hasn't moved at all. For example, there is the rise of the Ku Klux Klan. Superficially, it appears to indicate that whole areas of the Republic have gone over to Methodist voodooism with a bang, and that civilization is barred out of them as effectively as the Bill of Rights is barred out of a Federal court. But actually all it indicates is that the remoter and more forlorn yokels have risen against their betters—and that their uprising is as hopeless as it is idiotic. Whenever the Klan wins, the fact is smeared all over the front pages of the great organs of intelligence; when it loses, which is at least three times as often, the news gets only a few lines. The truth is that the strength of the Klan, like the strength of the Anti-Saloon League and that of the Methodist-Baptist *bloc* of moron churches, the pa of both of them, has always been greatly overestimated. Even in the most barbarous reaches of the South, where every village is bossed by a Baptist dervish, it met with vigorous challenge from the start, and there are not three Confederate States today in which, on a fair plebiscite, it could hope to prevail. The fact that huge hordes of Southern politicians jumped into night-shirts when it began is no proof that it was actually mighty; it is only proof that politicians are cowards and idiots. Of late all of them have been seeking to rid themselves of the tell-tale tar and feathers: they try to ride the very genuine wave of aversion and disgust as they tried to ride the illusory wave of popularity. As the Klan falls everywhere, the Anti-Saloon League tends to fall with it—and the evangelical churches are strapped tightly to both corpses.

This connection, when it was first denounced, was violently denied by the Baptist and Methodist ecclesiastics, but now everyone knows that it was and is real. These ecclesiastics are responsible for the Anti-Saloon League and its swineries, and they are responsible no less for the Klan. In other words, they are responsible, directly and certainly, for all the turmoils and black hatreds that now rage in the bleak regions between the State roads—they are to blame for every witches' pot that now brews in the backwoods of the Union. They have sowed enmities that will last for years. They have divided neighbors, debauched local governments and enormously multiplied lawlessness. They are responsible for more crime than even the wildest foes of the saloon ever laid to its discredit, and it is crime, in the main, that is infinitely more anti-social and dangerous. They have opposed every honest effort to compose the natural differences between man and man, and they have opposed ˙˙ry attempt to meet ignorance and prejudice with enlightenment. Alike, in the name of God, they have advocated murder and they have murdered sense. Where they flourish no intelligent and well-disposed man is safe, and no sound and useful idea is safe. They have preached not only the bitter, savage morality of the Old Testament; they have also preached its childish contempt of obvious facts. Hordes of poor creatures have followed these appalling rogues and vagabonds of the cloth down their Gadarene hill: the result, in immense areas, is the conversion of Christianity into a machine for making civilized living impossible. It is wholly corrupt, rotten and abominable. It deserves no more respect than a pile of garbage.

What I contend is that hundreds of thousands of poor simpletons are beginning to be acutely aware of the fact—that they are not nearly so stupid as they sometimes appear to be—above all, that there is much more native decency in them than is to be found in their ecclesiastical masters. In other words, I believe that they tire of the obscenity. One glances at such a State as Arkansas or such a town as Atlanta and sees only a swarm of bawling Methodists; only too easily one overlooks the fact that the bawling is far from unanimous. Logic is possible, in its rudiments, even to the *Simiidæ*. On the next step of the scale, in the suburbs, so to speak, of *Homo sapiens,* it flourishes intermittently and explosively. All that is needed to set it off is a suitable yell. The first chautauquan who looses such a yell against the True Faith will shake the Bible Belt like an earthquake, and, as they say, mop up. Half his work is already done for him. The True Faith, the only variety of the True Faith known to those hinds, is already under their rising distrust and suspicion. They look for the Ambassador of Christ, and they behold a Baptist elder in a mail-order suit, describing voluptuously the Harlot of Babylon. They yearn for consolation, and they are invited to a raid on bootleggers. Their souls reach out to the eternal mystery, and the evening's entertainment is the clubbing of a fancy woman. All they need is a leader. Christianity is sick all over this pious land. The Christians have poisoned it. One blast upon a bugle horn, and the mob will be ready for the wake.

[*American Mercury,* November 1924]

SERVICES FOR THE DAMNED

I

One of the crying needs of the time, in this imperial Republic, is for a
suave and soothing burial service for the admittedly damned. I speak as one
who has of late attended the funeral orgies of several such gentlemen, each
time to my æsthetic distress. The first of them, having a great abhorrence
of rhetoric, left orders that not a word was to be said. The result was two
gruesome moments: when six of us walked into his house in utter silence
and carried him out, and when we shoved him, in the same silence, into
the crematory. The whole business was somehow unnatural and even a
shade indecent: it seemed a brutal thing to dispatch so charming a fellow
in so cavalier a fashion. The second funeral was even worse. The deceased
was a Socialist of the militantly anti-clerical variety, and threatened, on his
death-bed, to spout obscenities from his coffin if a clergyman were
admitted to the house of mourning. His widow accordingly asked two of
his Socialist friends to address the assemblage. Unluckily, both of them
were in their cups, and their harangues, in consequence, were very painful.
One of them traced the career of Karl Marx in immense detail; the other,
after first denouncing Dr. Coolidge, read half a dozen cantos of dreadful
poetry out of the *Freethinker*.[7] The third funeral was conducted by the
Freemasons, who came in plug hats and with white aprons over their cow-
catchers. Their burial service was long, and full of pseudo-theological fus-
tian. As for me, I'd rather have been planted by a Swedenborgian, whiskers
and all. Or even by a mullah of the Ethical Culture Society.

What is needed, and what I bawl for politely, is a service that is free
from the pious but unsupported asseverations that revolt so many of our
best minds, and yet happily graceful and consoling. It will be very hard, I
grant you, to concoct anything as beautiful as the dithyrambs in the Book
of Common Prayer. Who wrote them originally I don't know, but whoever did it was a poet. They put the highly improbable into amazingly lus-
cious words, and the palpably not-true into words even more caressing and
disarming. It is impossible to listen to them, when they are intoned by a
High Church rector of sepulchral gifts, without harboring a sneaking wish
that, by some transcendental magic, they could throw off their poetical
character and take on the dignity and reliability of prose—in other words,

that the departed could be actually imagined as leaping out of the grave on the Last Morn, his split colloids all restored to their pristine complexity, his clothes neatly scoured and pressed, and every molecule of him thrilling with a wild surmise. I have felt this wish at the funerals of many virtuous and earnest brethren, whose sole sin was their refusal to swallow such anecdotes as the one in 2 Kings 2:23–24.[8] It seems a pity that men of that sort should be doomed to Hell, and it seems an even greater pity that they should be laid away to the banal chin-music of humorless Freemasons and stewed Socialists.

But, so far as I know, no suitable last rites for them have ever been drawn up. Between the service in the Book of Common Prayer (and its analogues, nearly all of them greatly inferior) and the maudlin mortuary dialogues of the Freemasons, Ku Kluxers, Knights of Pythias and other such foes to beauty there is absolutely nothing. Even the professional agnostics, who are violently literary, have never produced anything worthy to be considered: their best is indistinguishable from the text of a flag-drill or high-school pageant. Thus the average American skeptic, when his time comes to return to earth, is commonly knocked off with what, considering his prejudices, may be best described as a razzing. His widow, disinclined to risk scandal by burying him without any ceremonies at all, calls in the nearest clergyman, and the result is a lamentable comedy, creditable neither to honest faith nor to honest doubt. More than once, in attendance upon such an affair, I have observed a sardonic glitter in the eye of the pastor, especially when he came to the unequivocal statement that the deceased would infallibly rise again. Did he secretly doubt it? Or was he poking fun at a dead opponent, now persuaded of the truth of revelation at last? In either case there was something unpleasant in the spectacle. A suitable funeral service for doubters, full of lovely poetry but devoid of any specific pronouncement on the subject of a future life, would make such unpleasantnesses unnecessary.

We have the poets for the job, and I incline to suspect that their private theological ideas fit them for it. Skepticism, in fact, runs with their trade. Most Americans, as everyone knows, give their ecclesiastical affiliations in *Who's Who in America*—especially Congressmen, pedagogues, bank presidents and uplifters. But not the poets. The sole exception, so far as I can make out, is Vachel Lindsay, who reports that he is a member of the "Christian (Disciples) Church," a powerful sect in the No-More Scrub-

Bulls Belt. Even Edgar Albert Guest is silent on the subject, though he mentions the fact that he is a 33° Mason. Frost, George Sterling, Robinson, Sandburg and Masters keep suspiciously mum.[9] I suggest that they meet in some quiet saloon and draw up the ritual I advocate. Let Masters be chairman of the committee: he is a lawyer as well as a poet, and may be trusted to keep within the statutes. And let Sterling be the boss consultor.

II

There is some need, too, for a marriage service for the damned, and at different times attempts have been made to supply it. But all such works seem to emanate from Radicals showing a characteristic lack of humor—and humor is as necessary to a marriage service as poetry is to a funeral service: a fact that the astute authors of the Book of Common Prayer did not overlook. However, the need here is not pressing, for in most American States civil marriage is sufficient, and heretics may be safely united without going before a rhetorician at all. Court clerks and police magistrates perform the job, mumbling unintelligibly out of a mysterious book, perhaps only a stolen Gideon Bible, hollowed to hold cigarettes. The main thing is to pay the fee. Marriages after midnight cost double, and if the bridegroom has the fumes of wine in his head he is apt to lose his watch as well as his liberty.

There are, as I say, marriage services drawn up by antinomians for the use of unbelievers, but they are full of distressing defects. Their lack of humor I have mentioned. Still worse, they are full of indignation—against the promise to obey, against the common theory that a wife is bound to give some supervision to her husband's household, against the convention that she shall adopt his surname. It is hard to give serious attention to such grim notions at a time immemorially viewed as festive and jocose. One hears frequently of wedding guests getting tight: not long ago a Methodist pastor in Missouri was protesting against it publicly. But when they are drawn into sociological controversy it is too much. Such revolutionary wedding services, in point of fact, have never gained much popularity. Now and then a pair of Socialists resorts to one, but even Socialists appear to prefer the harsh, mechanical offices of a court clerk.

Nor is there any active demand for a non-theological christening service. I am constantly amazed, as a bachelor, by the number of children growing up, in these iconoclastic modern days, without any formal naming at all. Not only do heretics spurn the ceremony; even professing Christians often neglect it. In my own nonage practically all babies, at least of the more respectable tribes of the race, were christened. There was a general feeling that failing to put them through was, in some obscure way, a tort against them—that it would bring them bad luck, and perhaps lead to legal difficulties in after life. It is so believed to this day nearly everywhere in Europe, and for sound reasons. Whenever a citizen in those decaying lands comes into contact with the state, which is very often, its agents demand his baptismal certificate as well as his birth certificate. So far, the imbeciles at Washington have not come to that, but it must be plain that they will come to it soon or late, and when the time is finally upon us there will be trouble for all those Americanos whose naming is now trusted to acclamation. They will have to dig up senile aunts and uncles, and produce affidavits that they were known to everyone as so-and-so at some date far in the past, just as they now have to get such affidavits, more often than not, when they want passports. The bureaucracy grinds slowly, but it grinds exceeding fine. Recruited from the mentally deficient, it runs to circular insanities. Let it be proved tomorrow that some John Doe, suspected of favoring the recognition of Russia, was actually baptized Johannes, and it will be sufficient excuse for requiring all of us to prove that we are legally entitled to the names we sign to checks.

III

But all these are side issues. The main thing is that the poets, though most of them seem to have departed from the precincts and protection of Holy Church and her schismatic colonies—since when has a first-rate American poet written a hymn?—have failed, so far, to rise to the occasion when, even among heretics, poets are most pressingly needed. I have suggested that they meet in one of their temples and remedy the lack gloriously, but I don't insist, of course, that their service for the doubting dead be wholly original. The authors of the Book of Common Prayer, though they were poets of great talent, certainly did not trust only to their private inspiration. They borrowed copiously from the old missals, and they borrowed, too, directly from Holy Writ. What they concocted finally was a composite, but it was very discreetly and delicately put together, and remains impregnable to this day, despite many furious efforts to embellish and undo it.

All I propose is that the committee of poets imitate them, but with an avoidance of strophes objectionable in doctrine. Isn't there material enough in the books? There is enough, and to spare. I point to the works of Walt Whitman, now at last passing freely through the mails—to those parts, of course, of a non-erotic and non-political nature. I point to certain memorable stanzas of William Cullen Bryant. I point to Blake, Tennyson, Milton, Shelley, Keats, even Swinburne: what gaudy stuff for the purpose is in "Ave Atque Vale," *Tristram of Lyonesse* and *Atalanta in Calydon!*[10] There is here a sweet soothing, a healing reassurance, a divine booziness—in brief, all the stuff of A No. 1 poetry. It would bring comfort, I believe, to many a poor widow who now groans as the Freemasons intone their balderdash or blushes as a Socialist orator criticizes Omnipotence for permitting stock dividends—it would bring her a great deal more comfort, certainly, than the positive statement, made defiantly by the unwilling rector of the parish, that her departed John, having been colloidal and imperfect, has now become gaseous and immortal. Such a libretto for the unescapable last act would be humane and valuable. I renew my suggestion that the poets fall upon it at once.

[*American Mercury,* December 1926]

IMMUNE

The most curious social convention of the great age in which we live is the one to the effect that religious opinions should be respected. Its evil effects must be plain enough to everyone. All it accomplishes is (*a*) to throw a veil of sanctity about ideas that violate every intellectual decency, and (*b*) to make every theologian a sort of chartered libertine. No doubt it is mainly to blame for the appalling slowness with which really sound notions make their way in the world. The minute a new one is launched, in whatever field, some imbecile of a theologian is certain to fall upon it, seeking to put it down. The most effective way to defend it, of course, would be to fall upon the theologian, for the only really workable defense, in polemics as in war, is a vigorous offensive. But the convention that I have mentioned frowns upon that device as indecent, and so theologians continue their assault upon sense without much resistance, and the enlightenment is unpleasantly delayed.

There is, in fact, nothing about religious opinions that entitles them to any more respect than other opinions get. On the contrary, they tend to be noticeably silly. If you doubt it, then ask any pious fellow of your acquaintance to put what he believes into the form of an affidavit, and see how it reads. . . . "I, John Doe, being duly sworn do say that I believe that, at death, I shall turn into a vertebrate without substance, having neither weight, extent or mass, but with all the intellectual powers and bodily sensations of an ordinary mammal; . . . and that, for the high crime and misdemeanor of having kissed my sister-in-law behind the door, with evil intent, I shall be boiled in molten sulphur for one billion calendar years." Or, "I, Mary Roe, having the fear of Hell before me, do solemnly affirm and declare that I believe it was right, just, lawful and decent for the Lord God Jehovah, seeing certain little children of Beth-el laugh at Elisha's bald head, to send a she-bear from the wood, and to instruct, incite, induce and command it to tear forty-two of them to pieces." Or, "I, the Right Rev. ———, bishop of ———, D.D., LL.D., do honestly, faithfully and on my honor as a man and a priest, declare that I believe that Jonah swallowed the whale," or *vice versa,* as the case may be.

No; there is nothing notably dignified about religious ideas. They run, rather, to a peculiarly puerile and tedious kind of nonsense. At their best, they are borrowed from metaphysicians, which is to say, from men who devote their lives to proving that twice two is not always or necessarily four. At their worst, they smell of spiritualism and fortune-telling. Nor is there any visible virtue in the men who merchant them professionally. Few theologians know anything that is worth knowing, even about theology, and not many of them are honest. One may forgive a Socialist or a Single Taxer on the ground that there is something the matter with his ductless glands, and that a Winter in the south of France would relieve him. But the average theologian is a hearty, red-faced, well-fed fellow with no discernible excuse in pathology. He disseminates his blather, not innocently, like a philosopher, but maliciously, like a politician. In a well-organized world he would be on the stone-pile, along with the lawyer. But in the world as it exists we are asked to listen to him, not only politely, but even reverently, and with our mouths open!

[*American Mercury,* March 1930]

SEARCHING HOLY WRIT

If one is to believe what one hears, the Bible is the corner-stone of the Constitution and the sole guide and excuse for being of the Republic. As the Supreme Court has put it, this is a Christian nation. The laws, alas, bear out that disquieting theory: in all their moral aspects they lean most heavily, not upon the needs of man but upon the supposed desires of God. If all this be true—and I am certainly not one to dispute it—then it becomes a marvel that the Book which rules us all is so imperfectly studied. Not a single theologian of the first class has appeared in the United States for a century past, nor is there a native school of exegetes of any appreciable dignity or authority. To imagine American Bible scholars producing a work as sound and searching as *Christianity in the Light of Modern Knowledge* by the Archbishop of York and his associates,[11] would strain the psyche almost as much as to imagine the Supreme Court making an intelligent contribution to the science of jurisprudence. Our typical theologian is not a scholar at all, but a politician, and our Bible schools are almost unanimously in the hands of fools.

Those who, by reason of their loose lives, are unfamiliar with the matter, would do well to get a set of the International Sunday-School Lessons, say for the current year, and one or two of the popular commentaries thereon. These Sunday-School Lessons are taught every week in practically all of the Protestant Sunday-schools of the land, always with the aid of one of the commentaries. The latter reduce a rich and noble literature to the level of a series of flabby tracts. The two Jahvehs—the bellicose and salty old barbarian of the Old Testament and the metaphysical but amiable Greek of the New—are alike transformed into a sort of amalgam of Federal judge, reformed rabbi and Presbyterian investment securities banker. The voluptuous strophes of the Song of Solomon, perhaps the most fleshly hymn to love ever written, become arguments in favor of Clean Living, the Sermon on the Mount is squeezed into the Methodist Book of Discipline, and the magnificent twelfth chapter of Romans is butchered to make a Prohibitionist holiday. Vandalism could scarcely go further, and yet it is only after such curry-combing and boiling in mercurochrome that the Bible is laid before the Protestant infantry of the land.

This seems a sad state of affairs, and every American of decent tastes and feelings must deplore it. For the Bible, despite all its contradictions and absurdities, its barbarisms and obscenities, remains grand and gaudy stuff, and so it deserves careful study and enlightened exposition. It is not only lovely in phrase; it is also rich in ideas, many of them far from foolish. One somehow gathers the notion that it was written from end to end by honest men—inspired, perhaps, but nevertheless honest. When they had anything to say they said it plainly, whether it was counsel that enemies be slain or counsel that enemies be kissed. They knew how to tell a story, and how to sing a song, and how to swathe a dubious argument in specious and disarming words. They were privy to all the tricks of poets, orators, evangelists, politicians, historians, college presidents, insurance solicitors, executive secreraries. They had everything except humor, and maybe they had humor too, as I have often suspected after reading 2 Kings 2:23–24, and Matthew 1:1–16.[12] No secular authors have ever surpassed them in cunning and address, not even Shakespeare, not even Homer, not even Dr. Henry van Dyke or Edgar A. Guest, or Dr. Irving Babbitt. Seeking to save the world from Hell, they failed; but they at least gave it a superb literature.

This literature is now taught to the young by a corps of solemn and unintelligent pedagogues of both sexes, themselves dependent for light upon glosses composed by theological eunuchs. It is an absurdity almost without parallel in human history. The Bible deserves to be taught by teachers who are not afraid of it, and have actually read it. It deserves to be set before the young, not as a bugaboo for enforcing the moral ideas of nitwits, but as the rich storehouse of human wisdom and folly, strength and weakness, hope and despair that it really is. But where are the teachers for the job? How are they to be recruited and trained? Once more I can only advise a resort to prayer.

[*American Mercury,* July 1930]

THE AMERICAN RELIGION

As every schoolboy knows, the course of biological evolution is marked by a steady increase of functional differentiation among the cells. In the lowest organisms, though they may consist of immense aggregations of cells, all are substantially alike, and if one could hear one of them speak one would hear all of them. But in the highest organisms there are wide differences, and in man they are not only wide but also very numerous. How many separate and distinct kinds of cells make up the human body I don't know, and neither does anyone else, but certainly it must be many thousands. In the liver alone there are hundreds, each as unlike its fellows as a Congressman is unlike a holy Christian martyr. The neurons which make up the nerves are so different from the cells which float in the blood plasm that it is hard to believe that they descend from a single zygote. Nor is it easy to think of the cells of the *lens crystallina* and those of a wart as the offspring of the same fertilized ovum. Here nature pants and sweats for specialization, and very often it is carried to astonishing lengths.

So in the social organism. Human society simply repeats the history of the living creature. It begins with all individuals acting pretty much alike. There are males and females, but that is about all. Every man practises all the arts that any man knows, and every woman can do what all her sisters do. But as culture develops so does differentiation. There come to be kings and subjects, philosophers and laborers, traders and artists, farmers and priests, doctors and lawyers, and so on almost *ad infinitum*. In the most advanced societies such differences are as wide and dramatic as those between the different classes of cells in the body. If there is any likeness between, say, a Huxley on the one hand and a Mississippi Baptist on the other, it is a likeness mainly of gross anatomy; functionally, and especially psychologically, they differ almost as much as a whale and a June-bug. Not only is the Baptist incapable of doing any of the things that make a Huxley what he is; he is also incapable of imagining Huxley doing them, just as a June-bug is incapable of imagining a whale swallowing Jonah.

But neither in the physical organism or in the social organism does this specialization go unchallenged. Now and then, in a human body otherwise apparently healthy, certain lowly varieties of cells run amuck and begin assaulting their betters: their aim is to bring the whole body down to their own vulgar and incompetent level. The result is what is called a cancer. In the social organism the parallel phenomenon is called democracy. The aim of democracy is to destroy if possible, and if not, then to make ineffective, the genetic differences between man and man. It begins in the political domain—by setting up the doctrine that one man's opinion about the common affairs of all is as good as any other man's—but it always tries to extend itself to other and higher domains. In a democratic society it is more hazardous than elsewhere to show any oddity in conduct or opinion. Whoever differs from the general is held to be inferior, though it may be obvious, by any rational standard, that he is really superior. People who live under democracy tend to wear the same kind of hats, to eat the same food, to laugh at the same jokes, and to admire the same mountebanks. They become, as the phrase has it, standardized. Their laws lay heavy penalties on any man whose taste in reading, in drinking or in any other private avocation differs from that of his neighbors. Life tends to be regimented and unpleasant, and everyone is more or less uneasy.

In the United States, where democracy has gone further than anywhere else, this levelling tendency is frequently remarked. There was a time, for example, when the Americans spent a lot of time debating political theories, and developed a great many new ones, but of late they are so much of the same mind that the difference between the two chief parties is scarcely discernible. A Democrat in Georgia believes precisely what a Republican in Kansas believes; if they continue to vote against one another it is only because they are too stupid to notice their complete agreement. And as in politics, so in every every other field of thought and action. There is no longer any substantial difference between man and man. All decent Americans believe that it is better to boost than to knock, that the radio is a wonderful invention, that all communists come from Russia and ought to be sent back there, that the public schools do a great work, and that the best cure for anything that happens to ail one is a dose of aspirin. On all such matters there is a steady approach to unanimity. It becomes a grave indecorum to question anything that is generally believed.

Of late this movement has begun to show itself even in the field of religion, where for centuries past there has been nothing but quarrel and turmoil. Theoretically, to be sure, the old animosity between sect and sect is still alive, and now and then, as in the national campaign of 1928, it takes on a melodramatic reality;[13] nevertheless, I believe that it is slowly dying, and that in another century or so it will be pretty well forgotten. Not only will the various varieties of Protestants then lie down together in relative amity; there will also be a truce between the Protestants as a whole and the Catholics. The result, I believe, will be a common American religion, based mainly upon Wesleyan ideas but borrowing a great deal from Latin practises. Two influences will bring it in. On the one hand the Protestants of the land, as they gradually grow civilized, will tire of the vulgarity of evangelism and turn to something more dignified and self-respecting. And on the other hand, the Catholics will tire of their allegiance to Rome, and set up shop on their own, as the faithful of the Near East did in the year 1054,[14] and as the French came near doing toward the close of the Seventeenth Century. Once these revolutions are permitted by God, actual union will become possible.

The learned ex-Jesuit, Dr. E. Boyd Barrett, believes that the Catholics of the United States are already drifting away from Rome, though most of them are probably still unaware of it. He points out that the Roman theory of government and the American theory are hopelessly at odds, and that American Catholics are outraged in some of their dearest beliefs every time the former is stated, say in one of the recurrent papal encyclicals. The contention scarcely needs argument. During the Smith-Hoover combat various Catholic theologians tried to reconcile the two theories, but they never got far enough to make even Al himself understand them. The obvious fact is that the American theory is incurably repugnant to Rome, and that on some near to-morrow it may be categorically condemned. When that time comes the way will be open for a new schism.

But there is something more. A good many American Catholics, even now, may be unpleasantly conscious of the conflict in this department, and eager to throw off Rome, but such a wish is surely not common in the American hierarchy. Its members are faithful to Rome, and they will probably remain faithful to the last ditch. Nevertheless, they also, at least by residence, are Americans, and if they do not succumb to the American theory of government, they plainly succumb to a multitude of other American notions. There was a time when, if a bishop spoke, one could tell at once from what he said whether he was a Catholic or a Protestant. But that time is no more. With one cardinal archbishop damning Einstein as a corruptor of youth and another entering into an alliance with the Methodists and Presbyterians to drive all ideas out of the theater, it becomes increasingly difficult to mark the point where John Wesley ceases to be a heretic and becomes a saint.

This Methodization of Holy Church in the Republic has gone a good deal further than most people seem to think. It has, within the space of two generations, changed the whole character of the Roman hierarchy. Once it was made up chiefly of pious and courtly souls of the general character of Cardinal Gibbons, but today it is full of go-getters who are almost indistinguishable from their Wesleyan brethren. They carry on the enterprises of the church by mass production methods, and do not hesitate to bulge out into secular affairs. One hears from them increasingly in the halls of legislation, and many of them cherish schemes to improve and save non-Catholics at wholesale and even by force. It is, I think, a significant change, and I can only ascribe it to the effects of living in a Methodist land and breathing evangelical air. Many of these right rev. brethren, no doubt, are quite unaware of their own transformation, but there it is all the same.

But if they thus yield to the Wesleyan heretics, then the Wesleyan heretics respond by a mad shinning up the slopes of Canossa. Here, again, what is going on is too little observed. With Bishop Cannon constantly in the limelight, such men as Bishop O'Connell are overlooked. But even Bishop Cannon offers plenty of evidence of the change going on. On the one hand, he has not held a revival for years, and on the other hand he has boldly proposed a revision of the traditional Methodist code of ethics. Sitting in Washington, with one eye on the White House and the other on Capitol Hill, he moves further and further from the circuit rider of yesterday and more and more toward the Roman cardinal. Nor is he alone in that progress, nor is it confined to such novelties as he himself has introduced. Even more significant is the abandonment of conversion by orgy among Methodists generally, and the increasing popularity of ritual. There was a time when a Methodist service was almost indistinguishable from an auction sale, but today sixteen thousand of the brethren in holy orders pine publicly for the Book of Common Prayer as it was revised by Wesley in 1784, and in many of their tabernacles they go through ceremonies almost as stately as a hanging, and some of them have even taken to burning candles.

As a neutral in theology, I express no formal opinion about these changes. Naturally enough, I incline toward those which make for decorum rather than for those which make for unpleasantness, and so, if I took a side, it would probably be what now seems to be the Wesleyan side. But fortunately there is no need to do so, for the process cannot be influenced by either praise or blame. It is a function of the general standardization now going on in the United States. Fifty years ago, or even thirty years ago, anyone who predicted that Democrats and Republicans would ever be brought together on a common platform would have been set down a lunatic, but the thing has actually happened, and the country seems little the worse for it. It will take longer to bring on amity among Christians, for it is God's will that they should hate one another with a blistering and implacable hatred. Nevertheless, that will may be changed at any time, and, as I have tried to set forth, I suspect that it is being changed even now. Children born to-day may see the beginnings of a genuine state church in the Republic, with a hierarchy of live wires and a purely American theology. I regret that I am too old to wait for it, for if it comes it will be a lulu.

[*American Mercury,* May 1931]

QUOD EST VERITAS?

WHAT IS THERE LEFT TO BELIEVE? By Herbert Parrish. $2.50. 277 pp. New York: *The Sears Publishing Company.*

THE CATHOLIC FAITH, by Paul Elmer More. $4. 312 pp. Princeton, N.J.: *The Princeton University Press.*

HAS SCIENCE DISCOVERED GOD? Edited by Edward H. Cotten. $3.50. 308 pp. New York: *The Thomas Y. Crowell Company.*

JESUS THROUGH THE CENTURIES, by Shirley Jackson Case. $3. 382 pp. Chicago: *The University of Chicago Press.*

THE GREAT AMPHIBIUM, by Joseph Needham. $1.75. 180 pp. New York: *Charles Scribner's Sons.*

WITHIN, by Thomas L. Masson. $2.50. 325 pp. New York: *The Sears Publishing Company.*

THE GROWTH OF THE IDEA OF GOD, by Shailer Mathews. $2.50. 237 pp. New York: *The Macmillan Company.*

SOCIAL SUBSTANCE OF RELIGION, by Gerald Heard. $3.50. 318 pp. New York: *Harcourt, Brace & Company.*

A RABBI TAKES STOCK, by Solomon Goldman. $2.50. 247 pp. New York: *Harper & Brothers.*

AS A JEW SEES JESUS, by Ernest R. Trattner. $2. 232 pp. New York: *Charles Scribner's Sons.*

SINCE CALVARY, by Lewis Browne. $3.50. 443 pp. New York: *The Macmillan Company.*

SCIENCE REDISCOVERS GOD, by Donald Campbell Macfie. $3. 275 pp. New York: *Charles Scribner's Sons.*

EVOLUTION AND THEOLOGY, by Ernest C. Messenger. $2.50. 313 pp. New York: *The Macmillan Company.*

THE WORLD OF THE NEW TESTAMENT, by T. R. Glover. 233 pp. New York: *The Macmillan Company.*

THE KINGDOM OF GOD IN THE NEW TESTAMENT, by Ernest F. Scott. 197 pp. New York: *The Macmillan Company.*
THE DEVIL IN LEGEND AND LITERATURE, by Maximilian Rudwin. $3. 354 pp. Chicago: *The Open Court Publishing Company.*
THE STORY OF THE DEVIL, by Arturo Graf. $3. 296 pp. New York: *The Macmillan Company.*

With perhaps two exceptions all of these authors show a bias in favor of supernaturalism: either they are theologians expounding the arcana of their trade or pious laymen arguing that those arcana are somehow superior to the demonstrable facts of the laboratory. It is curious to note that the theologians, who might be expected reasonably to strut and spout a bit, show a far more modest and engaging spirit than the laymen, and are at least ten times as persuasive. I pick out two volumes at random, and set them side by side. The one is *What Is There Left to Believe?* by Dr. Parrish, an Anglican priest and a lecturer on theology; the other is *Has Science Discovered God?* a symposium by a posse of scientists headed by Dr. Robert A. Millikan, Sir Arthur Eddington, Dr. William McDougall, Dr. Edwin G. Conklin and Sir Oliver Lodge. The difference is enormous, and instantly apparent. Dr. Parrish presents his ideas simply clearly and in a modest spirit, confessing frankly to dubieties when he has them, but yielding nothing of his basic *credo.* He is fair to his opponents, and does them the honor of assuming that they are intelligent, and deserve to be answered in a rational manner. Now turn for contrast to the tome of Millikan and company, and for example to an essay entitled "A Biologist's Religion" by Dr. Conklin, who pursues that art and mystery at Princeton. Thus:

> No one can furnish scientific proof of the existence or nature of God, but atheism leads to fatalism and despair while theism leads to faith and hope and love. . . . Science cannot solve the great mysteries of our existence—why we are, whither we are bound, what it all means. Faith alone assures us that there is a definite purpose in all experience. This knowledge makes life worth living and service a privilege.

This, remember, is not a quotation from the late William Jennings Bryan, or from Aimée Semple McPherson, or from Bishop Manning, or from any other such comic character; it is from the professor of biology at a great American university. What could be more puerile? What could be more completely ridiculous? I'd like to have from Dr. Conklin a list of the other biologists who subscribe to his rubbish. And another list of those who, *dis*believing in it, are plunged into "fatalism and despair," and hold that life is not worth living, and find it impossible to save their fellow men. While he is at it, let him also send me something else, to wit, a clear statement, fetched out of that theism which leads to "faith and hope and love," as to "why we are, whither we are bound, and what it all means." I'd like to know precisely what "the definite purpose" is "in all experience." On this point, indeed, I have always yearned for light—so far in vain, but certainly without anything properly describable as despair. It would be immensely satisfying to receive a clear answer from a man trained to scientific exactness of exposition.

Dr. Conklin's thesis is so weak, alas, that he finds it quite impossible to stick to it. What I have quoted with blushes for him is from his last page; on an earlier page he admits naïvely that "neither Mark Twain nor any other philosopher of despair could avoid the instinct to work for human betterment." Certainly there is a discrepancy between this and the idea that only faith—in what? in whom?—can make "service a privilege." It might be well for Dr. Conklin to recall briefly a man of his own trade who had no faith whatever and yet labored through a long life for the enlightenment and betterment of the human race—a man who laughed at all the divinities, beginning with the Yahweh of the Old Testament and running down to General William Booth of the Salvation Army, and yet never yielded to despair, a man who confessed openly that he did not know and could not imagine "why we are, whither we are bound, and what it all means," and yet did a man's work in the heat of the day and was probably more responsible than anyone else for enabling Dr. Conklin to do his. I allude, of course, to Thomas Henry Huxley. How he would have snorted over the stale camp-meeting bilge of the Millikans and Conklins! How he would have yelled with rage to see the logic of the backwoods evangelist invading the laboratory!

Dr. More, also a Princeton pedagogue, gives almost as sad an exhibition in *The Catholic Faith,* though he is much more competent as an arguer. He has been one of the leaders of the New Humanist movement in literary criticism, now falling into decay, and gives away, somewhat innocently, its animus, which was and is mainly theological. Unless I misread him, the Inner Check which the sophomore Taines and Coleridges were lately talking of so shrilly is simply a check on logic, that godless art. One pursues the facts for a certain space, and then one suddenly hauls up and returns to the International Sunday-School Lessons. Thus Dr. More himself first proves elaborately that "the revelation, if revelation there be, in the Bible" is of a most "imperfect character," and then proceeds placidly to swallow it. But not, of course, all of it. There are parts of it that gag him, and there are implications of it that gag him yet worse. For example, he simply cannot get down the infallibility of the Pope, and so he finds himself a Catholic, not in the sense in which Archbishop Cannon and Cardinal Hayes alike use the word, but only in the sense in which it is used by High Church Episcopalians. Even so, his rejection of the papal claim seems to be grounded less upon a logical process than upon an instinctive fear of what he calls the Demon of the Absolute. He prefers the twilight, where nothing is clearly defined, and even the awful truths of Holy Writ take on a pleasantly vague and literary character. The late Cardinal Newman, it appears, was an almost perfect Humanist, in the Harvard-Princeton sense, when he wrote "Lead Kindly Light," but then "his courage failed him, and in his anguish for the perfect light he bowed down to the Demon," which is to say, to the Pope. Dr. More will have nothing to do with His Holiness. He plainly likes the style and appellation of Catholic, but he wants it to be understood that he is not that kind.

I am always shocked, reading the works of pious intellectuals, to discover how little humor they have. Dr. More exhibits that lack very painfully in a chapter discussing the relations between Buddhism and Christianity. It is full of solemn and approving quotations from the Buddhist scriptures, most of them sheer nonsense. I offer as an example the following from the 115th *sutta* of the Majjhima Nikâya:

From Ignorance spring the Factors of Mentality,
From the Factors of Mentality springs Consciousness,
From Consciousness springs Name-Form (mind and body),
From Name-Form springs the Sixfold Seat (the five organs of sense and
    the central organ),
From the Six-Fold Seat springs Contact,
From Contact springs Sensations,
From Sensations spring Thirst (craving, desire),

From Thirst springs Attachment,
From Attachment springs Becoming,
From Becoming springs Birth,
From Birth spring Old Age, Death, Pain, Lamentation, Sorrow, Trouble,
  Despair.

It is obvious that all this is no more than a banal juggling with words, signifying nothing. It has no sense as psychology, it has no sense as philosophy, and it is even idiotic as theology. That New Thoughters[15] should mouth such grandiose hooey is perhaps understandable, but that it should be soberly set forth and discussed by a professor at Princeton is surely most remarkable. Dr. More seems to be a glutton for it. A few pages further on he embellishes his book with another dose, this time the Eightfold Path to the Cessation of Sorrow:

1. Right opinion (otherwise translated views).
2. Right purpose (intention, aspirations).
3. Right speech.
4. Right action.
5. Right employment (means of livelihood, *Wandeln, vita*).
6. Right endeavor (effort, *Mühn, sforzo*).
7. Right mindfulness (*sati,* otherwise translated memory, conscience, attention, meditation, contemplation, insight, thought).
8. Right collectedness (*samâdhi,* meditation, ecstasy, *Einigung, Konzentration, raccoglimento*).

It is interesting to hear from Dr. More that right opinion is "otherwise translated views," but he neglects, unfortunately, to tell us what difference there is, if any, between opinion and views. Nor does he explain what the difference is between right action and right employment, or between right purpose and right endeavor. Nor how conscience and attention, by any conceivable aberration of translators, may be made equal to the same word, whatever it is in the original. Nor, indeed, what all this pompous rumble-bumble is about. Does anyone seriously believe that right speech can produce a cessation of sorrow? It should be added in fairness that Dr. More, as a good "Catholic," rejects Buddhism at the end, thus departing at last from the New Thoughters. He has an "admiring reverence" for its founder, but believes he failed because he missed hearing about "the dogma of the Incarnation." Lacking that dogma, the religion he devised at such pains and with so brutal a torture of words remains no more than "the most convincing argument that truth to be clearly known waits upon revelation."

It is pleasant to leave this mooniness for the clearer thinking of the professional theologians. Dr. Parrish's perspicuous and perspicacious *What Is There Left to Believe?* I have already noticed briefly. Dr. Mathews in *The Growth of the Idea of God,* Dr. Case in *Jesus through the Centuries* and Dr. Scott in *The Kingdom of God* present interesting, dispassionate and well-informed accounts of the development of Christian doctrine, Dr. Glover in *The World of the New Testament* attempts successfully a useful historical reconstruction, and the three rabbis, Messrs. Trattner, Browne and Goldman, make ponderable contributions to an understanding of the position of religion in the civilized world today. There is merit, too, in the two studies of the Devil legend by Messrs. Graf and Rudwin, though neither is a theologian. And there is an instructive example of theological casuistry at its best in Dr. Messenger's *Evolution and Theology.*

Dr. Messenger is one of those learned priests who have actually read the Fathers, and what is more, read them attentively. He gathers from his studies that there is really no reason why any Catholic, however pious, should doubt the main facts of organic evolution, even including the evolution of man. He holds, of course, as a dutiful son of Holy Church, that the creation of the soul was something else again—that it is impossible to imagine it developing out of the lowly psyche of orang-outang, baboon or gorilla. But when that concession is made to revelation, there is nothing left to upset a biologist. Adam was not confected by Yahweh as a sculptor confects a clay model; on the contrary, he plainly developed out of the primordial slime by slow and painful stages, and there is nothing contrary to faith or morals in holding that, in the earlier of those stages, he was something less than human. The manufacture of Eve out of Adam's rib gives Father Messenger rather more difficulty, but he is still not quite daunted. Nor is he indisposed to admit that there may have been men before Adam, and that *Homo neandertalensis* may have been one of them. At the end, unfortunately, after filling two hundred eighty pages with impressive arguments that human evolution is probably a fact, he remembers that he is a priest, and resorts to caution. After all, no one knows precisely what Holy Church thinks on the subject. It has reprimanded a few scientifically inclined clerics for going too far, but it has never formally repudiated Darwin. But on some near tomorrow one of the Sacred Congregations at Rome, manned by Italian gentlemen hostile to Modernism in all its forms, may issue a blast against the evolutionary hypothesis, and so make believing in it a dangerous matter *post mortem*. Father Messenger therefore advises every good Catholic "to suspend his judgment on the matter at the present moment." But what he thinks himself is made very plain.

The remaining tomes are unimportant. Mr. Needham's *The Great Amphibium* consists of four lectures delivered before lay Bible students in England, and is far more literary than theological. Mr. Macfie's *Science Rediscovers God* is an effort by one who "does not believe in the theory of continuous evolution" to reconcile science and what remains of Christian theology. *Within*, by Mr. Masson, is a sort of text-book of the New Thought, more frank than Dr. More's, but even more dubious. In one place Mr. Masson undertakes to advise a friend who has succumbed to the filthy, immoral and un-Christian vice of smoking. He says:

> We have no power in our human wills. When we understand that fully and that all power comes from God, why, then it is quite easy to stop smoking, for the reason that you cannot function from the Spirit and also smoke. The two things don't go together. To stop smoking cigarettes, therefore, Love God. The more you love Him the sooner smoking will depart from you, and this without any backing and filling on your part.

Mr. Masson used to be editor of *Life* and later on was a member of the editorial staff of the *Saturday Evening Post*. His book seems to be intended quite seriously. I commend it as auxiliary reading to Dr. More's students at Princeton.

Finally comes Mr. Heard's *Social Substance of Religion*. Mr. Heard sees religion as a sort of mediator between the sharply selfish interests of the individual and the larger interests of group and race. What he calls "charitic love" has always "ranged outward," he says, "desiring to embrace the infinite." This charitic love has been most evident in such sectarians as the Moravians and Quakers, but it will increase in the general population as man goes forward. "If," says Mr. Heard, a sound basic unit is first founded, if the individual is shown the first step out of himself (and it is certainly the most difficult), we may build up a hierarchy of wholes, a real feudal system of intense loyalties, not imposed, but built up by the imperative overplus emotional needs of each group for a wider compass, as inevitable and as natural, once the process has been soundly started, as are the precipitations of crystals, or the coral animalcules' accumulated rise of reef toward the surface of the sea.

It may be so, but I am constrained to add that I find myself doubting it.

[*American Mercury,* April 1932]

III

PROTESTANTS
AND CATHOLICS

RELIGIOUS PREJUDICE

The learned brethren of the Latin rite now protest bitterly every time the Ku Klux has at them; if they were as shrewd as they are reputed to be they would be far less disturbed. For the truth is that the Catholic Church in the Republic would be greatly benefited by a heavy bombardment—the heavier, indeed, the better. What ails it where it happens to be strong, say in New York, is a blatant and somewhat ridiculous complacency. It tends to assume that it is beyond all reasonable criticism, and that its fiats have all the force of law. Hence its frequent descent into such absurdities as its effort to suppress the birth-controllers and its idiotic support of the Comstock "clean books" bill[1]—a piece of legislation quite as dishonest and quite as vicious as the Southern statutes which require country sheriffs to search all nunneries once a year, to make sure that no nuns are held against their will.

The Church bears criticism very badly, and frequently hits below the belt in its rejoinders. This is especially true in America, where the hierarchy is largely made up of men unfamiliar with the punctilio. The fact explains the fear in which it is held by the overwhelming majority of American newspaper editors. Not one American newspaper out of a hundred ever ventures to print anything against its enterprises, however dubious, or even against its personnel, however lawless. The immunity it enjoys is not unlike that enjoyed by the Jews twenty years ago, when practically all American editors were under the thumbs of Jewish advertisers. That old immunity, I believe, was broken down by the Jews themselves. They grew so bombastic and oppressive in their demands and pretensions that they suddenly found themselves face to face with a vigorous anti-Semitic movement, and presently even newspaper editors gathered some courage from it.

It is my contention that this anti-Semitic movement has done them a great deal of good—that their position is actually more secure to-day, with attacks upon them going on openly, than it was when all they heard about themselves was flattering. First of all, it enables them to see clearly who their enemies are, and to plan their defense intelligently. Secondly, it makes them privy, in so far as they have sense, to their faults, and inspires them to mend their ways. Thirdly, it serves as a test of their leaders, and gives them a means of distinguishing between the good and the bad. Their most conspicuous leaders, in the days of their immunity, were bad ones—noisy rabbis of the newspaper interview species, professional charitymongers with active press-agents, advertisers with the manners of mule drivers and gang bosses. Such vermin, I believe, built up a prejudice against the whole race. The Jews to-day, under heavy fire, show a tendency to supplant them with better men, and the change will be to their lasting benefit.

I am myself almost completely devoid of religious prejudices. I may have a slight prejudice against Christians in general, but it is dispersed and feeble. I can't imagine myself laying any burden upon a man, or denying him any common right, on the sole ground that he is a Christian. Nevertheless, I can't dodge the fact that many other men, otherwise quite as creditable to the Creator as I am, are full of such prejudices, nor can I rid myself of the notion that they ought to be free to voice them. The fact that a Catholic respects and agrees with his bishop is no reason why I should respect or agree with him, or say I do when I do not. If I am compelled to do so by a social convention I not only suffer injury myself; I also do injury to the bishop. For his job in this world is not to go about in an armor of cotton wool; his job is to deal with realities in the heat of the day. One of the chief of these realities is the impression that he and the Church make on the circumambient heathen. How can he know what it is unless the heathen are free to rage?

In the specific controversy between the Ku Klux and the Catholics I incline frankly toward the Catholics, if only because they have more courage and are, on the whole, decent~~ ~nd more intelligent men. It is hard for me to imagine anyone believing in an archbishop, but it is a thousand times harder for me to imagine anyone believing in the Imperial Wizard. For that very reason I welcome the war that the Klan now makes upon Holy Church, and herewith give it three cheers. The Kluxers can do no harm, I believe, to what is sound and good in the Church. They are too obviously idiotic to have any hope of convincing fair men against the weight of the evidence. But they are still not so idiotic that their onslaught is wholly without effect—when it is apposite and honest. They will penetrate, now and then, to genuine truths; they will unveil actual weaknesses. The Church, if it is wise, will not protest, but seek quietly to remedy those weaknesses.

Meanwhile, the show from the sidelines is excellent, and I advocate it also on that ground. No combat set in this world ever grows more furious and extravagant than a combat between Christians. They seem to have a special talent for hatred, almost a vocation. Perhaps the fact that their creed denounces it specifically and is mainly concerned with putting it down— perhaps this fact has its significance for practitioners of the Freudian necro- mancy. In any case, I enjoy such slaughters immensely, and hence hope that they will go on. In the course of them many a false-face and bed-sheet is pulled off, and many a fraud is burnt by the pitiless sun. It is a salubrious sport, and, as I have said, diverting. Of it one may say what one may say of all other varieties of war: that the offensive is more charming than the defensive. Neither side is very impressive when it bawls against the libels of the other. But both are thrilling when they lay on.

[*American Mercury,* September 1924]

THE DECLINE OF PROTESTANTISM

That Protestantism in this great Christian realm is down with a wasting disease must be obvious to every amateur of ghostly pathology. The de- nominational papers are full of alarming reports from its bedside, and all sorts of projects for the relief of the patient. One authority holds that only more money is needed to work a cure—that if the Christian exploiters and usurers of the country would but provide a sufficient slush fund, all the vacant pews could be filled, and the baptismal tanks with them. Another authority argues that the one way to save the churches of the Only True

Faith is to close all other places of resort and amusement on the Sabbath, from delicatessen shops to road-houses, and from movie parlors to jazz palaces. Yet another proposes a mass attack by prayer, apparently in the hope of provoking a miracle. A fourth advocates a vast augmentation of so-called institutional effort, *i.e.,* the scheme of putting bowling alleys and courting cubicles into church cellars, and of giving over the rest of every sacred edifice to debates on the Single Tax, boxing matches, baby shows, mental hygiene clinics, lectures by converted actors, raffles, non-voluptuous dances and evening classes in salesmanship, automobile repairing, birth control, interior decoration and the art and mystery of the realtor. A fifth, borrowing a leaf from Big Business, maintains that consolidation and reorganization are what are needed—that the existence of half a dozen rival churches in every American village profits the devil a great deal more than it profits God. This last scheme seems to have won a great deal of support among the pious. At least a score of committees are now trying to draw up plans for concrete consolidations, and even the Southern and Northern Methodists, who hate each other violently, are in peaceful but somewhat suspicious negotiation.

On the merits of these conflicting remedies I attempt no pronouncement, but I have been at some pains to look into the symptoms and nature of the disease. My report is that it seems to me to be analogous to that malady which afflicts a star in the heavens when it splits into halves and they go slambanging into space in opposite directions. That, in brief, is what appears to be the matter with Protestantism in the United States today. One half of it is moving, with slowly accelerating speed, in the direction of Rome; the other is sliding down into voodooism. The former carries the greater part of Protestant money with it; the latter carries the greater part of Protestant enthusiasm, or, as the word now is, pep. What remains in the middle may be likened to a torso without either brains to think with or legs to dance—in other words, something that begins to be professionally attractive to the mortician, though it still makes shift to breathe. There is no lack of life on the higher levels, where the more solvent Methodists and the like are gradually transmogrified into Episcopalians, and the Episcopalians gradually shin up the bastions of Holy Church, and there is no lack of life on the lower levels, where the rural Baptists, by the route of Fundamentalism, the Anti-Saloon League and the Ku Klux, rapidly descend to the dogmas and practises of the Congo jungle.

But in the middle there is desiccation and decay. Here is where Protestantism was once strongest. Here is the region of the plain and godly man, fond of devotion but distrustful of every hint of orgy—the honest fellow who suffers dutifully on Sunday, pays his share and hopes for a few kind words from the pastor when his time comes to die. He stands today on a burning deck. It is no wonder that Sunday automobiling begins to get him in its clutches. If he is not staggered one day by his pastor's appearance in surplice and stole, he is staggered the day following by a file of Ku Kluxers marching up the aisle. So he tends to absent himself from pious exercises, and the news goes about that there is something the matter with the churches, and the denominational papers bristle with schemes to set it right, and many up-and-coming pastors, tiring of preaching and parish work, get excellent jobs as the executive secretaries of these schemes, and go about the country expounding them.

II

The extent to which Protestantism, in its upper reaches, has succumbed to the temptations of Rome seems to be but little apprehended by the majority of connoisseurs. I was myself unaware of the whole truth until last Christmas, when, in the pursuit of a quite unrelated inquiry, I employed agents to attend all the services held in the principal Protestant basilicas of an eminent American city.

The substance of their reports, in so far as they related to churches patronized by the well-to-do, was simple: they revealed a headlong movement to the Right, an almost precipitate flight into the arms of Rome. Six so-called Episcopal churches held midnight services on Christmas Eve in obvious imitation of Catholic midnight masses, and one of them actually called its service a "solemn high mass." Two invited the nobility and gentry to processions, and a third concealed a procession under the name of a pageant. One offered Gounod's St. Cecilia mass on Christmas morning, and another the Messe Solennelle by the same composer; three others, somewhat more timorous, contented themselves with parts of masses. One, throwing off all pretense and euphemism, summoned the faithful to no less than three Christmas masses, naming them by name—two low and one high. All six had candles, and two employed incense.

But that was not the worst. Two Presbyterian churches and one Baptist church, not to mention five Lutheran churches of different synods, had choral services in the dawn of Christmas morning, and the service attended by the only one of my agents who got up early enough—it was in a Presbyterian church—was made gay with candles, and had a palpably Roman smack. Yet worse: a rich and conspicuous Methodist church, patronized by the leading Wesleyan wholesalers and moneylenders of the town, boldly offered a "medieval carol service." Medieval? What did that mean? The Middle Ages ended on July 16, 1453, at 12 o'clock meridian,[2] and the Reformation was not launched by Luther until October 31, 1517, at 10:15 A.M. If medieval, in the sense in which it was here used, does not mean Roman Catholic, then I surely went to school in vain. My agent, born a Methodist, reported that the whole ceremony shocked him excessively. It began with trumpet blasts from the church spire and it ended with an "Ave Maria" by a vested choir! Candles rose up in glittering ranks behind the chancel rail, and above them glowed a shining electric star. God help us all, indeed! What next? Will the rev. pastor, on some near tomorrow, defy the lightnings of Jahveh by appearing in alb and dalmatic? Will he turn his back upon the faithful? Will he put in a telephone booth for auricular confession? I shudder to think of what old John Wesley would have said about that vested choir and that shining star. Or Bishop Francis Asbury.

Here, of course, I do not venture into the contumacy of criticizing; I merely marvel. A student of the sacred sciences all my life, I am well learned in the dogmas and ceremonials of the sects, and know what they affect and what they abhor. Does anyone argue that the use of candles in public worship would have had the sanction of the Ur-Wesleyans, or that they would have consented to Blasmusik and a vested choir? If so, let the sciolist come forward. Down to fifty years ago, in fact, the Methodists prohibited Christmas services altogether, as Romish and heathen. But now we have ceremonies almost operatic, and the sweet masses of Gounod are just around the corner! As I have said, the Episcopalians—who, in most American cities, are largely ex-Methodists or ex-Presbyterians, or, in New York, ex-Jews—go still further. In three of the churches attended by my agents Holy Communion was almost indistinguishable from the Catholic mass. Two of these churches, according to information placed at my disposal by the police, are very fashionable; to get into one of them is almost as difficult as ordering a suit of clothes from Poole. But the richer the Episcopalian, the more eager he is to forget that he was once baptized by public outcry or total immersion. The Low Church rectors, in the main, struggle with poor congregations, born to the faith but deficient in buying power. As bank accounts increase the fear of the devil diminishes, and there arises a sense of beauty. This sense of beauty, in its practical effects, is identical with the work of the Paulist Fathers.

Now even the Methodists who remain Methodists begin to wobble. Tiring of the dreadful din that goes with the orthodox Wesleyan demonology, they take to ceremonials that grow more and more stately and voluptuous. The sermon ceases to be a cavalry charge and becomes soft and *pizzicato*. The choir abandons "Throw Out the Life-Line" and "Are You Ready for the Judgment Day?" and toys with Handel. The rev. pastor throws off the uniform of a bank cashier and puts on a gown. It is an evolution that has, viewed from a tree, a certain merit. The stock of nonsense in the world is sensibly diminished and the stock of beauty is augmented. But what would the old-time circuit-riders say of it, imagining them miraculously brought back from hell?

III

So much for the volatilization that is going on above the diaphragm. What is in progress below? All I can detect is a rapid descent to mere barbaric devil-chasing. In all those parts of the Republic where Beelzebub is still as real as Babe Ruth or Dr. Coolidge, and men drink raw fusel oil hot from the still—for example, in the rural sections of the Middle West and everywhere in the South save a few walled towns—the evangelical sects plunge into an abyss of malignant imbecility, and declare a holy war upon every decency that civilized men cherish. First the Anti-Saloon League and now the Ku Klux Klan have converted them into vast machines for pursuing and butchering unbelievers. They have thrown the New Testament overboard, and gone back to the Old, and particularly to the bloodiest parts of it. Their one aim seems to be to break heads, to spread terror, to propagate hatred. Everywhere they have set up enmities that will not die out for generations. Neighbor looks askance at neighbor, the land is filled with spies, every man of the slightest intelligence is suspect.

What is the effect of all this upon the Christian who retains some measure of sanity, the moderate and peaceable fellow—him called by William Graham Sumner the Forgotten Man?[3] He is silent while the bombs burst and the stink bombs go off, but what is he thinking? I believe that he is thinking strange and dreadful thoughts—thoughts that would have frozen his own spine a dozen years ago. He is thinking, *imprimis,* that there must be something in this evolution heresy, after all, else Methodist bishops and other such foes to sense would not be so frantically against it. And he is thinking, secondly, that perhaps a civilized man, in the last analysis, would not be worse off if Sherman's march were repeated by the Papal Guard. Between these two thoughts Protestantism is being squeezed, so to speak, to death.

[*American Mercury,* March 1925]

SHOCK TROOPS

THE JESUIT ENIGMA, by E. Boyd Barrett. $4. 351 pp. New York: *Boni & Liveright.*

If this thoughtful and valuable book gets any notice at all from the literati of the Latin rite, it will probably be only abuse—the inevitable reply, from that quarter, to any man who proposes, however honestly and judiciously, to discuss the weaknesses of Holy Church. But that abuse cannot dispose of the manifest fact that Dr. Barrett knows what he is talking about, and deserves to be heard. For twenty years he was himself a Jesuit, and during that time his scholarship—he is a psychologist—shed credit upon the order, and he was in excellent repute both within and without its ranks. When he withdrew at last, it was not because of any apostasy to the faith. On the contrary, he apparently retained his belief in all the salient Catholic doctrines, and actually offered himself for service as an ordinary priest. What drove him out was simply his conviction that the Society of Jesus offered an impossible environment to a man of his intellectual curiosity and integrity. Its atmosphere of repression, of deliberate obscurantism, of petty intrigue, of childish spying and tale-bearing choked him, and so he departed.

He opens his book with a brief sketch of Jesuit history, proceeds to a somewhat elaborate description of Loyola's celebrated *Spiritual Exercises* and the Jesuit Constitutions,[4] the two ruling documents of the order, and then launches into a long discussion of Jesuit practises. There is no tedious scandal-mongering in his story. He believes that the Jesuit rule regarding dealings with women is unworkable, and he shows that it is frequently evaded, but that evasion he pictures as due to necessity, not to looseness. For most Jesuits, as priests and as men, he apparently has high respect. But he is convinced that their education tends to make them narrow and bigoted, that the dreadful discipline under which they live breaks down their self-reliance and self-esteem and makes them mere cogs in an ecclesiastical machine, and that preferment among them, instead of going to the strongest men, only too often goes to the most complaisant. The Jesuit system of espionage, as he describes it, is really quite appalling. But it is not directed, as Ku Kluxers believe, against Methodist bishops, members of Congress and the Federal judiciary; it is directed solely against Jesuits. They live under a surveillance that would irk prisoners in a penitentiary. They literally have no privacy whatever, even of thought, and the method adopted for keeping watch over them offers obvious temptations to men with a talent for persecution. Accused, a Jesuit never knows his accusers. Punished, he is forbidden even to demand a trial.

Dr. Barrett offers many examples of the unpleasant workings of this system. It has the inevitable effect, he says, of shutting off the free play of ideas within the order, and it is responsible for the generally hackneyed and uninspiring character of Jesuit thinking. The members of the Society shine only in safe fields. They make capital astronomers, meteorologists and so on, but where ideas are in conflict they are chained up by a medieval and inflexible philosophy. What that confinement amounts to was shown when Dr. Barrett, on coming to America from Ireland, was invited to contribute some articles on the new psychology to the Jesuit weekly, *America*. His articles, it would seem, were harmless enough, and the editor at the time, Father Tierney, S. J., began printing them. But presently they were stopped by orders from above, and to this day Dr. Barrett has had no explanation of that cavalier affront. Obviously, the new psychology, as banal as it is, was thought to be too heady for the customers of *America*. That the editors of the weekly (many of them able men) cannot do their work effectively under such conditions is plain enough; the fact sufficiently explains the failure of their magazine, which started out with high promise and no little uproar, to make any impression whatever upon American thought. A rival weekly, the *Commonweal,* edited by Catholic laymen, has got further in two or three years than *America* has got in twelve or fifteen. Yet it remains the best that the Jesuits have ever offered in this country. It measures them as fairly and as cruelly as the *War Cry* measures the Salvation Army.[5]

Dr. Barrett's description of the Jesuit scheme of education is devastating. Himself a doctor of a secular university, he is in a singularly favorable position for judging it. It is in the main, he says, a witless ramming in of flyblown nonsense. Nothing is taught objectively; everything must be turned to the glory of the Church, and especially of the Jesuit order. The philosophy on tap is strictly Thomistic, and was abandoned by non-Catholic philosophers, save as an interesting curiosity, centuries ago. All the modern philosophers of any account, even including Kant and Hegel, are under the ban. The sciences are approached in a gingery fashion; literature is simply Catholic literature. Worse, the pedagogical method is medieval and the teachers are often unprepared. Dr. Barrett himself, a psychologist, was put to teaching sociology at Georgetown University, despite his protests that he knew nothing of the subject. When he was relieved of that impossible duty at last, it was to be made professor of catechism. Finally, he was allowed "one short course of psychology toward the latter half of the school year." It was after this that he resigned from the order, and applied to Cardinal Hayes for assignment as a parish priest. In vain! The long arm of the Black Pope reaches out from Rome. No ex-Jesuit may join any other order or serve as a secular priest. Shortly after Dr. Barrett resigned a friend sent a letter to him at Georgetown. It was returned marked "Unknown."

His case is impressive, but it seems to me that he yet forgets something—that, in the last analysis, he seriously misunderstands the order he served for so many years. He appears to see it, ideally, as a sort of intellectual aristocracy within the Church, grounded in learning by a harsh, laborious and relentless process and devoted to widening learning's bounds. It is, I believe, nothing of the sort. Founded by a soldier, it remains essentially military, not scholarly. Its aim is not to find out what is true, but to defend and propagate what Holy Church says is true. All the ideas that it is officially aware of are fixed ideas: it knows of no machinery for changing them, and wants to hear of none. For a Jesuit to engage in free speculation would be as incongruous and as shocking as it would be for General Pershing to flout the ideals of the Elks. The black-robed and romantic brethren have a quite different function. It is to spread out fanwise where the Catholic ranks are thinnest, and there do battle for the Church—for God too, of course, but principally for the Church. They are at their best on the remotest frontiers. In Catholic countries they are suspect; more than once, indeed, they have been thrown out. But where the faithful are few and far between and the enemies of Peter rage and roar, there they yet use their ancient weapons effectively, and are mighty soldiers of the Lord. As soldiers, they deserve a far easier testing than Dr. Barrett gives to them. A psychologist by trade, with a leaning toward psychoanalysis, he prods into their heads a bit too scientifically. Let him try to figure out what a competent Freudian would have made of St. Louis, or the Cid, or Washington, or even Robert E. Lee. The very hallmark of the military mind is repression. The moment soldiers begin to think the war is over, and there is Bolshevism. If Dr. Barrett had his way the Jesuits would be marching upon Rome (as they came near doing once before), and His Holiness, like his colleague of the Quirinal, would be a gilded prisoner in a very tight cage.

[*American Mercury,* January 1928]

THE I.Q. OF HOLY CHURCH

If only because it is manifestly more honest, intelligent and urbane than any of the dominant Protestant sects, the Catholic church usually enjoys a good press in the United States. Ku Kluxers allege that this is because newspaper and magazine editors are afraid of its ire, but that is not altogether true. Some of the more bullet-headed Irish bishops may occasionally try to put down a critic by force, but not often. The commoner method is simple remonstrance, and not infrequently is so artfully employed that the offender is persuaded, and emerges from the experience convinced that the church and its agents are excessively amiable, enlightened, sagacious and high-toned.

This judgment, alas, is somewhat over-sanguine. There are undoubtedly many shrewd fellows among the Catholic clergy, and there are many more who are charming and amusing, but the church as a church, like any other ecclesiastical organization, is highly unintelligent. It is forever making thumping errors, both in psychology and in politics, and despite its occasional brilliant successes among sentimental pseudo-intellectuals, as in England, and among the *Chandala,*[6] as in America it seems destined to go downhill hereafter. Consider its position in the world today. After 1800 years of uninterrupted propaganda, during 1500 of which it was virtually unopposed in Christendom, scarcely a dozen really first-rate men subscribe to its ideas, and not a single first-rate nation!

Its poverty in this respect is well demonstrated by its almost comical excess of enthusiasm whenever a stray member of the intelligentsia succumbs. Reading the Catholic papers—I allude, of course, to the more intelligent of them, not to the dismal diocesan rags—an uninformed person might easily gather the impression that Hilaire Belloc is the greatest historian who ever lived, and G. K. Chesterton the most profound metaphysician. Both men, obviously, are immensely clever, but the Catholic Hazlitts are not content to say so much: they must make them universal geniuses. Similarly, at least on this side of the water, the late Joyce Kilmer is converted into a poet comparable to Whitman or Browning, and the late Bertram C. A. Windle becomes a scientist almost equal to Pasteur, Koch, Darwin or Johannes Müller. The thing proceeds to the lowest and most grotesque levels. Even Harvey Wickham, among Catholic critics, is usually spoken of as if he were a grand and incomparable fellow, glorious alike to the True Religion and the human race.

This gurgling, it seems to me, is injudicious. A more moderate rejoicing would be far more convincing. And a more moderate reviling would probably do more damage to the church's chief current enemies—the birth controllers and the physical scientists. The war upon birth control, as it is commonly carried on by virgin bishops, is not only unfair, but also ridiculous, for it is based upon theological postulates that no educated man could conceivably accept. There is, I believe, a lot to be said against the birth-controllers—for example, on the score of their false pretenses: they really know no more about preventing conception than any corner druggist. But their Catholic critics, so far as I know, have never said it. Instead, they ground their case upon a dogmatism that is offensive to every intellectual decency, and try to dispose of their opponents by denouncing them as mere voluptuaries. This last is sheer nonsense. The principal birth-controllers are as serious as so many witch-burners, and the theory that they are voluptuaries is easily refuted by looking at one of them, preferably a female.

The war upon modern science, carried on in Boston by Cardinal O'Connell and elsewhere by ecclesiastics even less prudent, is quite as silly. Its sole effect must be to make every enlightened Catholic blush. And in the long run, if he be of a reflective habit, it must make him wonder whether he really belongs in the Roman camp. Every Catholic of that sort, the world being what it is, has a hard enough time already to hold his faith:

it is opposed not only by a multitude of objective evidences but also by the inner spirit of his day and generation. Certainly it does not help him to be told that Belloc is a great historian and that Gibbon was an ass, that Kilmer was a good poet and Hardy a bad one, and that Windle was superior to Einstein. Nor does it help him to be taught solemnly that the hatching of rachitic and syphilitic children is an act of merit, *ad maiorem Dei gloriam.*

[*American Mercury,* September 1930]

INFANTS IN HELL

CHILDREN AND PURITANISM, by Sandford Fleming. $2.50. 236 pp. New Haven: *The Yale University Press.*

Dr. Fleming is professor of church history and religious education at the Berkeley Baptist Divinity School in California, and the present work is an abbreviation of a dissertation written "in partial fulfilment of the requirements for the degree of doctor of philosophy" at the Yale Graduate School, apparently under the Faculty of Divinity. It is thus reasonable to assume that he is a man of pious habit and friendly to the Christian revelation, and that assumption is supported by various somewhat mellifluous passages in his exposition. Nevertheless, ... has managed to write one of the most appalling indictments of the New England Puritans ever got upon paper, and it is made only the more damning by its total lack of indignation. Not once does he pause to cuss them out. Instead, he simply sets forth the evidence that he has gathered, and most of it comes out of their own mouths.

What lay at the bottom of their savagery, of course, was their idiotic belief in Calvinism—beyond question the most brutal and barbaric theology ever subscribed to by mortal man, whether in or out of the African bush. Its essence was a florid and obscene concept of Hell, and the believer was kept in a lather of fear by his uncertainty whether he would escape it or land in it. There was really no way for him to find out which way he was headed, for he was taught that the bloody Jahveh who operated it chose candidates in a completely capricious and irrational fashion. The best of men might be damned to an eternity of fire, and the worst might be saved by the divine grace. A little child, cut short in its first innocent squawks, might begin at once a trillion years of boiling in brimstone, and an ancient sinner, with ten wives and forty concubines behind him, might be greeted *post mortem* by the massed brass bands of Heaven, and ushered to a soft and permanent seat on the right hand of its despotic Proprietor. This was the Calvinist doctrine of election, the center of the Puritan system.

Obviously, there were some holes in it, considered from the practical sacerdotal standpoint. If no man could tell whether his destiny was Heaven or Hell, and nothing that he could do could change it, then why should he bother to be good? Why not eat, drink and be merry, and trust Jahveh to turn up the right card? The question had come up in theology before— for Calvinism was old long before Calvin was born—and various answers had been made to it. The Puritan answer was to hint that the same Jahveh who had decided every man's fate in the dark backward and abysm of time might be induced, by proper devices, to change His mind. He could not be moved, of course, by simple rectitude, for rectitude was, by definition, something that He disregarded. But perhaps He could be shaken by what came to be called a conviction of sin—that is, by a wild and all-consuming terror of His Hell. Inasmuch as the main purpose of that Hell was to alarm, He would probably be pleased by evidence that it was working. Thus Puritan preaching devoted practically all of its energies to terrorizing the faithful. If it could scare them enough their agonies might attract the notice of Jahveh, and He might be induced to let them go in consideration of their painful tribute to His awful puissance.

The logic here is somewhat lame, and no doubt the Puritans made frequent efforts to improve it, but this is substantially what they appear to have taught, if one may estimate it by their acts. When they came to apply it to children they at once encountered serious technical difficulties. Children, by their theory, could be damned just as readily as adults, but it was manifestly a hard job to instill into them that conviction of sin which offered the only apparent way out. A hard job, yes, but only in its early stages. Down to the age of two or three a child was almost resistant to theological processes, and if it died one could only hope for the best. But after that the simpler concepts, and especially the concept of Hell, became more or less intelligible to it, and by the time it came to five or six years it could smell the brimstone with the oldest gaffer. So the Puritan divines tackled it early, bent upon taking quick advantage of the first sign of theological capacity, and if it happened to be of a nature favorable to their science they had it howling in terror before it knew its letters. Some of their greatest feats of professional derring-do were such scarings of little children, and when they achieved a good one they commonly made a record of it, that other virtuosi might be suitably edified, and it might be remembered in the profession.

Dr. Fleming shows that this horrifying theology, surviving the enlightenment of the Eighteenth Century, was still cherished during the first decades of the Nineteenth, and that it was not until the publication of Horace Bushnell's *Views of Christian Nurture* in 1847 that it really began to break up. As a matter of fact, there is some steam in it even to this day, if not in New England, then in the remoter reaches of the Christian South. Most of the evangelists yet in practise down there—and a good many are left, despite the gradual decay of their trade—do not baptize until the candidate reaches the age of discretion, but their definition of the age of discretion is very loose, and few of them would reject a child of eight who was searching the Scriptures by day and seeing things at night. At their revivals, in fact, they give a large part of their energy to scaring children, and some of them have developed a very effective technique. From this generalization, I think, the Holy Rollers should be excepted, but that is only because the Holy Roller cantods are largely sexual, and candidates who have not reached puberty make difficult material.

Dr. Fleming warns his readers that his picture of "Puritan life and thought is not complete"—that he is concerned "only with a part of the religious life of the early generations of New England." He should have added that what he describes is quite typical of the rest. Puritanism, in its essence, was sheer brutality; there was absolutely no beauty in it, and very little decency. It revolved around the fear of Hell, and nothing else. In late years there have been many defenses of the Puritans on the ground that, for all the rigors of their theology, they yet lived more or less normal lives, and were not unacquainted with the sempiternal arts of thieving, forestalling, fighting, wine-bibbing and fornication. But all that this comes to is the confession that many of them were hypocrites. Granted. So are many of their heirs and assigns today. But the fact remains that they hung on to their theology as long as possible, and that, if they had had their way, it would still be an intolerable cultural burden upon New England, as what remains of it is a burden upon the rural South and Middle West.

There was, in fact, nothing admirable in it—nothing whatever. It was completely vile. The salvation of New England was achieved by its enemies, which is to say, by skeptics, the heralds of civilization at all times and everywhere. The Puritans tried desperately to put them down, but failed in the long run, as theologians always must fail. Revealed religion is still fighting hard for life in the world, but it is doomed. The day can't be far off when all men pretending to be civilized will look back upon it as they now look back upon witchcraft, human sacrifice and cannibalism.

[*American Mercury*, August 1933]

IV

FUNDAMENTALISTS AND EVANGELICALS

A DAY WITH BILLY SUNDAY

One William T. Ellis, an author, lately filled the *Bulletin* of the Authors' League with moving bellows against a publisher, alleging atrocities of the classical sort, but worse. The name of this Ellis arrests me; I seem to remember him as one who loves his fellow men to distraction, and gallops to save them from hell for modest honoraria. Isn't he the same, in fact, who is staff expert in piety to the Philadelphia *North American,* that loveliest flower of consecrated journalism? Isn't he Ellis the jitney Savonarola, the emblem wholesaler in Sunday-school lessons, the endless perspirer for the Uplift, the author of *Men and Missions* and other great doxological works? Isn't he the ecstatic one who hymned the late vice crusade in lascivious Atlanta—now, alas, almost forgotten!—as "more fun than a fleet of airships," and urged the moral sportsmen of other towns to go to it? I suspect that he is, and if so I have venerated him for years. Let a tear fall for him. If he does not gild his tale of woe, his hornswoggling was cruel, indeed. . . .

But enough of this grand young man. He appears in the chronicle only incidently, and as complaining of his royalties on his *magnum opus, Billy Sunday: The Man and His Message.* This great critical biography, he says, has sold 300,000 copies within a year!—and is still going like coca-cola in "dry" Georgia! . . . Har, har, me luds! Where are your best-sellers now? What becomes of McCutcheon, MacGrath, Chambers, the Glyn? Who will now whisper the figures for *Pollyanna, Trilby, Eben Holden, Dora Thorne?*[1] More, this Ellis tome is but one of several on the same subject. I have another before me; it is *The Real Billy Sunday,* by the Rev. Dr. Ram's Horn Brown, and if the signs and portents go for anything, it has sold even better than the Ellis book. The plates, indeed, show signs of usage; it has been rolled off by the hundred thousand. And in the city where I bought it, just outside the gates of Dr. Sunday's vast arena of God, the official bookseller told me that it was the best-seller of them all, and worth ten times the dollar that he asked for it.

Nevertheless, the fellow had a heart and so offered me *lagniappe.* He was sworn on the Four Gospels, he said, to sell the book for no less than a dollar, but if I would take it without parley, passing over the Ellis book, he would give me something instructive as makeweight. This something as makeweight turned out to be a gaudy pamphlet entitled *Fighting the Traffic in Young Girls, or, War on the White Slave Trade,* by Ernest A. Bell, "secretary of the Illinois Vigilance Association, superintendent of Midnight Missions, etc." Another great tussler for rectitude. The Ellis, no doubt, of Cook County. The beyond-Parkhurst. But himself, it would appear, rather daring, and to the evil-minded, perhaps even somewhat racy. Several of the full-page half-tones give us flaming views of brothel parlors, with the resident staff at persiflage with the visiting fireman; another shows the exterior of "a gilded palace of sin," with a stained glass *porte-cochère;* yet another (a photograph) shows a plump *geisha,* in skirts almost as short as a débutante's, in the lewd act of plaiting her hair. In a fourth appears "the white slave clearing-house," with a gospel meeting going on across the street. In a fifth we are introduced to a lady uplifter "pleading with a lost one to give up her sinful life," the "lost one" being by far the better looking. In a sixth we see a white slave trader plying his abominable arts upon a simple country girl in an ice-cream parlor. In a seventh—

But I spare you any further carnalities in effigy. The text of the work is horrifying enough. Not only Dr. Bell himself, but various other virtuosi, each of learning and cunning, encourage the popping eyeball. One of them is the Hon. Edwin W. Sims, district attorney in Chicago during the palmy days of the white slave uproar,[2] and secretary to the immortal Chicago Vice Commission, whose report was barred from the mails by super-uplifters at Washington. The unctuous Sims protests that he has "strong personal feelings against appearing in print in connection with a subject so abhorrent," but swallows them in order to warn all country girls that "the ordinary ice-cream parlor is very likely to be a spider's web." Another "expert" is Principal D. F. Sutherland, "of Red Water, Texas," who tells the sad story of the kidnapping of Estelle Ramon, of Kentucky, and of her rescue by the valiant William Scott, an old beau. Many more are mentioned on the title-page, but I fail to find their contributions inside. The explanation appears in an advertisement on the back cover. This advertisement shows that the present volume is no more than a sort of bait or pilot for a larger work of the same title, the which sells to connoisseurs at a dollar and a half. ("Fastest selling book of the age! Agents wanted! Write for terms and outfit!") A chance for the young gentlemen of the Y.M.C.A. to dedicate themselves to Service. Pornography for the plain people. . . . Too late, alas, too late! The copyright of the oleaginous Bell is dated 1910. That was the golden age of vice crusading, the year of unparalleled harvests for the snouting fraternity. To-day only the old-fashioned believe in white slavery; there are other bugaboos for the progressive. No wonder Dr. Sunday's bookseller was so free with his *lagniappe!* . . .

As for the actual Sunday book, dated 1914, it already tells an old story, for the sweating doctor has since done such press-agenting as not even a whole library of books could do, and his public eminence in these States is scarcely less exalted than that of Col. Roosevelt, Jess Willard, Henry Ford and the Kaiser. Dr. Horn-Brown reviews his career in phrases of laudation—a career of double distinction, for he was a celebrated baseball-player before he became the American St. Paul. (Joseph Smith, William Miller, Mary Baker G. Eddy, John Alexander Dowie, Sam Jones, William A. Sunday: we have produced some noble theologians!) His paternal grandfather was a Pennsylvania Dutchman named Sontag, but on the distaff side he stems from Lord William Corey, "who married the only daughter of Sir Francis Drake." The family of Corey de Pittsburgh de Reno is apparently the *jüngerer Linie.* Bill, our present hero, was converted in Chicago at the Pacific Garden Mission, in 1886 or thereabout, and after getting clear of his baseball contracts became assistant secretary of the Chicago Y.M.C.A. Then he got a job as advance man for J. Wilbur Chapman, an itinerant evangelist. When Chapman retired, in 1896, Sunday took over his trade, and has since gone steadily ahead. For fifteen years he worked the water-tanks, snaring the sinful tobacco chewers for the heavenly choir. Then he struck out for bigger game, and today he performs only in the main centers of population. He has saved Philadelphia, Baltimore, Kansas City and

Pittsburgh; he is headed for Boston, Chicago and New York. He has been lavishly praised by the President of the United States, is a Freemason and a Doctor of Divinity, and has enjoyed the honor of shaking me by the hand.

So much for the facts of his career, and the book of Dr. Horn-Brown. In laborious preparation for the review of that book I went to hear the whooping doctor himself. I found him vastly more interesting than any tome that these old eyes have rested upon in many a day. He was engaged, as I entered his vast bull-ring for the first time, in trying to scare a delegation of Civil War veterans into some realization, however faint, of the perils of hell, and when I took my seat in the pen reserved for the *literati*, directly under the eaves of his pulpit, I was sprinkled copiously with the dew of his frenzy. On it came, dribble, dribble, splash, splash, every time he executed one of his terrifying revolutions. It was like holding the bottle for a Russian dancer with a wet sponge strapped to his head. Of a sudden he would rush to the edge of the platform—his pulpit is as long as a barroom, but is without rails—, scream hysterically, and then bring himself up with a jolt and spin 'round like a top, his arms flung out and saline globules leaping from his brow in a pelting shower. He shed, I daresay, at least eight ounces of sweat between 7:45 and 9:00 P.M., and though he mopped his brow constantly and tried to be polite, a good deal of it escaped into the air, and so begemmed my critical gown. . . . Revolting details, but the love of all truth is above all prudery!

Of the *sforzando* doctor's actual discourse, that night or on the other nights I heard him, I have only a faint memory. Some sweet mush about the joys of heaven, with dogs and children playing on the grass; a long review of the life and times of King Solomon, with incidental railings against money; the orthodox arguments against ethyl alcohol, of no effect upon my thirst; high words against deacons who roll their eyes on Sunday and rob the widow on Monday; the joys of hell in detail, with not a singe omitted—all the orthodox camp-meeting stuff, howled from a million stumps by Methodist dervishes since the days of Wesley, and before them by Puritans of one sort or another since the croaking of the captive in Herod's rain-barrel. Out of all this I could get nothing; it was as empty of ideas as an editorial in the Boston *Transcript*. But away with ideas, and their pursuit. It was not by ideas that the downpouring doctor bemused those sinful veterans, and white-faced shop girls, and quaking Sunday school teachers, and staggered fat women; it was by his sheer roar and outcry. He survives in the cortex, not intellectually or visually, but purely aurally—as an astounding and benumbing noise, a riot of unearthly sound, an ear-torturing cacophony. Time and again he would have to pause for breath. Time and again he would make a megaphone of his hands to give the yell more pedal. Time and again you could see the elect in the front rows shrink and quiver beneath the gargantuan wallop of his shouts. I have fought through four wars; I have been a boilermaker; I have heard *Feuersnot*.[3] But never have I eared such a flabbergasting caterwauling; never have I suffered such a racking of the fenestra rotunda. It penetrates the capital ivory like a bullet, and sets up a raging pyemia. Sunday tells the simplest anecdote with the triumphant yelp of Satan sighting another archbishop in the chute. He utters such bald words as "Yes" and "No" with all the withering passion that the Old Guard put into its naughty reply at Waterloo. In the midst of a quite banal sentence his voice flies off into a shrill falsetto, and he clubs the side of his desk as if it were the very door of hell.

No wonder the candidates down in the arena are raised to incandescence, and begin screaming to be saved! Imagine the balcony scene in *Romeo and Juliet* with Juliet bellowing like Klytämnestra in the last round of *Electra*,[4] and Romeo howling up at her like an auctioneer, and both swinging Indian clubs, and revolving like pinwheels, and sweating like the colored waiters in a Pullman diner! Imagine "Nearer, My God, to Thee" accompanied by anvils, tom-toms, ophicleides, bass-drums and artillery, and a committee sticking pins into the tenors to make them squeal! No wonder the frontal celluloid is pierced and set afire! No wonder the devil flees in alarm, and takes refuge in some quiet Unitarian church! . . . Losing, alackaday, not much! Robbed of very little appetizing stock! The converts, indeed, are but feeble specimens of God's handiwork. Those I saw seemed anthropoid, but no more. In all my life I have never looked into more stupid and miserable faces. At least half of the aspirants for harps were adolescent and chlorotic girls; most of the males were of the sort one finds in water-front missions and at Salvation Army Christmas dinners. Even an osteopath, glancing at the former, would have noted a deficiency in haemoglobin, a disturbance below the diaphragm and above the neck, a profound veneration for moving picture actors. Some of them seemed to be flirting with tuberculosis; many of them had heads of curious shape and eyes that did not match; nearly all looked pitifully poor and wretched and godforsaken. Of such, perhaps, are the kingdom of heaven. They, too, have immortal souls, as much so as Claude

Debussy, General Carranza or the Hon. Josephus Daniels. Let us hope, at all events, that somewhere or other they will get square meals, and less work, and a chance to be care-free, and sinful, and happy.

Such is my memory of four nights of the Rev. Dr. Billy Sunday, now the emperor and pope of all our uplifters, the beyond-Gerald Stanley Lee, the super-Herbert Kaufman, the Augustine of American theology, the heir of Bryan, Dowie and Barnum. Let it stand as a review of Dr. Horn-Brown's instructive book, the which I commend to your study. Buy a couple of copies. Give one to your pastor, that honest man. But if it sets him to whooping like Sunday, then I advise you, in all charity, to have your gunmen do execution of the *lex non scripta* upon him. You will never stand such *fortissimos*—as a steady diet. Now and then, like laparotomy or mania-à-potu, a benign stimulant, but not for every Sunday! . . .

[*Smart Set,* July 1916]

FUNDAMENTALISM: DIVINE AND SECULAR

Those optimists who plan to put down fundamentalism by educating *Homo boobiens* are on all fours, it seems to me, with that simpleton of fable who sought to lift himself over a stile by pulling at his boot straps. *Homo boobiens* is a fundamentalist for the precise reason that he is uneducable. That is to say, he is quite unable to grasp the complex evidences upon which the civilized minority bases its heresies, and so he seeks refuge in the sublime simplicities of revelation. Is Genesis incredible? Does it go counter to the known facts? Perhaps. But do not forget to add that it is divinely simple—that even a Tennessee judge can understand it.

Perhaps the process is a bit clearer on another plane: I choose that of medicine. As everyone knows, scientific medicine has made more progress since the middle of the last century than it had made in the fifty centuries preceding. Today it is rapidly divesting itself of what remains of its old superstitions; it is becoming scientific in the exact sense, and year by year its practical efficacy, its capacity to cure disease, is greater. Yet in the very time of its greatest progress it is confronted by ever increasing hordes of quacks. The very day that news of insulin is in the newspapers *Homo boobiens* seeks treatment for his diabetes from a chiropractor.

Why? The reason seems to me to be simple. When an ignorant man goes to a doctor, he wants not only treatment but also enlightenment and consolation. He wants to know what is the matter with him and how it is to be cured. Now try to imagine a medical man explaining to him the nature of diabetes and the action of insulin. If you can imagine it, then you have an imagination indeed. The whole thing is inordinately complex. The explanation must be itself explained. To get to the bottom of it, to understand it in any true sense, is a sheer impossibility to a man not specially trained, and that training may be given only to men of unusual intelligence. But any moron can understand the explanation of the chiropractor. It is idiotic, but, like most things that are idiotic, it is also beautifully simple. So the moron grasps it—and cherishes it.

Something of the same sort goes on in the department of divinity. The clodhopper's objection to the hypothesis of evolution is not primarily that it is heathenish; that, indeed, is only an afterthought. His primary objection is that it is complicated and unintelligible—in the late Martyr Bryan's phrase, that it is "stuff and nonsense." In order to understand it a man must have a sound grounding in all the natural sciences; he must bring to the business an immense and intricate knowledge. And in order to get that grounding he must have a mind capable of taking it in.

Obviously, such minds are not common—that is, viewing the population as a whole. In the cities, where the sharpest fellows congregate, they may run to four or five per cent of the total, but in the back reaches of the land, where the population has been degenerating for generations, they are probably far below one per cent. The fact was brilliantly on display at the late trial of the infidel Scopes at Dayton, Tenn. What impressed me most, watching that trial through long sweaty days, was the honest bewilderment of the assembled yokels. They simply could not understand the thing that Scopes was accused of teaching. Its veriest elements were as far beyond their comprehension as the music of Bach or the theory of least squares.

Nor was it only the obvious peasants who showed that pathetic puzzlement. The judge on the bench was plainly flabbergasted. His questions were those of a man completely ignorant and, what is more, of one completely unable to learn. When Darrow attempted to explain the A B C of the evolutionary hypothesis to him he sat there with his mouth open, blinking his eyes uneasily. The thing was beyond his powers, and so he quite naturally concluded that it was senseless and against God. An explanation of the nature and causes of diabetes would have dismayed and alarmed him in exactly the same manner.

The central difficulty lies in the fact that all of the sciences have made such great progress during the last century that they have got quite beyond the reach of the average man. There was a time when this was not so. Even down to the end of the eighteenth century any man of ordinary intelligence could understand every scientific concept in good repute, even in astronomy. In medicine the thing was quite simple. Read the memoirs and biographies of the period—for example, Boswell's *Johnson*—and you will find every sick man disputing with his doctor as an equal, and often driving the good man into an uncomfortable corner.

But with the dawn of the nineteenth century all that began to change. Chemistry slowly took on the character of an exact science; physics, stimulated by the discovery of electricity, made vast and rapid progress; geology began to stand on its own legs; biology was born. More important, the sciences began to interchange facts and ideas; it was no longer possible for a zoölogist, say, to be ignorant of chemistry, or for a pathologist to neglect physics. There followed an era of synthesis, culminating dramatically in Darwin's publication of *The Origin of Species,* and science was reborn.

Simultaneously it threw off all its old diffidence, its ancient subservience to general opinion, and especially to theological opinion. The earliest scientists of the new order had to step very softly; the whole world was yet a sort of Tennessee. But the later revolutionists promulgated their heresies boldly, and met the ensuing uproar bravely. In England it was Huxley who led them; in every civilized country there was another like him. When the battle was over science was free at last, for the first time in the history of man. Since then no scientist, coming upon new knowledge in his laboratory or in the field, has had to pause before announcing it to sound out the bishop.

This freedom, as everyone knows, has immensely increased what may be called the momentum of scientific research. Discoveries have followed one another at a rapid pace, and some of them have been of the first importance. There is scarcely a science that has not been completely revolutionized since 1860, and to the old ones many new ones have been added. Thus the body of scientific knowledge has grown immensely, and as it has grown it has taken on an ever greater and greater complexity. No man of today could hope to sweep the whole field of the sciences, as many men did so lately as 1850. And no man can take in all that even one science has to say without long and difficult training, and a special aptitude for that sort of knowledge.

Meanwhile, man in general has lagged far behind. He remains, indeed, precisely where he was when all this tremendous advance began. His mind is simple; his talents are few. In the days when the sciences themselves were simple, he could be made, perhaps, to understand their elements—in other words, he was educable. But today the thing is quite beyond him. No conceivable training could convert an ice wagon driver into a pathologist or a hillbilly into a mathematical physicist. But the former may become a chiropractor and the latter may become a rustic judge. And there we are.

The fundamental fallacy is the assumption that all this is not true—that *Homo boobiens* is still capable of grasping anything and everything that goes on in the world. It is an imbecility, and hence dear to pedagogues. They are responsible, at bottom, for fundamentalism. Half-educated themselves, they have sought to crowd an impossible education upon their victims. The young moron in the village high school must be taught geology, paleontology, biology—all completely incomprehensible to him, and both incomprehensible and sinister to his pa. No wonder his pa sounds the fire alarm, rushes to the village tabernacle and appeals for succor to the Lord Jehovah!

[*Chicago Sunday Tribune,* September 20, 1925]

EVANGELICAL IGNORAMUSES

Under Prohibition, Fundamentalism and the complex ideals of the Klan there runs a common stream of bilge: it issues from the ghostly glands of the evangelical pastors of the land. The influence of these consecrated men upon the so-called thinking of the American people has been greatly underestimated by fanciers; in fact, most of the principal professors of such forms of metabolism overlook it altogether. Yet it must be obvious that their power is immense, and that they exert it steadily and with great gusto. It was not primarily the Christian faithful of the backwoods who fastened Prohibition upon us; it was the rustic *curés* working upon the Christian faithful, whose heat, in turn, ran the State legislators amok. If the *curés,* clinging to 1 Timothy 5:23,[5] had resolved to spare light wines and beer, we'd have them today, not behind the arras but in the full glare of rectitude. Here, as always in our moral Republic, scriptural exegesis preceded the uplift, and gave it its punch. While the agents of the brewers and distillers were fatuously bribing legislators, and paying higher and higher prices as session succeeded session, the Prohibitionists were out in the Bryan Belt organizing the country ecclesiastics. Once the latter had steam up the rest was only a matter of choosing the time. It came conveniently in the midst of war's alarms, at a moment of mystical exaltation. If history says that William H. Anderson, Wayne B. Wheeler and company turned the trick then history will err once more. It was really turned by a hundred thousand Methodist and Baptist pastors.

As I say, the doings of these gentlemen of God have been investigated but imperfectly, and so too little is known about them. Even the sources of their power, so far as I know, have not been looked into. My suspicion is that it has developed as the influence of the old-time country-town newspapers has declined. These newspapers, in large areas of the land, once genuinely molded public opinion. They attracted to their service a shrewd and salty class of rustic philosophers; they were outspoken in their views and responded only slightly to prevailing crazes. In the midst of the Bryan uproar, a quarter of a century ago, scores of little weeklies in the South and Middle West kept up a gallant battle for sound money and the Hanna idealism. There were red-hot Democratic papers in Pennsylvania, and others in Ohio; there were Republican sheets in rural Maryland, and even in Virginia. The growth of the big city dailies is what chiefly reduced them to puerility. As communications improved every yokel got dragged into the glittering orbits of Brisbane, Dr. Frank Crane and Mutt and Jeff. The rural mail carrier began leaving a 24-page yellow in every second box. The hinds distrusted and detested the politics of these great organs, but enjoyed their imbecilities. The country weekly could not match the latter, and so it began to decline. It is now in a low state everywhere in America. Half of it is boiler-plate and the other half is crossroads gossip. The editor is no longer the leading thinker of his dunghill; instead, he is commonly a broken and despairing man, cadging for advertisements and hoping for a third-rate political job.

His place has been taken by the village pastor. The pastor got into public affairs by the route of Prohibition. The shrewd shysters who developed the Anti-Saloon League made a politician of him, and once he had got a taste of power he was eager for more. It came very quickly. As industry penetrated the rural regions the new-blown Babbitts began to sense his capacity for safeguarding the established order, and so he was given the job: he became a local Billy Sunday. The old-line politicians, taught a lesson by the Anti-Saloon League, began to defer to him in general, as they had yielded to him in particular. He was consulted about candidacies; he had his say about policies. The local school-board soon became his private preserve. The wandering cony-catchers of the tin-pot fraternal orders found him a useful man. He was, by now, a specialist in all forms of public rectitude, from teetotalism to patriotism. He was put up on days of ceremony to sob for the flag, vice the county judge, retired. When the Klan burst upon the peasants all of his new duties were synthesized. He was obviously the chief local repository of its sublime principles, theological, social, ethnological and patriotic. In every country town in America today the chief engine of the Klan is a clerk in holy orders. If the Baptists are strong, their pastor is that engine. Failing Baptists, the heroic work is assumed by the Methodist parson, or the Presbyterian, or the Campbellite. Take away these sacerdotal props and the Invisible Empire would fade like that of Constantine.

II

What one mainly notices about these ambassadors of Christ, observing them in the mass, is their colossal ignorance. They constitute, perhaps, the most ignorant class of teachers ever set up to lead a civilized people; they are even more ignorant than the county superintendents of schools. Learning, indeed, is not esteemed in the evangelical denominations, and any literate plowhand, if the Holy Spirit inflames him, is thought to be fit to preach. Is he commonly sent, as a preliminary, to a training-camp, to college? But what a college! You will find one in every mountain valley of the land, with its single building in its bare pasture lot, and its faculty of half-idiot pedagogues and broken-down preachers. One man, in such a college, teaches oratory, ancient history, arithmetic and Old Testament exegesis. The aspirant comes in from the barnyard, and goes back in a year or two to the village. His body of knowledge is that of a street-car motorman or a movie actor. But he has learned the *clichés* of his craft, and he has got him a long-tailed coat, and so he has made his escape from the harsh labors of his ancestors, and is set up as a fountain of light and learning.

It is from such ignoramuses that the American peasantry gets its view of the cosmos. Certainly Fundamentalism should not be hard to understand when its sources are inspected. How can the teacher teach when his own head is empty? Of all that constitutes the sum of human knowledge he is as innocent as an Eskimo. Of the arts he knows absolutely nothing; of the sciences he has never so much as heard. No good book ever penetrates to those remote "colleges," nor does any graduate ever take away a desire to read one. He has been warned, indeed, against their blandishments; what is not addressed solely to the paramount business of saving souls is of the devil. So when he hears by chance of the battle of ideas beyond the sky-rim, he quite naturally puts it down to Beelzebub. What comes to him, vaguely and distorted, is unintelligible to him. He is suspicious of it, afraid of it—and he quickly communicates his fears to his dupes. The common man, in many ways, is hard to arouse. It is a terrific job to ram even the most elemental ideas into him. But it is always easy to scare him.

That is the daily business of the evangelical pastors of the Republic. They are specialists in alarms and bugaboos. The rum demon, atheists, Bolsheviki, the Pope, bootleggers, Leopold and Loeb—all these have served them in turn, and in the demonology of the Ku Klux Klan all have been conveniently brought together. The old stock company of devils has been retired, and with it the old repertoire of sins. The American peasant of today finds it vastly easier to claw into heaven than he used to. Private holiness has now been handed over to the Holy Rollers and other such survivors from a harsher day. It is sufficient now to hate the Pope, to hate the Jews, to hate the scientists, to hate all foreigners, to hate whatever the cities yield to. These hatreds have been spread in the land by rev. pastors, chiefly Baptists and Methodists. They constitute, with their attendant fears, the basic religion of the American clodhopper today. They are the essence of the new Christianity, American style.

III

Their public effects are constantly underestimated until it is too late. I ask no indulgence for calling attention again to the case of Prohibition. Fundamentalism, in its various forms, sneaks upon the nation in the same disarming way. The cities laugh at the yokels, but meanwhile the politicians take careful notice; such mountebanks as Peay of Tennessee and Blease of

South Carolina have already issued their preliminary whoops. As the tide rolls up the pastors will attain to greater and greater consequence. Already, indeed, they swell visibly, in power and pretension. The Klan, in its early days, kept them discreetly under cover; they labored valiantly in the hold, but only lay go-getters were seen upon the bridge. But now they are everywhere on public display, leading the anthropoid host. At the great outpouring in Washington a few months ago—which alarmed the absentee Dr. Coolidge so vastly that he at once gave a high Klan dignitary a federal office of trust and profit—there were Baptist mullahs all over the lot, and actually more in line, I daresay, than bootleggers or insurance solicitors.

The curious and amusing thing is that the ant-like activity of these holy men has so far got little if any attention from our established publicists. Let a lone Red arise to annoy a barroom full of Michigan lumberjacks, and at once the fire alarm sounds and the full military and naval power of the nation is summoned to put down the outrage. But how many Americanos would the Reds convert to their rubbish, even supposing them free to spout it on every street-corner? Probably not enough, all told, to make a day's hunting for a regiment of militia. The American moron's mind simply does not run in that direction; he wants to keep his Ford, even at the cost of losing the Bill of Rights. But the stuff that the Baptist and Methodist dervishes have on tap is very much to his taste; he gulps it eagerly and rubs his tummy. I suggest that it might be well to make a scientific inquiry into the nature of it. The existing agencies of sociological snooting seem to be busy in other direction. There are elaborate surveys of some of the large cities, showing how much it costs to teach a child the principles of Americanism, how often the average citizen falls into the hands of the cops, how many detective stories are taken out of the city library daily, and how many children a normal Polish woman has every year. Why not a survey of the rustic areas, where men are he and God still reigns? Why not an attempt to find out just what the Baptist dominies have drilled into the heads of the Tennesseeans, Arkansans and Nebraskans? It would be amusing—and instructive.

And useful. For it is well, in such matters, to see clearly what is ahead. The United States grows increasingly urban, but its ideas are still hatched in the little towns. What the swineherds credit today is whooped tomorrow by their agents and attorneys in Congress, and then comes upon the cities suddenly with all the force of law. Where do the swineherds get it? Mainly

from the only publicists and metaphysicians they know: the gentlemen of
the sacred faculty. It was not the bawling of the mountebank Bryan, but
the sermon of a mountain Bossuet that laid the train of the Scopes case and
made a whole State forever ridiculous. I suggest looking more carefully
into the notions that such divine ignoramuses spout.

[*American Mercury,* November 1925]

SISTER AIMÉE

I

This rev. sister in God, I confess, greatly disappointed me. Arriving in Los
Angeles out of the dreadful deserts of Arizona and New Mexico, I naturally made tracks to hear and see the town's most distinguished citizen. Her
basilica turned out to be a great distance from my hotel, far up a high hill
and in the midst of a third-rate neighborhood. It was a cool and sunshiny
Sunday afternoon, the place was packed, and the whisper had gone around
that Aimée was heated up by the effort to jail her, and would give a gaudy
show. But all I found myself gaping at, after half an hour, was an orthodox
Methodist revival, with a few trimmings borrowed from the Baptists and
United Brethren—in brief, precisely the sort of thing that goes on in the
shabby suburbs and dark back streets of Baltimore, three hundred nights of
every year. I caught myself waiting for Dr. Crabbe to pop up, to shake
down the boobs for the Anti-Saloon League—or Dr. Howard A. Kelly, to
tell what Bible-reading has done for him.

Aimée, of course, is richer than most evangelists, and so she has got
herself a plant that far surpasses anything ever seen in shabby suburbs. Her
temple to the One God is immensely wide—as wide, almost, as the Hip-
podrome in New York—and probably seats 2,500 customers. There is a full
brass band down in front, with a grand piano to one side of it and an organ
to the other. From the vast gallery, built like that of a theater, runways run
along the side walls to what may be called the proscenium arch, and from
their far ends stairways lead down to the platform. As in many other evangelical churches, there are theater seats instead of pews. Some pious texts
are emblazoned on the wall behind the platform: I forget what they say.
There are no stained-glass windows. The architecture, in and out, is other-

wise of the Early Norddeutscher-Lloyd Rauchzimmer school, with modifications suggested by the filling-stations of the Standard Oil Company of New Jersey. The whole building is very cheaply made. It is large and hideous, but I don't think it costs much. Nothing in Los Angeles appears to have cost much. The town, save for a few brilliant spots—for example, the Elk clubhouse and one or two theaters—is inconceivably shoddy.

II

As I say, Aimée has nothing on tap to make my eyes pop, old revival fan that I am. The proceedings began with a solemn march by the brass band, played about as well as the average Salvation Army band could have done it, but no better. Then a brother from some remote outpost filed down the aisle at the head of a party of fifty or sixty of the faithful. They sang a hymn, the brother made a short speech, and then he handed Aimée a check for $500 for her Defense Fund. A quartet followed, male, a bit scared, and with Camp Meade haircuts. Two little girls then did a duet, to the music of a ukulele played by one of them. Then Aimée prayed. And then she delivered a brief harangue.

I could find nothing in it worthy of remark. It was the time-honored evangelical hokum, made a bit more raucous than usual by the loudspeakers strewn all over the hall. A brother who seemed to be a sort of stage manager shoved the microphone of the radio directly under Aimée's nose. When, warmed by her homiletic passion, she turned this way and that, he followed her with the microphone. It somehow suggested an attentive deck-steward, plying his useful art and mystery on a rough day. Aimée wore a long white robe, with a very low-cut collar, and over it there was a cape of dark purple. Her thick hair, piled high in a curious coiffure, turned out to be of mahogany brown. I had heard that it was a flaming red.

The rest of the orgy went on in the usual way. Groups of four, six, eight or twenty got up and sang. A large, pudgy, soapy-looking brother prayed. Aimée herself led the choir in a hymn with a lively tune and very saucy words, chiefly aimed at her enemies. Two or three times more she launched into brief addresses. But mostly she simply ran the show. While the quartets bawled and the band played she was busy at a telephone behind the altar or hurling orders in a loud stage-whisper at sergeants and corporals on the floor. Obviously a very managing woman. A fixed smile stuck to her from first to last.

III

What brought this commonplace and transparent mountebank to her present high estate, with thousands crowding her tabernacle daily and money flowing in upon her from whole regiments of eager dupes? The answer, it seems to me, is as plain as mud. For years she had been wandering about the West, first as a sideshow barker, then as a faith healer, and finally as a cow-town evangelist. One day, inspired by God, she decided to try her fortune in Los Angeles. Instantly she was a roaring success. And why? For the plain reason that there were more morons collected in Los Angeles than in any other town on earth—because it was a pasture foreordained for evangelists, and she was the first comer to give it anything low enough for its taste and comprehension.

The osteopaths, chiropractors and other such quacks had long marked and occupied it. It swarmed with swamis, spiritualists, Christian Scientists, cyrstal-gazers and the allied necromancers. It offered brilliant pickings for real estate speculators, oil-stock brokers, wire-tappers and so on. But the town pastors were not up to its opportunities. They ranged from melancholy High Church Episcopalians, laboriously trying to interest retired Iowa alfalfa kings in ritualism, down to struggling Methodists and Baptists, as earnestly seeking to inflame the wives of the same monarchs with the crimes of the Pope. All this was over the heads of the trade. The Iowans longed for something that they could get their teeth into. They wanted magic and noise. They wanted an excuse to whoop.

Then came Aimée, with the oldest, safest tricks out of the pack of Dr. Billy Sunday, Dr. Gipsy Smith and the rest of the consecreted hell-robbers. To them she added some passes from her circus days. In a month she had Los Angeles sitting up. In six months she had it in an uproar. In a year she was building her rococo temple and her flamboyant Bible College, and the half-wits were flocking in to hear her from twenty States. Today, if her temple were closed by the police, she could live on her radio business alone. Every word she utters is carried on the air to every forlorn hamlet in those abominable deserts, and every day the mail brings her a flood of money.

IV

The effort to jail her has disingenuousness in it, and the more civilized Angelenoas all sympathize with her, and wish her well. Her great success raised up two sets of enemies, both powerful. One was made up of the other town clergy, who resented her raids upon their customers. The other was composed of the town Babbitts, who began to fear that her growing celebrity was making Los Angeles ridiculous. So it was decided to bump her off, and her ill-timed morganatic honeymoon with the bald-headed and wooden-legged Mr. Ormiston offered a good chance.

But it must be manifest to any fair observer that there is very little merit in the case against her. What she is charged with, in essence, is perjury, and the chief specification is that, when asked if she had been guilty of unchastity, she said no. I submit that no self-respecting judge in the Maryland Free State, drunk or sober, would entertain such a charge against a woman, and that no Maryland grand jury would indict her. It is unheard of, indeed, in any civilized community for a woman to be tried for perjury uttered in defense of her honor. But in California, as everyone knows, the process of justice is full of unpleasant novelties, and so poor Aimée, after a long and obscene hearing, has been held for trial, and will go before a petit jury some time in January.

The betting odds in the Los Angeles saloons are 50 to 1 that she will either hang the jury or get a clean acquittal. I myself, tarrying in the town, invested some money on the long end, not in avarice, but as a gesture of sympathy for a lady in distress. The local district attorney has the newspapers on his side, and during the progress of Aimée's hearing he filled one of them, in the chivalrous Southern California manner, with denunciations of her. But Aimée herself has the radio, and I believe that the radio will count most in the long run. Twice a day, week in and week out, she caresses the anthropoids of all that dusty, forbidding region with her evangelical coos. And twice a day she meets her lieges of Los Angeles face to face, and has at them with her lovely eyes, her mahogany hair, her eloquent hips and her lascivious voice. It will be a hard job, indeed, to find twelve men and true to send her to the hoosegow. Unless I err grievously, God is with her.

[*Baltimore Evening Sun,* December 13, 1926]

THE MISSIONARIES

I

If, as seems likely, the emerging Chinese celebrate the end of their *Frei-heitskrieg* by heaving all the Christian missionaries into the sea, the sacrifice will put a brilliant, if somewhat shocking finish to one or the most grotesque episodes of the modern era.[6] The effort to convert China, indeed, seems likely to go down into history as the least successful enterprise ever undertaken by civilized man. Its failure, after centuries of effort, actually exceeds that of Prohibition. Since the Nestorians first entered the country, far back in the Sixth Century, not a hundred Chinamen of any dignity or influence have ever succumbed to the missionaries' zeal, and among the gabble the number of converts has never gone beyond one-half of one per cent of the total population.

Here I allow everything to missionary enthusiasm, which only too often takes the form of palpable exaggeration. Every Chinese boy or girl who goes to a mission school is counted as a professing Christian, and even as a fanatic, though everyone knows that nine-tenths of them, once they have got what they want, revert to their ancestral theology. Among the unlettered coolies (apparently a Chinese distortion of the word coolidges) the percentage of bogus converts is probably still higher. Every time there is a famine, and soup-houses are opened by the missionaries, hundreds of thousands of the starving begin a feverish study of the International Sunday-School Lessons, but as soon as the grocery-stores resume traffic they forget all that they have learned and are pagans once more.

This has happened over and over again. In poor districts, I daresay, the same Chinaman has been converted four or five times, and during different famines has been Romanist, Hard-shell Baptist, High Church Episcopalian, Missouri Synod Lutheran and Seventh Day Adventist. The Adventists have been very active in China of late years, and many of the missionaries rescued from Nanking two weeks ago were of their persuasion. Thus it is probable that large numbers of the peasants of the surrounding country, craving vitamins in evil times, became convinced that Saturday was the one and only true Sabbath, and that going to church on Sunday was somehow loose and in bad taste, like reading Goethe on the Fourth of

July. But this conviction, no doubt, has now been obliterated by the Canton equivalent of the Creel Press Bureau.[7]

II

It is the common theory that the Chinese reject Christianity because, compared to the indigenous religions of their country, it is mystical, illogical and incredible. The doctrine of the Trinity is frequently mentioned as a chief cause of their doubts, and they are also said to find it difficult, if not downright impossible, to accept the New Testament miracles. But I see no reason to believe all this. As a matter of fact, the religions of China, even on their upper levels, are quite as mystical and illogical as Christianity, and further down they are simply farragoes of demonological nonsense. What the average Chinese coolie (or coolidge) believes is quite as idiotic as what a Tennessee Christian believes.

Thus it is not a theological difficulty that incommodes the work of the missionaries. Even an educated Chinaman, I suspect, would find little to daunt him in Presbyterianism, or Catholicism, though he might buck at some of the fancier dogmas of the Seventh Day Adventists. The real difficulty probably lies in the field of Christian ethics, where it lies, too, for most Caucasian skeptics. It is the missionary himself, rather than his magic, that offends the Chinaman. For it is a gross trespass upon common decency, by the Chinese code, to be a missionary at all. That is, it is indecent to press one's opinion, wnether ghostly or secular, upon another, and especially indecent when he shows signs of not being willing to listen.

The poor missionaries are thus doomed to offend all their potential customers every time they open their mouths, for it is of the essence of their art and mystery that they cannot wait for invitations to expound the Gospel according to their lights, but must roam around with the Book in hand, banging every head in sight. Their motive, of course, is impeccable: they believe that every Chinaman they fail to fetch will sweat in Hell through all eternity, and they yearn to save him, even against his will. But in this world, as everyone knows, worthy purposes are seldom a sufficient excuse for bad manners. The missionary, in Chinese eyes, is a bounder and a nuisance, and so he is doomed to go on bellowing in what may be called a hostile vacuum—save only when a dire belly-need induces those who dislike him to be polite to him.

III

In late years the missionaries in China (and elsewhere) have embellished and facilitated their theological labors by adding medical and surgical services. The value of these services, I believe, is somewhat in dispute among faunal naturalists: by reducing the death-rate (if they have actually done so) they have probably only accelerated the problem of subsistence. But that objection, it is likely, is not often heard from the persons directly benefited. To these persons the advantage of getting cured of gallstones or leprosy or barber's itch to-day is more than sufficient compensation for the burden of having to be converted to Christianity in order to eat to-morrow.

Nevertheless, I believe that this medical service, however laudable in itself, has only increased the unpopularity of the missionaries among the more thoughtful Chinese. What they see in it is only a dodge to make proselyting easier. A new necessity is attached to the old theological design, and the one cannot be obtained without yielding to the other. Here again the apparent device of the missionaries violates Chinese notions of fairness, courtesy and common decency. Even in America, where almost anything is considered decent that brings home the bacon, this device would probably cause murmurs. Suppose all the hospitals of the United States were in charge of persons advocating free love, free speech, unrestricted submarine warfare or some other such abhorrent heresy, and that a tract advocating it were handed out with every dose of castor oil? Would the scheme be popular, or would it be resented?

Of late there has been a movement to supply China with hospitals free from ecclesiastical control, but those maintained by the missionaries are still in a majority, and during the recent uproars, as everyone knows, they were favorite targets of attack. The Chinese do not want to abolish them: they simply want to turn the missionaries out of them. That desire may be sinful, but I think it would be hard to prove that it is unnatural.

IV

Hitherto the Christian Powers have stood behind the missionaries—perhaps not often for pious motives, but at all events very vigorously. So-called outrages upon them, *i.e.,* quite natural efforts, with the only means at hand, to get rid of them, have provoked many punitive expeditions, and even formal wars, and I think it may be said very fairly that they have been the cause of the deaths of at least ten times as many heathen as they have ever saved. At the present time the thirty thousand or more white and Japanese troops in the Shanghai-Nanking region are largely engaged in protecting them, and it was in their behalf that the American and British commanders recently threatened, in the gallant Christian manner, to bombard a town full of unarmed men, women and children.

But this business, I fear, cannot go on in China much longer. The Chinese sicken of it, and are beginning to be strong enough to resist it. They see that the missionary is not only a most unpleasant theological propagandist, but also that he is the advance agent of all sorts of commercial exploiters, and even of military assassins. He has brought them some of the so-called boons of Western civilization, but he has not brought them all, nor are they convinced that he has brought them the best. The rest they propose to get for themselves, in their own way and without any accompaniment of hymn singing and moral snuffling. If the missionaries will retire gracefully, shouting polite hosannas, well and good; if they linger, they will be heaved out.

Who will blame the Chinese? Certainly not any man with experience of evangelical fervor at home. It is one of the basic weaknesses and one of the salient curses of the Christian scheme of things. Man will never be wholly civilized until he ceases to intrude his snout into the shy, mysterious, highly private recesses of his brother's soul.

[*Baltimore Evening Sun,* April 4, 1927]

THE IMPREGNABLE ROCK[8]

Thinking of the theological doctrine called Fundamentalism, one is apt to think at once of the Rev. Aimée Semple McPherson, the Rev. Dr. Billy Sunday and the late Dr. John Roach Straton. It is almost as if, in thinking of physic, one thought of Lydia Pinkham or Dr. Munyon. Such clowns, of course, are high in human interest, and their sincerity need not be impugned, but one must remember always that they do not represent fairly the body of ideas they presume to voice, and that those ideas have much better spokesmen. I point, for example, to the Rev. J. Gresham Machen, D.D., Litt.D., formerly of Princeton and now professor of the New Testament in Westminster Theological Seminary, Philadelphia. Dr. Machen is surely no mere soap-boxer of God, alarming bucolic sinners for a percentage of the plate. On the contrary, he is a man of great learning and dignity—a former student at European universities, the author of various valuable books, including a Greek grammar, and a member of several societies of savants. Moreover, he is a Democrat and a wet, and may be presumed to have voted for Al in 1928. Nevertheless, this Dr. Machen believes completely in the inspired integrity of Holy Writ, and when it was questioned at Princeton he withdrew indignantly from those hallowed shades, leaving Dr. Paul Elmer More to hold the bag.

I confess frankly, as a life-long fan of theology, that I can find no defect in his defense of his position. Is Christianity actually a revealed religion? If not, then it is nothing; if so, then we must accept the Bible as an inspired statement of its principles. But how can we think of the Bible as inspired and at the same time as fallible? How can we imagine it as part divine and awful truth and part mere literary confectionery? And how, if we manage so to imagine it, are we to distinguish between the truth and the confectionery? Dr. Machen answers these questions very simply and very convincingly. If Christianity is really true, as he believes, then the Bible is true, and if the Bible is true, then it is true from cover to cover. So answering, he takes his stand upon it, and defies the hosts of Beelzebub to shake him. As I have hinted, I think that, given his faith, his position is completely impregnable. There is absolutely no flaw in the argument with which he supports it. If he is wrong, then the science of logic is a hollow vanity, signifying nothing.

His moral advantage over his Modernist adversaries, like his logical advantage, is immense and obvious. He faces the onslaught of the Higher Criticism without flinching, and yields nothing of his faith to expediency or decorum. Does his searching of Holy Writ compel him to believe that Jesus was descended from David through Joseph, as Matthew says, and yet begotten by the Holy Ghost, as Matthew also says, then he believes it calmly and goes on. Does he encounter witches in Exodus, and more of them in Deuteronomy, and yet more in Chronicles, then he is unperturbed. Is he confronted, in Revelation, with angels, dragons, serpents and beasts with seven heads and ten horns, then he contemplates them as calmly as an atheist looks at a chimpanzee in a zoo. For he has risen superior to all such trivial details, the bane of less devout and honest men. The greater marvel swallows all the lesser ones. If it be a fact, as he holds, that Yahweh has revealed the truth to His lieges on this earth, then he is quite as willing to accept and cherish that truth when it is odd and surprising as when it is transparent and indubitable. Believing, as he does, in an omnipotent and omniscient God, maker of heaven and earth, he admits freely that that God probably knows more than he himself knows, both of the credible and the incredible, though he is a member of both Phi Beta Kappa and the American Philological Association.

It must be plain that the Modernists are in a much weaker position. The instant they admit that only part of the Bible may be rejected, if it be only the most trifling fly-speck in the Pauline Epistles, they admit that any other part may be rejected. Thus the divine authority of the whole disappears, and there is no more evidence that Christianity is a revealed religion than there is that Mohammedanism is. It is idle for such iconoclasts to say that one man—usually the speaker—is better able to judge in such matters than other men, for they have to admit in the same breath that no man's judgment, however learned he may be, is infallible, and that no man's judgment, however mean he may be, is negligible. They thus reduce theology to the humble level of a debate over probabilities. Such a debate it has become, in fact, in the hands of the more advanced Modernists. No two of them agree in all details, nor can they conceivably agree so long as one man, by God's inscrutable will, differs from all other men. The Catholics get rid of the difficulty by setting up an infallible Pope, and consenting formally to accept his verdicts, but the Protestants simply chase their own tails. By depriving revelation of all force and authority, they rob their so-called religion of every dignity. It becomes, in their hands, a mere romantic imposture, unsatisfying to the pious and unconvincing to the judicious.

I have noted that Dr. Machen is a wet. This is somewhat remarkable in a Presbyterian, but certainly it is not illogical in a Fundamentalist. He is a wet, I take it, simply because the Yahweh of the Old Testament and the Jesus of the New are both wet—because the whole Bible, in fact, is wet. He not only refuses to expunge from the text anything that is plainly there; he also refuses to insert anything that is not there. What I marvel at is that such sincere and unyielding Christians as he is do not start legal proceeding against the usurpers who now disgrace the name. By what right does a Methodist bishop, in the face of John 2:1–11, Matthew 11:19 and Timothy 5:23,[9] hold himself out as a follower of Jesus, and even as an oracle on

Jesus's ideas and desires? Surely there is libel here, and if I were the believer that Dr. Machen is I think I'd say that there is also blasphemy. I suggest formally that he and his orthodox friends get together, and petition some competent court to restrain the nearest Methodist congregation from calling itself Christian. I offer myself as a witness for the plaintiffs, and promise to come well heeled with evidence. At worst, such a suit would expose the fraudulence of the Methodist claim and redound greatly to the glory and prosperity of the true faith; at best, some judge more intelligent and less scary than the general might actually grant the injunction.

[*American Mercury*, December 1931]

V

SPIRITUALISM, THEOSOPHY, AND CHRISTIAN SCIENCE

THE SPIRIT WORLD

Although I believe in ghosts no more than I believe in Eamon de Valera, Mrs. Fiske and cures for neuralgia in the eyeball, some of the arguments currently vouchsafed by skeptics against them do not entirely persuade me. One of the favorite of these arguments, the chief in fact, is, for example, that, if spirits really exist and can get into communication with the living, why don't they tell something worth while instead of confining themselves to such obvious pieces of news as: Uncle Henry is very happy in Heaven and Casanova is not among those present. Let us say that the ghost speaking is that of Mr. Sigmund Dusenblatt, late of Dusenblatt, Kraus and Glaubman, Inc., Ladies' Wear, and late husband to Mrs. Amanda Dusenblatt, *née* Piesporter. The erstwhile M. Dusenblatt during his lifetime was assuredly no raconteur, no walking edition of the *Atlantic Monthly* and *Literary Digest,* no fellow of infinite jest, information and *esprit.* His conversations with the no less estimable Madame Dusenblatt while he was on earth and a patriotic and active citizen of the Republic were certainly nothing to provoke envy in the breast of a Benjamin Disraeli or an Edmund Gosse. They were confined, doubtless, to the perfectly obvious observations of perfectly obvious gentlemen like himself. Why, then, under these circumstances, should it be demanded of the M. Dusenblatt that, dead, he should suddenly become gifted with infinite wisdoms, perspicuities and philosophies that were utterly foreign to him when his soul still reposed in his corporeal body? When alive, the M. Dusenblatt undoubtedly sought to convey an emphatic point to his spouse, to his partners, the talented MM. Kraus and Glaubman, and to his head buyer, the statuesque and capable Miss Sheila O'Rourke, by pounding on a table. When dead, why should not the same M. Dusenblatt pursue the course that he pursued while alive and seek analogously to convey his convictions by a necessarily and inevitably somewhat less obstreperous tapping on a table?

Or take a ghost of fibre different from that of Mr. Dusenblatt. Say the shade of Mr. Herman C. Perkins, the eminent lawyer. Throughout his life, Mr. Perkins confined himself to subtle evasions, to thumping balderdash and to magnificent prevarications. Why then, now that he is dead, should his ghost suddenly turn turtle on him and seek not to evade? Why shouldn't his ghost go on lying and emitting profound nonsense just as Herman himself did while he was still in a state of eating mundane Schweitzer cheese sandwiches and drinking mundane bootleg liquor? If the ghost of Mr. Perkins, appearing in the darkened back parlor of Mme. Flora's flat in West One Hundred and Sixth Street, whispers to his trembling widow that he still loves her, why shouldn't his widow accept it as an unmistakably accurate proof of after-life, since surely Mr. Perkins told her the selfsame thing countless times during his life just after he had returned from important business in Atlantic City with a Follies girl?

Go a step farther. Indeed, go a thousand steps farther. Take the ghost of Napoleon Bonaparte. It is argued by the skeptics that if there really is such a thing as the ghost of Napoleon Bonaparte, that ghost should reasonably be expected to convey more piquant and important information to an expectant world than confining himself merely to the stereotyped spook intelligence that Little Bright Eyes can hear what it is trying to say, that there must be sympathy in the back parlor if it is to get its message across, and that this flabbergastingly important message (subsequently conveyed in the voice of a tenor with the No. 3 "Irene" company) is as follows: "It is true that I lost the Battle of Waterloo."

Now, what intelligent, logically minded person would reasonably expect the late Napoleon Bonaparte to do anything else? To expect his ghost, after all these years, to turn up in the rear of a two-room, bath and kitchenette apartment in Harlem and confide the inside secrets of his military campaigns to half a dozen former privates in the A.E.F. and their wives is surely to imagine a Napoleon Bonaparte without a sense of humor and deprived of all dignity by the majesty of death. Were he still alive and present in the same company is it conceivable that he would do otherwise than politely confine himself to the same trivialities that the skeptics object to in the case of his ghost? It is not.

The mistakes that these skeptics make, it seems to me, lies in assuming that death should completely alter the intrinsic nature of a man, that is, should occultly convert his spirit self into a completely different entity. If I, for instance, should die to-morrow from an overdose of wood alcohol and should turn up as an articulate vapor next Wednesday night in the dining-room of Madame Celeste's flat down in Greenwich Village, what sound reason should there be for expecting me to betray the fact that I have gone to Hell, that there are enough pretty girls down there to give me a very jolly time, and that if I had to live my life over again I should doubtless be just as great a jackass as I had been? Surely the residuum of spurious dignity, of hypocrisy and of talent for posturing that I had carried with me beyond the grave would restrain me from making any such honest and embarrassing admissions. I should certainly slyly content myself and support my late self-esteem with much of the hocus-pocus affected by me during my lifetime. I should distract and hornswoggle the assembled intelligentsia with all the familiar and reliable bosh about Wa-Wa, the Indian chief, and the spirit of Julius Cæsar, and should enjoy myself further by tipping the table, striking a tambourine, ringing a bell and—this most certainly—pinching the leg of the medium. This, after all, is more or less the sort of thing that amused me in life, this is the kind of thing, in the form of literary composition, with which during my life I tormented the yokelry, so why shouldn't I continue to have the same good time now that I was a ghost? Damned if I know.

[*Smart Set,* December 1922]

HOOEY FROM THE ORIENT

THE MYSTERIOUS MADAME, by C. E. Bechofer-Roberts. $3.50. 332 pp. New York: *Brewer & Warren.*

The madame of Mr. Bechofer-Roberts' title is the late Helena Petrovna Blavatsky (1831–91), *geb.* Hahn, founder and for sixteen years grand panjandrum of the Theosophical Society, and now a sort of goddess to all faithful customers of the cult. Her likeness to Mrs. Mary Baker G. Eddy must strike every connoisseur of the higher mountebankery. Both emerged from obscure and stupid family circles, both invented romantic biographies for themselves, both played heavily with love before giving it up as a bad job, both began their professional careers as conventional magicians and only gradually developed their own arcana, both were copious and shameless plagiarists, both suffered from life-long malaises, both were constantly beset by demons, both loved money and knew how to get it, both suspected their immediate followers of evil designs, and both have been purged *post mortem* of their plentiful blunders and rascalities, and elevated to what amounts substantially to sainthood.

La Eddy, on the whole, must be set down as the more respectable character. Her three marriages are hard to explain, and her stealings from Quimby and other such forerunners defy explanation altogether, but her New England upbringing saved her from the more gross and overt kinds of indecorum. La Blavatsky, a Russian of mixed Slavic and German ancestry, was a far rougher person. She smoked incessantly in a day when it was simply not done by ladies, she swore like a police lieutenant, and there is sound reason for believing that she once committed bigamy. But these peccadilloes add to her charm almost as much as they take away from her respectability. She was, indeed, a most salty and amusing old harridan, and Mr. Bechofer-Roberts has done a vivid portrait of her—very fairly and even humanely, but without losing anything of her picturesqueness. It well deserves to be put beside E. F. Dakin's recent portrait of Mrs. Eddy.

There seems to be little doubt that the Blavatsky was a fraud pure and unadulterated—a fraud deliberate, unconscionable and unmitigated. Mr. Bechofer-Roberts is disposed to believe that, toward the end, she was deluded by her own hocus-pocus, but I incline to think that his own evidence is against him. She started out in life as a professional spiritualist, and the banal tricks of that amusing trade were always her chief reliances. She materialized the forms of Koot Hoomi and her other preposterous mahatmas precisely as the hard-working mediums in back streets materialize the forms of Wah-Wah the Indian chief. That is to say, she had them confected of stuffed pillows and other such lowly stuff, and then danced them before her dupes in dark rooms. She had a cabinet with a sliding door in the back, and from it she produced letters from Tibet (all written in her own hand, with curious Russified letters) and other such marvels. Her books were all clumsy plagiarisms. In *Isis Unveiled* a diligent critic discovered two thousand passages borrowed from other treatises on occultism, not to mention seven hundred blunders "in names, words and numbers" and six hundred "mis-statements of fact." She was caught over and over again. Her very assistants exposed her more than once, with exact specifications. But she relied confidently upon the illimitable credulity of her followers, and was not disappointed. Like the patrons of Mrs. Eddy, they were insatiable gluttons for punishment. The more she was exposed, the more firmly they believed in her.

Thousands of them continue to do so to this day. Theosophy has never made the worldly success of Christian Science, but it still has a large following, both in Europe and in America, and every now and then the faithful are worked by some new operator, *e.g.,* the young Hindu who calls himself Krishnamurta, and who was but lately all over the front pages of the New York tabloids. The theosophical tenets are unanimously nonsensical. They are not merely dubious; they are downright insane. In part they are borrowed from the mooney speculations of such European mystics as Jakob Böhme, in part they come from the common claptrap of professional occultists (which is to say, of persons on a level, morally and intellectually, with corn-doctors at county fairs), and in part they are a stale and ignorant rehash of so-called oriental philosophy This oriental philosophy is the product of Hindus who believe that cows have souls, that adepts can fly through the air without the use of wings or gasoline, and that a man who permits his daughter to go unmarried so much as twenty-four hours beyond the onset of puberty is doomed to Hell. In brief, it is the product of degraded ignoramuses who make India a sewer of superstition.

How does it come that such imbecilities win converts in the West, and are even spoken of respectfully, now and then, by presumably learned men? There are two reasons. The first is that they are embodied in scriptures which also include a great deal of metaphysics—and metaphysics, to certain types of mind, always seems profound, even when it is palpable balderdash. The other is that not a few of the more ancient Indian ideas, working their way westward by way of Persia, Egypt and Greece, were embedded in Christianity by the Early Fathers, and have thus come to have a familiar and pious flavor. But they are just as silly in the Book of Revelation and in the lucubrations of Athanasius, Tertullian and Augustine as they are in the

Indian Vedas. To discuss them seriously is to turn one's back upon every intellectual decency. They are precisely equivalent to the philosophizing of phrenologists, chiropractors and Communists.

Mr. Bechofer-Roberts gives only passing attention to them: he devotes nearly all his attention to the racy character of La Blavatsky. It is to be hoped that he devotes another volume to a critical examination of the theosophist doctrine, as she set it forth authoritatively in *Isis Unveiled, The Secret Doctrine* and *The Stanzas of Dzyan*. To be sure, that would be a difficult job, for in large part these books are mere gibberish. Nevertheless, it would be worth undertaking, for thousands of fools accept their brummagem revelations as gospel, and they are thus instructive evidence of the incurable folly of mankind. One Blavatsky, indeed, tells far more about the human race than a whole herd of psychologists. Her works offer massive proof that, even in the midst of what seems to be civilization, Neandertal Man is still with us.

[*American Mercury,* November 1931]

ON CHRISTIAN SCIENCE

I

The followers of the inspired and polyandrous Mother Eddy have lately won a considerable victory in New York, where the Court of Appeals has decided that their consecrated sorcerers are not amenable to the Medical License Law, and may thus practise their magic upon the faithful without let or hindrance. The case was dragged from court to court and very bitterly fought, with the embattled Christian Scientists on the one side and the New York County Medical Society on the other. To the majority opinion, which was written by Chase, J., the following memorandum was added by Bartlett, C. J.:

> I would go further. I deny the power of the Legislature to make it a crime to treat disease by prayer.

The defeated pathologists of the Medical Society talk of carrying the case to the Supreme Court of the United States, but it is unlikely that many unprejudiced observers will quarrel with the decision of the Court of Appeals. The effort to put down Christian Science by law is one of the craziest enterprises upon which medical men waste their energies. It is based upon a superstition even sillier than that behind Christian Science itself: to wit, the superstition that, when an evil shows itself, all that is needed to dispose of it is to pass a law against it. This notion is fast making a burlesque of American legislation. It is responsible for an endless series of idiotic enactments, from Prohibition amendments to laws against card playing. One and all they are ineffective and ridiculous. One and all they foster an evil ten times worse than the evils they are aimed at.

II

In Maryland we have a shining example of the absurdity of legislating against the Eddyistas. Six or eight years ago, after various cases of bungling by Christian Science healers had got into the newspapers, the Legislature passed an act making it a misdemeanor for any such healer to accept a fee for his occult services. Obviously, it was the opinion of the master minds at Annapolis that this simple act would break up the business. But I doubt that its whole effect, during the entire time it has been upon the statute books, has been to deprive a single healer of a single patient or a single fee. Immediately it went into effect, the Eddyan magicians made a joke of it by announcing that they would cease to take fees, but would gladly accept "presents." Upon the increase of these "presents" they now pay the rent of expensive offices, ride about the city in luxurious Fords and erect gorgeous temples to the glory of their late prophetess. In brief, they laugh at the law, and the law deserves laughing at. Based ostensibly upon the sound assumption that Christian Science is a swindle, it is based actually upon the entirely false assumption that the law can protect people from their own perversity and imbecility.

The medical men of Maryland seem to recognize this fact, for they waste no time hunting down and prosecuting Christian Scientists under the statute. Their brethren of New York would do well to imitate them. Even if the Medical License act, after endless litigation, is sustained by the Supreme Court of the United States, they will never be able to enforce it. All it will ever accomplish, supposing it to be supported by the full military and naval power of the republic, will be to train the Christian Scientists in new tricks.

They will keep on practising their black art until hell freezes over. And their victims, immovably convinced that death is a delusion, will continue to enrich the embalmers at the old, old rate. A few professional spies and snouters will get a good living chasing them; a few doctors will pose in the papers as scourges of them; now and then one of them, betrayed by his rivals in the business, will roost a year or two in jail. But that is all. The net annual takings of the fraternity will not decrease 1 per cent. The number of the slain will not diminish by a single diabetic fat woman.

III

But Christian Science is a dangerous folly! Its practice by numskulls promotes the spread of infectious diseases! It works cruel hardships upon the children and other dependents of the fools who believe in it! True enough. But what are you going to do about it? Here in Maryland we have a simple and drastic law. But can we enforce it? Does it protect the neighbors of a Christian Scientist whose child is seized by infantile paralysis? Would it help us against a Christian Scientist sprinkled with smallpox? Nay! We can no more guard ourselves against such risks by law than we can guard ourselves against stupid doctors by law. They constitute, in truth, the irremovable hazards that life under civilization imposes upon all of us. They spring out of the fact that so-and-so-many persons out of every hundred are natural idiots—and the slings and arrows of those idiots we must learn to bear with as much grace as we can muster. The only practicable way to decrease the hazard is to diminish the number of idiots—and to me, at least, it seems that Christian Science is one of the most effective methods ever devised for accomplishing that business. Say what you will against it, it at all events bears more harshly upon those who believe in it than upon those who don't believe in it. Ah, that all the other manias of our fair commonwealth were as beautifully selective!

I stand under no supicion, I hope, of apologizing for Christian Science as a scheme of therapeutics, or of being under the slightest delusion as to its utility. The fact is that the idea behind it is one of the few human ideas in which I can find no sense or logic whatever. It is not merely erroneous; it is imbecile; I can't imagine anyone save a donkey giving a passing thought to it. But even a donkey, let us remember, is one of God's creatures, with pains and malaises like the rest of us, and if it gives him any ease to read gabble out of a silly book, then he should be allowed to read on. It will not cure him if he is ill, true enough; but, after all, he may not be actually ill, but merely in low spirits, and in need of reading matter within his limited capacities, and the touch of a white, velvety hand. If he pays through the nose for that recreation, whose place is it to object? Not mine, surely.

IV

As for the danger from infectious disease in Christian Science hands, I doubt that it amounts to much. The great majority of patients who fall into the net of the pussyfooted healers are not suffering from infectious diseases, nor even, indeed, from any other diseases of definite and accurately describable character, but from the obscure, mysterious complexes of symptoms against which scientific medicine is quite as ineffective as Christian Science itself. These sufferers are not a menace to the general populace. They groan along for years, passing from doctor to doctor, and finally falling into the hands of some suave healer. If they get better, as sometimes happens, the healer pockets his "present" and gives thanks to God; if they die, he blames it on the doctor who is hauled in at the last moment. Who is injured? The patient? He is agreeably dead. The healer? He has his "present." The doctor? He has his fat and vindictive fee. The public? It doesn't care a darn.

Moreover, there is no reason to believe that Christian Science healers treat any appreciable number of cases of infectious diseases, or that they make any worse mess of the business than a good many third-rate doctors—of which gentry, by the way, Baltimore has a far too plentiful ration. The average healer, when he sees a patient breaking out with smallpox, may be trusted, I take it, to remember an immediate engagement elsewhere; and so the victim falls into better hands and is forthwith removed to the pesthouse. As for the lesser maladies of that variety, it is improbable that their occasional treatment by a Christian Scientist does much harm, save to the patient. So long as our laws permit the home nursing of typhoid we can scarcely object to its Christian Science treatment. Most epidemics of infectious disease, it is likely, are set up by this home nursing; we only interfere with it when, as in the case at the polyomyelitis epidemic, there is public excitement. Tuberculosis is being nursed at this moment in thousands of Baltimore homes, and its transmission thus facilitated.

In truth, the number of cases in which Christian Science healers actually essay to treat infectious diseases by their magic would seem to be very small. Whenever one of them loses a patient, the fact is exposed by the physician who signs the death certificate, and a pother in the newspapers follows. Such pothers are few and far between. If there were more chances to make them, you may be sure that the Health Department would not forget its duties. Nay; the slick purveyors of the Eddyan buncombe do not like such trade. They have a care for their own hides, and besides, it is more profitable to tackle jobs that are easier. A child down with scarlet fever is visibly and horribly ill; its parents, whatever their faith in sorcery, demand quicker action than sorcery can offer. It is much more pleasant to monkey with the neurotic, the bughouse and the incurable, who are easily convinced that the hocus-pocus of *Science and Health* is doing them good, and get a lot of joy out of the mere chance to talk about their troubles.

V

As for the alleged sufferings of the helpless children of Christian Scientists, I do not let them interfere with my sinful happiness. On the surgical side, I believe that they are much exaggerated, for the great majority of Christian Scientists seek surgical aid whenever it seems to be necessary, and even the most ambitious healer, I venture, would not undertake to treat a compound fracture or a shoe button in the nose by petitioning the archangels. And on the medical side, it is difficult to discern any appreciable difference between the pains of having measles under allopathy and the pains of having measles under Christian Science. If, in point of fact, the child of a Christian Scientist undergoes cruel and unusual tortures in its nonage, then its sufferings are perhaps for the larger good, for it will come to maturity in full revolt against the foolishness of its parents, just as the sons of the reverend clergy so often come to maturity in revolt against the parental piety.

And if, on the other hand, the baleful forces of heredity overcome its bitter experience, then let us chalk it up to profit and loss in a philosophical spirit, and forget it. After all, a steady supply of such persons is necessary to the peace and joy of the world; the contemplation of them fills those of us who are wholly devoid of folly with a sweet and soothing sense of superiority, and gives us a reason for venerating our Creator. From our arctic heights of infallibility we look down upon them with agreeable sneers, and thank God that we are not as they are. Their tortures charm us; we attend their funerals with happy hearts. Human happiness is almost indistinguishable from this sense of superiority. The Christian Scientists attain to it by contemplating us, and we attain to it by contemplating the Christian Scientists—not forgetting the osteopaths, the initiators and referendors, the recallers of judges, the suffragettes and the prohibitionists. . . . A citizen of the republic stood on a street corner watching a preparedness parade. Observing his brother in the sweating procession, he threw back his head and bellowed, "What an ass!" At the same moment his brother caught sight of him and, stopping in his tracks, whooped "What a scoundrel!"

VI

Meanwhile, let us get over the silly notion that we can put down such manias as Christian Science by law. The progress of legislation in this country is fast heading us into trouble. We are already seeking, by statute, to prohibit and penalize a long string of private acts; we have begun to direct the same dangerous fury of the law against private ideas. The result is a gradual encroachment upon personal liberty, even a gradual denial of the right of free speech. Men are being denounced and hounded in the United States to-day, not because they are doing what is admitted to be wrong, but merely because they are thinking what is thought to be wrong. Error is converted into a felony; we are transforming the mob's fear of ideas into a sort of national philosophy. The end is bound to be disaster, for in the long run this tyranny of the cocksure will bear most harshly, not upon such poor fanatics as the Christian Scientists, but upon those men of intellectual enterprise and daring in whose hands, and in whose hands alone, everything approaching genuine progress reposes. We have already reached such a stage that no man of intellectual integrity and self-respect can hope to get far in the public service; our leaders in politics, with few exceptions, are simply mountebanks who echo the yells of the mob, and docilely take its orders. Let us beware lest we carry this sort of thing into other and more important fields of thought. However good one repressive law may seem to be, it is bound to be followed by others that are bad and worse. No man, once the mob gets moving, can say where it will stop.

I thus venture to raise a frail, feeble voice for the Christian Scientists, a fantoddish and amusing lot, but still with rights that should be respected. My argument for them is not altruistic in the least, but purely selfish. I should dislike to see them harassed by the law for two plain and sound reasons. One is that their continued existence soothes my vanity (and hence promotes my happiness) by proving to me that there are even worse fools in the world than I am. The other is that, if they were jailed to-morrow for believing in Christian Science, I should probably be jailed the next day for refusing to believe in something still sillier. Once the law begins to horn into such matters, I am against the law, no matter how virtuous its ostensible intent. No liberty is worth a hoot which doesn't allow the citizen to be foolish once in a while, and to kick up once in a while, and to hurt himself once in a while.

[*Baltimore Evening Sun,* October 23, 1916]

THE CAREER OF A DIVINITY

MRS. EDDY: *The Biography of a Virginal Mind.* by Edwin Franklin Dakin. $5. 553 pp. New York: *Charles Scribner's Sons.*

Mr. Dakin's sub-title, it seems to me, is rather far-fetched. The peculiar mixture of vapors and sagacities which marked Mrs. Eddy's sayings and doings from end to end of her long life showed few of the characters of the virginal mind. Rather it would be more plausible (without throwing the slightest doubt upon her virtue) to compare her peculiar wisdom to that of an ancient bordello-keeper, for in it a sharp sense of reality and a weakness for the occult were curiously mingled. She was seldom if ever taken in by concrete human beings, but there was never a time when she did not believe quite incredible things about the powers and principalities of the air.

In the sort of business woman to whom (perhaps in grossly bad taste) I venture to liken her, this sense of the transcendental takes the form of a shaking fear of black cats, opals, cross-eyed ice-men, blue-gum Negroes, policemen whose badge numbers contain 13 and enterprises begun on a Friday. In Mrs. Eddy it took the form of an incurable dread of malicious animal magnetism, or, as the flunkeys of her entourage made it, M.A.M. This M.A.M. pursued her during all the years of her prophesying, and even afflicted her after she had become a goddess. It came between her and her most faithful disciples; it brought down upon her the persecution of mesmerists, spiritualists, lawyers, newspaper reporters and other fiends from Hell; it haunted her days and made horrible her nights. She was a sharp woman, with all of a Yankee's talent for fetching the other fellow, but against M.A.M. she could do nothing. In the end, in fact, it finished her and maybe Christian Science with her.

Mr. Dakin, despite his inept sub-title, presents a capital biography of her—painstaking, shrewd, fair and very amusing. It is obvious that he takes no stock in her brummagem magic, but he seems to be convinced that she may have launched, nevertheless, an idea or two worth regarding. His account of her early days, and especially of her association with the celebrated Phineas P. Quimby, is full of a rich detail. She seems to have suffered from early girlhood from a combination of physical and psychical malaises. On the one hand she was frequently ill and on the other hand she was always revolting against the narrowness of her environment and her own humble place in it. The easiest way to the attention that she craved was to play the invalid, and this she did adroitly through many years, first at the expense of her father and mother, then at that of a married sister, and then at that of her three husbands.

Her first marriage was apparently happy and promised to restore her to normalcy, but her husband's death set her back, and soon thereafter she was going the round of the doctors. When they failed to cure her she moved on to the quacks, and thereafter, for a dozen years, she was the easy prey of all sorts of charlatans, including hypnotists. If Freudism had been known in those days she would have been one of its most eager customers. Failing it, she took to what has since become known as the New Thought, and eventually became a patient and pupil of its shining star, the aforesaid Quimby.

That the basic notions of Christian Science came from Quimby seems to be indubitable, despite her frantic denials in later years. If she added anything of importance it was simply the idea of malicious animal magnetism. Where she got this is uncertain, but probably it came from the itinerant mesmerists of her youth. When she set up shop as a healer and teacher it became a very important element in her theory, and in the long run it was destined to fill her own life with acute unhappiness. For despite her contention that disease was only an illusion, her ill health continued, and the temptation to blame it on M.A.M. was hard to resist. But who was launching this M.A.M.? At first she seemed uncertain, but finally she began putting the blame upon pupils who had set up in competition with her, and this habit she continued until the end of her days. Her historic break with her most eminent disciple, the celebrated Mrs. Augusta Stetson of New York, had its origin in fear quite as much as in jealousy. Someone had told her that Mrs. Stetson's pupils met daily to project waves in her direction, and she assumed quickly that they were malevolent. Her terror was extreme, and it kept with her until death. During her last years she maintained a staff of healers in her house to combat the M.A.M. issuing from these Stetsonites. They were on duty in sailor-like watches for the twenty-four hours of the day, but it was all in vain.

Mr. Dakin makes it plain that Mrs. Eddy had complete belief in her own magic. She had a low view, it appears, of most Christian Scientists, but she never had any serious doubt about Christian Science. Its conflicts with common experience and common sense did not daunt her, for she had the kind of mind which finds an easy refuge from such difficulties in sonorous words.

If, in the course of her incessant revisions of *Science and Health*, she occasionally modified her ideas, it was not because they had lost their hold on her, but simply because she wanted to bring them into harmony with the practical needs of a large and prosperous cult. She kept control of her church to the end, and its somewhat curious structure remains a monument to her sagacity to this day. Her principal aim, first and last, was to prevent the rise of rival prophets—to keep control of the whole organization in her own hands. This she achieved by devices of great ingenuity. The suspicion, once widely prevalent, that she was no more than a puppet in the hands of clever *entrepreneurs* is seen, in retrospect, to have been wholly without foundation. There was, in fact, no one in her church competent to grapple with her and beat her. It produced one woman of unusual capacities, Mrs. Stetson, but the men who came to place in it were mainly third-raters, and the Rev. Founder was more than a match for any of them or all of them. To this day the Board of Directors—the Sacred College of the organization—is made up of nobodies. As for the "judges," "professors" and other such ostensible big-wigs who roam the country lecturing on the Christian Science arcanum, and scaring provincial city editors into giving them columns of space, they are all on the level of Y.M.C.A. secretaries and the boob-catchers for the tin-pot fraternal orders.

As Mr. Dakin shows, the numerical strength of the Christian Scientists has always been greatly exaggerated. Their machine for getting publicity, designed by Mrs. Eddy herself, is so efficient that they seem to be of imposing importance, but in truth they constitute a very small sect, and its turn-over is probably very large. Its wealth is due to two facts. The first is that its theology professes to reward the believer with prosperity as well as with health, and that a certain proportion of seekers, giving this promise a trial, are bound to win. They give liberal thank-offerings to the church, whereas those who fail depart in choler and are heard of no more. The second reason why the sect is rich is that it frowns upon poor converts. They are not actually barred out, but they are certainly not welcomed, and so they tend to go to other cults, which treat them more politely and even hail their poverty as a proof of merit. But despite all its opulence, Christian Science is probably making very little progress. Its history, in the long run, will be that of all other such aberrations. It will make a noise for a while, and then it will suddenly vanish, to make way for something sweeter and worse.

Mr. Dakin's book is well ordered and competently written. He has been at pains to unearth the precise facts and he sets them forth carefully and pleasantly. The Christian Science press-agents, of course, will damn him as a slanderer, but that fact is unimportant. He has made a valuable contribution to American history.

[*American Mercury,* November 1929]

THE LID LIFTS AGAIN

I

Of censorships at least one pleasant thing may be said: that they never work. The brethren of Christian Science have been discovering it of late, following their imbecile attempt to suppress a life of Mrs. Eddy by Edwin F. Dakin, published by the Scribners. What inspired them to that attempt I don't know—maybe malicious animal magnetism radiating from the Scribner press-agent. Whatever the cause, they have let themselves in for a considerable embarrassment, and it will pursue them for a long while. On the one hand, they are being damned all over the lot for a gross and idiotic assault upon free speech and a free press, and on the other hand they have vastly augmented the sales of the book, and so helped to spread the poisons in it.

It is, by the way, a very amusing volume, and well worth reading. The author, Dakin, is by no means an enemy of La Eddy; on the contrary, he treats her most politely, and is at great pains to show that she was far superior to the ninth-rate sorcerers who have succeeded her. But he can no more tell her story without mentioning her occasional sharp practises than one could tell the story of Liszt without mentioning his warts. The result is a picaresque and exhilarating narrative, with frequent scenes of low comedy. No doubt the history of any other jitney Thomas Aquinas would be just as racy, but Dakin is not concerned with any other; he confines himself to the author of *Science and Health*. I commend his work to all lovers of humor without obscenity.

If the Christian Science Boy Scouts had said nothing about it, it would have gone on to the normal sale of such a book, and then been forgotten. But they tried to suppress it by intimidating booksellers—and now it is raging like a pestilence. The Scribners protest solemnly in the name of Magna Charta, the Bill of Rights and other such holy carcasses, but if they have any sagacity in them, which is overwhelmingly probable, they must be howling with mirth behind the door. Consider, for example, the present free and lovely puff. If they tried to buy it, the chief of the *Evening Sunpaper*'s military police, Capt. T. J. McCartney, would set upon them with bludgeons and bloodhounds. But here they get it for nothing.

II

It is, of course, not surprising that Christian Scientists should be injudicious, for it plainly takes a great capacity for fatuity to swallow the dreadful stuff in *Science and Health*. I have been a constant reader of it for twenty-five years, and find fresh humors in it at every reading, just as I find fresh beauties in 1 Timothy 5:23. Mr. Dakin hints broadly that Mrs. Eddy burgled the ideas in it from one Phineas P. Quimby, a primeval faith-healer, but if that be true it is unimportant, for she got a rakish charm into them that Quimby was quite incapable of. No better bootleg Bible has ever been written, not even the Book of Mormon. Some call it dull, but I do not find it so. More than once, it has helped me through the depression which always follows high-toned literary effort, as *Katzenjammer* follows dining with United States Senators.

But, as I say, it takes a high talent for folly to accept such blather as inspired, and so one may naturally expect Christian Scientists to be somewhat silly. That expectation is borne out every time they undertake to defend their superstition. Almost invariably they seek to do so by intimidating and terrorizing those who venture to criticize it, and almost invariably they come to grief. The Dakin case is surely not the first of its kind. Every time a newspaper prints anything about their doings they bombard it with protests—and every time they get into trouble with the coroner it is first-page stuff, with black and inflammatory headlines.

The really sad part of it is that they apparently believe that their scheme works—they are too stupid to see its complete failure. Yet it must be plain to every rational person that their position is much worse today than it was when they began. There was a time when the newspapers gave them, so to speak, the benefit of clergy, and treated them very politely, and lavished a lot of space on the maunderings of their traveling lecturers. But now even the meanest sheet deals with them in a cavalier manner, and they get precious little space that they do not pay for in hard cash.

III

Here in Maryland, it seems to me, they labor under disabilities that are unjust and ought to be removed. There is a statute, though most people seem to be unaware of it, which forbids their healers to take fees from customers. That statute is a disgrace to the Maryland Free State, and it is no less a disgrace because various eminent medical men are in favor of it, and have combated every effort to have it repealed. These big-wigs should be ashamed of themselves. All they accomplish by their law is to put themselves on the level of Prohibitionists, movie censors, Blue Sunday advocates and other such vain and disgusting persons. For the Christian Science magicians get their fees, law or no law, and what is more, they deserve to get them.

Why, indeed, shouldn't anyone who believes in their magic be at liberty, as Dr. Coolidge would say, to hire it? Why should they be forced into a sort of bootlegging? I can imagine no reason. My private belief is that Christian Science is unmitigated buncombe, and I can pretend to a considerably more intimate acquaintance with it than is common outside the fold; nevertheless, I believe that anyone who thinks otherwise should be free to cherish his belief, and to act upon it. What is freedom worth if it doesn't include the right to be wrong? And who is to decide, easily and irrevocably, what is right and what is wrong? Certainly not parties at interest.

A great deal of suspiciously noisy sympathy is wasted upon the children of Christian Scientists. The theory seems to be that they die daily in great agony, and that their parents are inhuman. I doubt it. Now and then it may happen, but surely not often. If it did, we'd hear a great deal more from the coroner. What happens normally is that the parents fool with a healer for a while, and then, if the child seems really ill, send posthaste for a doctor. Every doctor has had that experience, and most of them enjoy it immensely. The child gets the most assiduous of attention, and if it so be God's will it recovers, and its parents heave *Science and Health* out of the window.

IV

The occasional death of such a child is a melancholy business, but it is certainly not as melancholy as the death of a child of enlightened parents. The latter may conceivably grow up into a useful and even brilliant maturity; the former is almost inevitably doomed to be what the vulgar call a sucker. The brains it inherits have large sinuses in them, and those sinuses, in the years to come, will be the natural habitats of nonsense. If it does not believe in Christian Science, like its parents, then it will believe in Socialism, the Single Tax, chiropractic, Prohibition, the Second Coming or some other such blowsy staff. For despite all the hooplahs of the behaviorists, it remains a massive and beautiful fact, firmly rooted in the divine will, that intelligent children do not issue from numskull parents.

This thirst for the palpably not true is not uncommon in this world, nor is it confined to Christian Scientists. It is to be observed, in some measure, in all of us, and in great multitudes it takes on a powerful virulence. Why should a man be harassed by law for believing in the mumbo-jumbo, of Mrs. Eddy when his brother is quite free to believe in the Kellogg Peace Treaties, or in osteopathy, or in stock-market tips, or in spiritualism, or in rabbit-feet? Are there laws against poets? Apparently not yet. Nevertheless, every poet spends his whole time disseminating what everyone knows to be untrue. The instant, indeed, he loosed a fact he would cease to be a poet.

What we need in this world is more freedom for odd and foolish people. They make life pleasanter than it would be without them, and they do no harm. Nothing could be more disagreeable than a world in which everyone was discreet, prudent, sage, astute, wise. It would be as horrible as a house of correction. The clowns make the show, whether it be political, theological, æsthetic or scientific. Not the least gifted among them are the Christian Scientists. They are immensely amusing when they try to straighten a deviated septum by reading out of a book. They are ten times as amusing when, borrowing a folly from their enemies, they try to put down the ensuing laugh.

[*Baltimore Evening Sun,* December 16, 1929]

CHRISTIAN SCIENCE TECHNIQUE

I

On December 16 last, writing in this place, I described and denounced the effort of certain Christian Scientists, some of them in official station in their so-called church, to pre⸻ ⸻ the sale of a life of Mrs. Eddy by Edwin F. Dakin, published by the Scribners. A short while afterward I left the country and was gone until very recently. During my absence, on January 2, there appeared in *The Evening Sun* a letter of protest from Mr. Frank K. Poe, "Christian Science Committee on Publication for the State of Maryland." From it I take the following strophes:

> Mr. Mencken . . . states that Christian Scientists are trying to suppress Mr. Dakin's book "by intimidating booksellers." In this I believe Mr. Mencken is misinformed. As Committee on Publication for the State of Maryland it is one of my duties to interview booksellers and . . . I have never made this fact an occasion for threat or intimidation. . . . If individual Christian Scientists, acting on their own initiative, have attempted to intimidate booksellers for selling this book, it is to be regretted. . . .

Not only is it to be regretted; it has been done—and Mr. Poe must be very well aware of the fact. Three weeks before he wrote his letter, and five days before my article was published, sufficient evidence of it to convince any fair man was printed in the *New Republic* by Craig F. Thompson.[1] That evidence only showed that "individual Christian Scientists" in places as far separated as Burlington, Vt., and Portland, Ore., had been going about trying to scare booksellers into refusing to sell the book; it also showed that at least one Christian Science "church"—the Third, of Kansas City—had attempted a direct onslaught upon the publishers. And it showed too that this action was based frankly and avowedly upon a canon of the Christian Science Church Manual, making it obligatory upon all believers in the Eddyan revelation to boycott every "publishing house or bookstore" selling books offensive to that revelation.

II

That Mr. Poe, in the discharge of his curious duty "to interview booksellers," has offered no "threat or intimidation" to the booksellers of Baltimore I can well believe, for I am acquainted with most of them, and the fact that he is still on his legs is plain proof of the fact. I can't imagine any of them submitting to any such brow-beating. They would not only resist it with dreadful yells; they would also resist it with their fists and hooves. But in other cities, where the tradition of freedom is less lively, their colleagues submitted cravenly, and the result was serious interference with the sale of the book. "During October and November," says the Scribners, "it had so diminished that for a few weeks it appeared as though the attempt . . . would succeed."

Mr. Poe would have us believe that this interference was confined to polite remonstrance, and that it thus kept itself within the plain rights of the Christian Scientists. It is simply not so. The Scribners, in a pamphlet entitled *The Blight That Failed*, offer incontrovertible proof of that. They not only show that booksellers were belabored with open threats of boycott; they also show that some of those threats succeeded. And they show that, in more than one case, they were made by representatives of the local Christian Science "churches" in their official capacity. Thus it is silly for Mr. Poe to try to put the blame on "individual Christian Scientists." The boycott was attempted officially, and it was soundly grounded upon a mandate of the Church Manual, which, according to the Third Church, Kansas City, "governs every branch Church of Christ, Scientist, throughout the world."

Fortunately, the Scribners were not to be intimidated. They not only refused to withdraw the book; they proceeded to advertise it extensively, and to make public all the facts that they could gather about the effort to boycott dealers selling it. Moreover, they called up their lawyers, and let it be known that they were contemplating action to the courts. The result was a swift change of tune at Christian Science G.H.Q. On December 23 there appeared in the *Christian Science Sentinel* a statement which disclaimed any intent to boycott the book, passed over the mandate of the Manual in discreet silence, and advised all customers of Mrs. Eddy to remember her admonition: "Meekness and temperance are the jewels of love, set in wisdom. Restrain untempered zeal." And during the week or two that followed the various regional press-agents of the cult worked their local papers for virtuous denials like that which Mr. Poe got into *The Evening Sun.*

III

The whole episode, viewed in retrospect, takes on a comic character. The job before the Christian Scientists was to discourage the reading of a book which, in a most amusing and persuasive manner, told the truth about Mrs. Eddy—and in particular, the truth about her bold stealing of ideas from other necromancers, her unseemly rows with her early followers and her frantic lust for power and money. They saw clearly that the volume, read generally, would do immense damage to Christian Science, and they tried to dispose of it at a single wallop. But they failed miserably—and now it is being read by thousands who would never have heard of it if they had kept quiet.

For some time to come, I daresay, they will be more careful. Another book that must give them great grief—*Our New Religion*, by the Right Hon. H. A. L. Fisher, Warden of New College, Oxford—has just come out, but I get no news of any effort to suppress it.[2] Soon or late, however, they will probably try the trick again, for it is of the eternal nature of theological fanatics to do such things, and, moreover, they have succeeded in the past more than once. The Georgine Milmine biography, the best before Mr. Dakin's, was disposed of long ago, and copies of it are now hard to come by.[3] So with the memoirs of Adam Dickey,[4] and so with various lesser works. In 1921 they actually caused the publishers of the Cambridge History of American Literature to withdraw one of the volumes thereof and delete a chapter.

What happened this time was simply that they tried to blackjack the wrong publisher. The house of Scribner is old and rich and justly proud of its high position; it is, in truth, quite as much a national institution as the house of Morgan. Its heads are very enlightened men: one of them is a trustee of Princeton and a director of the Association Against the Prohibition Amendment. When the attempt was made to scare them they naturally showed fight, and the issue of that fight was a cruel and inglorious defeat for the janissaries of the Divine Good. A less firmly intrenched house might have yielded supinely. It is upon that fact that the Christian Scientists—and all other browbeaters of their sort—rely.

IV

Cowardice, indeed, is the hallmark of Americans. "More than any other people," said Wendell Phillips, "we are afraid of one another." Nevertheless, there is some improvement in that department, and even the newspapers, which are the natural citadels of cowardice, show it. Time was when the Christian Scientists worked them in a magnificent manner, grabbing column after column of space on the ground that their advertisements of their healing business were religious news, but that time is past. Today they still get into the letter columns with their puerile sophistries and evasions, but it is not often, and it is seldom at any length.

If they hang on it is because, in other regions, they are still able to score an occasional victory. As the Scribner evidence shows, not a few booksellers put the Dakin book under the counter last November, alarmed by the mysterious consequences that were threatened if they refused. And no doubt it was taken out of many one-horse Carnegie libraries in the little towns, and perhaps also in one or two big cities. But on the whole the Christian Scientists are going downhill. The "church" sadly misses the charming impudence and fine Italian hand of Mother Eddy. Her heirs and assigns are a rabble of fifth-raters, lacking both imagination and common sense. They have a hard time holding their dupes, and there is no sign that their business is increasing. If La Eddy had been alive it is pretty certain that she would have saved them from the disaster which issued from their foolhardy attempt upon the Scribners. As stupid as they are, they will probably learn something from the experience. The next time they will tackle softer lads.

[*Baltimore Evening Sun,* March 3, 1930]

VI

THE SCOPES TRIAL

THE TENNESSEF CIRCUS

I

It is an old and bitter observation that, in armed conflicts, the peacemaker frequently gets the worst of it. The truth of the fact is being demonstrated anew in the case of the Tennessee pedagogue accused of teaching Evolution. No matter what the issue of that great moral cause, it seems to me very unlikely that either of the principal parties will be greatly shaken. The Evolutionists will go on demonstrating, believing in and teaching the mutability of living forms, and the Ku Klux theologians will continue to whoop for Genesis undefiled. But I look for many casualties and much suffering among the optimistic neutrals who strive to compose the controversy—that is, among the gentlemen who believe fondly that modern science and the ancient Hebrew demonology can be reconciled.

This reconciliation will take place, perhaps, on that bright day when Dr. Nicholas Murray Butler and the Hon. Wayne B. Wheeler meet in a saloon under a Baptist church, and drink *Brüderschaft* in a mixture of Clos Vougeot and coca-cola. But not before. For the two parties, it must be manifest, are at the farthermost poles of difference, and leaning out into space. If one of them is right at all, then the other is wrong altogether. There can be no honest compromise between them. Either Genesis

---

161

embodies a mathematically accurate statement of what took place during the week of June 3, 4004 B. C. or Genesis is not actually the Word of God. If the former alternative be accepted, then all of modern science is non-sense; if the latter, then evangelical Christianity is nonsense.

This fact must be apparent, I believe, to everyone who has given sober and prayerful thought to the controversy. It should be especially apparent to those who now try to talk it away. I have, I confess, a great suspicion of such persons. When they pretend to be scientists it always turns out on inspection that they are only half-scientists—that no fact, however massive, is yet massive enough to keep them off the mourners' bench. And when they pretend to be Christians they are always full of mental reservations, which is to say, they are full of secret doubts, heresies and hypocrisies.

II

When I say Christians, of course, I mean Christians of the sort who accept the Bible as their sole guide to the divine mysteries, and are forced, in con-sequence, to to take it exactly as it stands. There are also, of course, persons of the name who subscribed to warier and more sophisticated cults, each with its scheme for ameliorating the disconcerting improbability of certain parts of Holy Writ. Some of these cults get around the difficulty by denying that any sort of belief whatever, save perhaps in a few obvious fun-damentals, is necessary to the Christian way of life—that a Christian is properly judged not by what he believes, but by what he does. And others dispose of the matter by setting up an authority competent to "interpret" the Scriptures, *i.e.,* to determine, officially and finally, what they mean or ought to mean when what they say is obscure or incredible.

Of the latter cults the most familiar is the Roman Catholic. It does not reject or neglect the Bible, as the Ku Klux Protestants allege; it simply accepts frankly the obvious fact that the Bible is full of difficulties—or, as the non-believer would say, contradictions and absurdities. To resolve these difficulties it maintains a corps of experts specially gifted and trained, and to their decision, when reached in due form of canon law, it gives a high authority. The first of such experts, in normal times, is the Pope; when he settles a point of doctrine, *i.e.,* of Biblical interpetation, the faithful are bound to give it full credit. If he is in doubt, then he may summon a Council of the Church, *i.e.,* a parliament of all the chief living professors of the divine intent and meaning, and submit the matter to it. Technically, I believe, this council can only advise him; in practise, he usually follows the view of its majority.

The Anglican, Orthodox Greek and various other churches, including the Presbyterian, follow much the same plan, though with important differences in detail. Its defects are not hard to see. It tends to exalt ecclesiastical authority and to discourage the study of Holy Writ by laymen. But its advantages are just as apparent. For one thing, it puts down amateur theologians, and stills their idiotic controversies. For another thing, it quietly shelves the highly embarrassing question of the complete and literal accuracy of the Bible. What has not been singled out for necessary belief, and interpreted by authority, is tacitly regarded as not important.

III

Out of this plan flows the fact that the Catholics and their allies, in the present storm, are making much better weather of it than the evangelical sects. Their advantage lies in the simple fact that they do not have to decide either for Evolution or against it. Authority has not spoken upon the subject; hence it puts no burden upon conscience, and may be discussed realistically and without prejudice. A certain wariness, of course, is necessary. I say that authority has not spoken; it may, however, speak to-morrow, and so the prudent man remembers his step. But in the meanwhile there is nothing to prevent him examining all the available facts, and even offering arguments in support of them or against them—so long as those arguments are not presented as dogma.

The result of all this is that the current discussion of the Tennessee buffoonery, in the Catholic and other authoritarian press, is immensely more free and intelligent than it is in the evangelical Protestant press. In such journals as the *Conservator,* the new Catholic weekly, both sides are set forth, and the varying contentions are subjected to frank and untrammeled criticism. Canon de Dorlodot whoops for Evolution; Dr. O'Toole denounces it as nonsense.[1] If the question were the Virgin Birth, or the apostolic succession, or transubstantiation, or even birth control, the two antagonists would be in the same trench, for authority binds them there. Bill on Evolution authority is silent, and so they have at each other in the immemorial manner of theologians, with a great kicking up of dust.

The *Conservator* itself takes no sides, but argues that Evolution ought in be taught in the schools—not as an incontrovertible fact but as a hypothesis accepted by the overwhelming majority of enlightened men. The objections to it, theological and evidential, should be noted, but not represented as unanswerable.

IV

Obviously, this is an intelligent attitude. Equally obviously, it is one that the evangelical brethren cannot take without making their position absurd. For weal or for woe, they are committed absolutely to the literal accuracy of the Bible; they base their whole theology upon it. Once they admit, even by inference, that there may be a single error in Genesis, they open the way to an almost complete destruction of that theology. So they are forced to take up the present challenge boldly, and to prepare for a battle to the death. If, when and as they attempt a compromise, they admit defeat.

Thus there is nothing unnatural in their effort to protect their position by extra-theological means—for example, by calling in the law to put down their opponents. All Christians, when one of their essential dogmas seems to be menaced, turn instinctively to the same device. The whole history of the church, as everyone knows, is a history of schemes to put down heresy by force. Unluckily, those schemes do not work as well as they did in former ages. The heretic, in the course of time, has learned how to protect himself—even how to take the offensive. He refuses to go docilely to the stake. Instead, he yells, struggles, makes a frightful pother, bites his executioner. The church begins to learn that it is usually safest to let him go.

The Ku Klux Klergy, unfortunately for their cause, have not yet mastered that plain fact. Intellectually, they are still medieval. They believe that the devices which worked in the year 1300 will still work in 1925. As a life-long opponent of their pretensions I can only report that their fidelity to this belief fills me with agreeable sentiments. I rejoice that they have forced the fighting, and plan to do it in the open. My prediction is that, when the peanut shells are swept up at last and the hot-dog men go home, millions of honest minds in this great republic, hitherto uncontaminated by the slightest doubt, will have learned to regard parts of Genesis as they now regard the history of Andrew Gump.[2]

[*Baltimore Evening Sun,* June 15, 1925]

HOMO NEANDERTALENSIS

I

Such obscenities as the forthcoming trial of the Tennessee evolutionist, if they serve no other purpose, at least call attention dramatically to the fact that enlightenment, among mankind, is very narrowly dispersed. It is common to assume that human progress affects everyone—that even the dullest man, in these bright days, knows more than any man of, say, the Eighteenth Century, and is far more civilized. This assumption is quite erroneous. The men of the educated minority, no doubt, know more than their predecessors, and of some of them, perhaps, it may be said that they are more civilized—though I should not like to be put to giving names—but the great masses of men, even in this inspired republic, are precisely where the mob was at the dawn of history. They are ignorant, they are dishonest, they are cowardly, they are ignoble. They know little if anything that is worth knowing, and there is not the slightest sign of a natural desire among them to increase their knowledge.

Such immortal vermin, true enough, get their share of the fruits of human progress, and so they may be said, in a way, to have their part in it. The most ignorant man, when he is ill, may enjoy whatever boons and usufructs modern medicine may offer—that is, provided he is too poor to choose his own doctor. He is free, if he wants to, to take a bath. The literature of the world is at his disposal in public libraries. He may look at works of art. He may hear good music. He has at hand a thousand devices for making life less wearisome and more tolerable: the telephone, railroads, bichloride tablets, newspapers, sewers, correspondence schools, delicatessen. But he had no more to do with bringing these things into the world than the horned cattle in the fields, and he does no more to increase them to-day than the birds of the air.

On the contrary, he is generally against them, and sometimes with immense violence. Every step in human progress, from the first feeble stirrings in the abyss of time, has been opposed by the great majority of men. Every valuable thing that has been added to the store of man's possessions has been derided by them when it was new, and destroyed by them when they had the power. They have fought every new truth ever heard of, and they have killed every truth-seeker who got into their hands.

II

The so-called religious organizations which now lead the war against the teaching of evolution are nothing more, at bottom, than conspiracies of the inferior man against his betters. They mirror very accurately his congenital hatred of knowledge, his bitter enmity to the man who knows more than he does, and so gets more out of life. Certainly it cannot have gone unnoticed that their membership is recruited, in the overwhelming main, from the lower orders—that no man of any education or other human dignity belongs to them. What they propose to do, at bottom and in brief, is to make the superior man infamous—by mere abuse if it is sufficient, and if it is not, then by law.

Such organizations, of course, must have leaders; there must be men in them whose ignorance and imbecility are measurably less abject than the ignorance and imbecility of the average. These super-Chandala often attain to a considerable power, especially in democratic states. Their followers trust them and look up to them; sometimes, when the pack is on the loose, it is necessary to conciliate them. But their puissance cannot conceal their incurable inferiority. They belong to the mob as surely as their dupes, and the thing that animates them is precisely the mob's hatred of superiority. Whatever lies above the level of their comprehension is of the devil. A glass of wine delights civilized men; they themselves, drinking it, would get drunk. *Ergo,* wine must be prohibited. The hypothesis of evolution is credited by all men of education; they themselves can't understand it. *Ergo,* its teaching must be put down.

This simple fact explains such phenomena as the Tennessee buffoonery. Nothing else can. We must think of human progress, not as of something going on in the race in general, but as of something going on in a small minority, perpetually beleaguered in a few walled towns. Now and then the horde of barbarians outside breaks through, and we have an armed effort to halt the process. That is, we have a Reformation, a French Revolution, a war for democracy, a Great Awakening. The minority is decimated and driven to cover. But a few survive—and a few are enough to carry on.

III

The inferior man's reasons for hating knowledge are not hard to discern. He hates it because it is complex—because it puts an unbearable burden upon his meager capacity for taking in ideas. Thus his search is always for short cuts. All superstitions are such short cuts. Their aim is to make the unintelligible simple, and even obvious. So on what seem to be higher levels. No man who has not had a long and arduous education can understand even the most elementary concepts of modern pathology. But even a hind at the plow can grasp the theory of chiropractic in two lessons. Hence the vast popularity of chiropractic among the submerged—and of osteopathy, Christian Science and other such quackeries with it. They are idiotic, but they are simple—and every man prefers what he can understand to what puzzles and dismays him.

The popularity of Fundamentalism among the inferior orders of men is explicable in exactly the same way. The cosmogonies that educated men toy with are all inordinately complex. To comprehend their veriest outlines requires an immense stock of knowledge, and a habit of thought. It would be as vain to try to teach them to peasants or to the city proletariat as it would be to try to teach them to streptococci. But the cosmogony of Genesis is so simple that even a yokel can grasp it. It is set forth in a few phrases. It offers, to an ignorant man, the irresistible reasonableness of the nonsensical. So he accepts it with loud hosannas, and has one more excuse for hating his betters.

Politics and the fine arts repeat the story. The issues that the former throw up are often so complex that, in the present state of human knowledge, they must remain impenetrable, even to the most enlightened men. How much easier to follow a mountebank with a shibboleth—a Coolidge, a Wilson or a Roosevelt! The arts, like the sciences, demand special training, often very difficult. But in jazz there are simple rhythms, comprehensible even to savages.

IV

What all this amounts to is that the human race is divided into two sharply differentiated and mutually antagonistic classes, almost two genera—a small minority that plays with ideas and is capable of taking them in, and a vast majority that finds them painful, and is thus arrayed against them, and against all who have traffic with them. The intellectual heritage of the race belongs to the minority, and to the minority only. The majority has no more to do with it than it has to do with ecclesiastic politics on Mars. In so far as that heritage is apprehended, it is viewed with enmity. But in the main it is not apprehended at all.

That is why Beethoven survives. Of the 110,000,000 so-called human beings who now live in the United States, flogged and crazed by Coolidge, Rotary, the Ku Klux and the newspapers, it is probable that at least 108,000,000 have never heard of him at all. To these immortals, made in God's image, one of the greatest artists the human race has ever produced is not even a name. So far as they are concerned he might as well have died at birth. The gorgeous and incomparable beauties that he created are nothing to them. They get no value out of the fact that he existed. They are completely unaware of what he did in the world, and would not be interested if they were told.

The fact saves good Ludwig's bacon. His music survives because it lies outside the plane of the popular apprehension, like the colors beyond violet or the concept of honor. If it could be brought within range, it would at once arouse hostility. Its complexity would challenge; its lack of moral purpose would affright. Soon there would be a movement to put it down, and Baptist clergymen would range the land denouncing it, and in the end some poor musician, taken in the un-American act of playing it, would be put on trial before a jury of Ku Kluxers, and railroaded to the calaboose.

[*Baltimore Evening Sun,* June 29, 1925]

IN TENNESSEE

Always, in this great republic, controversies depart swiftly from their original terms and plunge into irrelevancies and false pretenses. The case of prohibition is salient. Who recalls the optimistic days before the Eighteenth Amendment, and the lofty prognostication of the dry mullahs, clerical and lay? Prohibition, we were told, would empty the jails, reduce the tax rate, abolish poverty and put an end to political corruption. Today even the Prohibitionists know better, and so they begin to grow discreetly silent upon the matter. Instead, they come forward with an entirely new Holy Cause.

What began as a campaign for a Babbitt's Utopia becomes transformed into a mystical campaign for Law Enforcement. Prohibition is a grotesque failure, but the fight must go on. A transcendental motive takes the place of a practical motive. One categorical imperative goes out and another comes in.

So, now, in Tennessee, where a rural pedagogue stands arraigned before his peers for violating the school law. At bottom, a quite simple business. The hinds of the State, desiring to prepare their young for life there, set up public schools. To man these schools they employ pedagogues. To guide those pedagogues they lay down rules prescribing what is to be taught and what is not to be taught. Why not, indeed? How could it be otherwise? Precisely the same custom prevails everywhere else in the world, wherever there are schools at all. Behind every school ever heard of there is a definite concept of its purpose—of the sort of equipment it is to give to its pupils. It cannot conceivably teach everything; it must confine itself by sheer necessity to teaching what will be of the greatest utility, cultural or practical, to the youth actually in hand. Well, what could be of greater utility to the son of a Tennessee mountaineer than an education making him a good Tennessean, content with his father, at peace with his neighbors, dutiful to the local religion and docile under the local mores?

That is all the Tennessee anti-evolution law seeks to accomplish. It differs from other regulations of the same sort only to the extent that Tennessee differs from the rest of the world. The State, to a degree that should be gratifying, has escaped the national standardization. Its people show a character that is immensely different from the character of, say, New Yorkers or Californians. They retain, among other things, the anthropomorphic religion of an elder day. They do not profess it; they actually believe in it. The Old Testament, to them, is not a mere sacerdotal whizz-bang, to be read for its pornography; it is an authoritative history, and the transactions recorded in it are as true as the story of Barbara Frietchie, or that of Washington and the cherry tree, or that of the late Woodrow's struggle to keep us out of the war. So crediting the sacred narrative, they desire that it be taught to their children, and any doctrine that makes game of it is immensely offensive to them. When such a doctrine, despite their protests, is actually taught, they proceed to put it down by force.

Is that procedure singular? I don't think it is. It is adopted everywhere, the instant the prevailing notions, whether real or false, are challenged.

Suppose a school-teacher in New York began entertaining his pupils with the case against the Jews, or against the Pope. Suppose a teacher in Vermont essayed to argue that the late Confederate States were right, as thousands of perfectly sane and intelligent persons believe that Lee was a defender of the Constitution and Grant a traitor to it. Suppose a teacher in Kansas taught that prohibition was evil, or a teacher in New Jersey that it was virtuous. But I need not pile up suppositions. The evidence of what happens to such a contumacious teacher was spread before us copiously during the late uproar about Bolsheviks. And it was not in rural Tennessee but in the great cultural centers which now laugh at Tennessee that punishments came most swiftly, and were most barbarous. It was not Dayton but New York City that cashiered teachers for protesting against the obvious lies of the State Department.

Yet now we are asked to believe that some mysterious and vastly important principle is at stake at Dayton—that the conviction of Professor Scopes will strike a deadly blow at enlightenment and bring down freedom to sorrow and shame. Tell it to the marines! No principle is at stake at Dayton save the principle that school-teachers, like plumbers, should stick to the job that is set before them, and not go roving about the house, breaking windows, raiding the cellar and demoralizing the children. The issue of free speech is quite irrelevant. When a pedagogue takes his oath of office, he renounces his right to free speech quite as certainly as a bishop does, or a colonel in the army, or an editorial writer on a newspaper. He becomes a paid propagandist of certain definite doctrines and attitudes, mainly determined specifically and in advance, and every time he departs from them deliberately he deliberately swindles his employers.

What ails Mr. Scopes, and many like him, is that they have been filled with subversive ideas by specialists in human liberty, of whom I have the honor to be one. Such specialists, confronted by the New York cases, saw a chance to make political capital out of them, and did so with great effect. I was certainly not backward in that enterprise. The liars of the State Department were fair game, and any stick is good enough to beat a dog with. Even a pedagogue, seized firmly by the legs, makes an effective shillelagh. (I have used, in my time, yet worse: a congressman, a psychiatrist, a birth-controller to maul an archbishop.) Unluckily, some of the pedagogues mistook the purpose of the operation. They came out of it full of a delusion that they were apostles of liberty, of the search for knowledge, of enlightenment. They have been worrying and exasperating their employers ever since.

I believe it must be plain that they are wrong, and that their employers, by a necessary inference, are right. In the whole history of the world no such pedagogue has ever actually increased the sum of human knowledge. His training unfits him for it; moreover, he would not be a pedagogue if he had either the taste or the capacity for it. He is a workingman, not a thinker. When he speaks, his employers speak. What he says has behind it all the authority of the community. If he would be true to his oath he must be very careful to say nothing that is in violation of the communal mores, the communal magic, the communal notion of the good, the beautiful and the true.

Here, I repeat, I speak of the pedagogue, and use the word in its strict sense—that is, I speak of the fellow whose sole job is teaching. Men of great learning, men who genuinely know something, men who have augmented the store of human knowledge—such men, in their leisure, may also teach. The master may take an apprentice. But he does not seek apprentices in the hill towns of Tennessee, or even on the East Side of New York. He does not waste himself upon children whose fate it will be, when they grow up, to become Rotarians or Methodist deacons, bootleggers or moonshiners. He looks for his apprentices in the minority that has somehow escaped that fate—that has, by some act of God, survived the dreadful ministrations of school-teachers. To this minority he may submit his doubts as well as his certainties. He may present what is dubious and of evil report along with what is official, and hence good. He may be wholly himself. Liberty of teaching begins where pedagogy ends.

[*Nation,* July 1, 1925]

MENCKEN FINDS DAYTONIANS FULL of SICKENING DOUBTS about VALUE of PUBLICITY

Dayton, Tenn., July 9.—On the eve of the great contest Dayton is full of sickening surges and tremors of doubt. Five or six weeks ago, when the infidel Scopes was first laid by the heels, there was no uncertainty in all this smiling valley. The town boomers leaped to the assault as one man. Here was an unexampled, almost a miraculous chance to get Dayton upon the front pages, to make it talked about, to put it upon the map. But how now?

Today, with the curtain barely rung up and the worst buffooneries to come, it is obvious to even town boomers that getting upon the map, like patriotism, is not enough. The getting there must be managed discreetly, adroitly, with careful regard to psychological niceties. The boomers of Dayton, alas, had no skill at such things, and the experts they called in were all quacks. The result now turns the communal liver to water. Two months ago the town was obscure and happy. Today it is a universal joke.

I have been attending the permanent town meeting that goes on in Robinson's drug store, trying to find out what the town optimists have saved from the wreck. All I can find is a sort of mystical confidence that God will somehow come to the rescue to reward His old and faithful partisans as they deserve—that good will flow eventually out of what now seems to be heavily evil. More specifically, it is believed that settlers will be attracted to the town as to some refuge from the atheism of the great urban Sodoms and Gomorrahs.

But will these refugees bring any money with them? Will they buy lots and build houses? Will they light the fires of the cold and silent blast furnace down the railroad tracks? On these points, I regret to report, optimism has to call in theology to aid it. Prayer can accomplish a lot. It can cure diabetes, find lost pocketbooks and restrain husbands from beating their wives. But is prayer made any more efficacious by giving a circus first? Coming to this thought, Dayton begins to sweat.

The town, I confess, greatly surprised me. I expected to find a squalid Southern village, with darkies snoozing on the horse-blocks, pigs rooting under the houses and the inhabitants full of hookworm and malaria. What I found was a country town full of charm and even beauty—a somewhat smallish but nevertheless very attractive Westminster or Belair.[3]

The houses are surrounded by pretty gardens, with cool green lawns and stately trees. The two chief streets are paved from curb to curb. The stores carry good stocks and have a metropolitan air, especially the drug, book, magazine, sporting goods and soda-water emporium of the estimable Robinson. A few of the town ancients still affect galluses and string ties, but the younger bucks are very nattily turned out. Scopes himself, even in his shirt sleeves, would fit into any college campus in America save that of Harvard alone.

Nor is there any evidence in the town of that poisonous spirit which usually shows itself when Christian men gather to defend the great doctrine of their faith. I have heard absolutely no whisper that Scopes is in the pay of the Jesuits, or that the whiskey trust is backing him, or that he is egged on by the Jews who manufacture lascivious moving pictures. On the contrary, the Evolutionists and the Anti-Evolutionists seem to be on the best of terms, and it is hard in a group to distinguish one from another.

The basic issues of the case, indeed, seem to be very little discussed at Dayton. What interests everyone is its mere strategy. By what device, precisely, will Bryan trim old Clarence Darrow? Will he do it gently and with every delicacy of forensics, or will he wade in on high gear and make a swift butchery of it? For no one here seems to doubt that Bryan will win—that is, if the bout goes to a finish. What worries the town is the fear that some diabolical higher power will intervene on Darrow's side—that is, before Bryan heaves him through the ropes.

The lack of Christian heat that I have mentioned is probably due in part to the fact that the fundamentalists are in overwhelming majority as far as the eye can reach—according to most local statisticians, in a majority of at least nine-tenths. There are, in fact, only two downright infidels in all Rhea county, and one of them is charitably assumed to be a bit balmy. The other, a yokel roosting far back in the hills, is probably simply a poet got into the wrong pew. The town account of him is to the effect that he professes to regard death as a beautiful adventure.

When the local ecclesiastics begin alarming the peasantry with word pictures of the last sad scene, and sulphurous fumes begin to choke even Unitarians, this skeptical rustic comes forward with his argument that it is foolish to be afraid of what one knows so little about—that, after all, there is no more genuine evidence that anyone will ever go to hell than there is that the Volstead act will ever be enforced.

Such blasphemous ideas naturally cause talk in a Baptist community, but both of the infidels are unmolested. Rhea county, in fact, is proud of its tolerance, and apparently with good reason. The Klan has never got a foothold here, though it rages everywhere else in Tennessee. When the first kleagles came in they got the cold shoulder, and pretty soon they gave up the county as hopeless. It is run today not by anonymous daredevils in white nightshirts, but by well-heeled Freemasons in decorous white aprons. In Dayton alone there are sixty thirty-second-degree Masons—an immense quota for so small a town. They believe in keeping the peace, and so even the stray Catholics of the town are treated politely, though everyone naturally regrets they are required to report to the Pope once a week.

It is probably this unusual tolerance, and not any extraordinary passion for the integrity of Genesis, that has made Dayton the scene of a celebrated case, and got its name upon the front pages, and caused its forward-looking men to begin to wonder uneasily if all advertising is really good advertising. The trial of Scopes is possible here simply because it can be carried on here without heat—because no one will lose any sleep even if the devil comes to the aid of Darrow and Malone, and Bryan gets a mauling. The local intelligentsia venerate Bryan as a Christian, but it was not as a Christian that they called him in, but as one adept at attracting the newspaper boys—in brief, as a showman. As I have said, they now begin to mistrust the show, but they still believe that he will make a good one, win or lose.

Elsewhere, North or South, the combat would become bitter. Here it retains the lofty qualities of the *duello*. I gather the notion, indeed, that the gentlemen who are most active in promoting it are precisely the most lacking in hot conviction—that it is, in its local aspects, rather a joust between neutrals than a battle between passionate believers. Is it a mere coincidence that the town clergy have been very carefully kept out of it? There are several Baptist brothers here of such powerful gifts that when they begin belaboring sinners the very rats of the alleys flee to the hills. They preach dreadfully. But they are not heard from to-day. By some process to me unknown they have been induced to shut up—a far harder business, I venture, than knocking out a lion with a sandbag. But the sixty thirty-second-degree Masons of Dayton have somehow achieved it.

Thus the battle joins and the good red sun shines down. Dayton lies in a fat and luxuriant valley. The bottoms are green with corn, pumpkins and young orchards and the hills are full of reliable moonshiners, all save one of them Christian men. We are not in the South here, but hanging on to the North. Very little cotton is grown in the valley. The people in politics are Republicans and put Coolidge next to Lincoln and John Wesley. The fences are in good repair. The roads are smooth and hard. The scene is set for a high-toned and even somewhat swagger combat. When it is over all the participants save Bryan will shake hands.

[*Baltimore Evening Sun,* July 9, 1925]

IMPOSSIBILITY OF OBTAINING FAIR JURY ENSURES SCOPES' CONVICTION, SAYS MENCKEN

Dayton, Tenn., July 10.—The trial of the infidel Scopes, beginning here this hot, lovely morning, will greatly resemble, I suspect, the trial of a prohibition agent accused of mayhem in Union Hill, N. J. That is to say, it will be conducted with the most austere regard for the highest principles of jurisprudence. Judge and jury will go to extreme lengths to assure the prisoner the last and least of his rights. He will be protected in his person and feelings by the full military and naval power of the State of Tennessee. No one will be permitted to pull his nose, to pray publicly for his condemnation or even to make a face at him. But all the same he will be bumped off inevitably when the time comes, and to the applause of all right-thinking men.

The real trial, in truth, will not begin until Scopes is convicted and ordered to the hulks. Then the prisoner will be the Legislature of Tennessee, and the jury will be that great fair, unimpassioned body of enlightened men which has already decided that a horse hair put into a bottle will turn into a snake and that the Kaiser started the late war. What goes on here is simply a sort of preliminary hearing, with music by the village choir. For it will be no more possible in this Christian valley to get a jury unprejudiced against Scopes than would be possible in Wall Street to get a jury unprejudiced against a Bolshevik.

I speak of prejudice in its purely philosophical sense. As I wrote yesterday, there is an almost complete absence, in these pious hills, of the ordinary and familiar malignancy of Christian men. If the Rev. Dr. Crabbe ever spoke of bootleggers as humanely and affectionately as the town theologians speak of Scopes, and even Darrow and Malone, his employers would pelt him with their spyglasses and sit on him until the ambulance came from Mount Hope. There is absolutely no bitterness on tap. But neither is there any doubt. It has been decided by acclamation, with only a few infidels dissenting, that the hypothesis of evolution is profane, inhumane and against God, and all that remains is to translate that almost unanimous decision into the jargon of the law and so have done.

The town boomers have banqueted Darrow as well as Bryan, but there is no mistaking which of the two has the crowd, which means the venire of tried and true men. Bryan has been oozing around the country since his first day here, addressing this organization and that, presenting the indubitable Word of God in his caressing, ingratiating way, and so making unanimity doubly unanimous. From the defense yesterday came hints that this was making hay before the sun had legally begun to shine—even that it was a sort of contempt of court. But no Daytonian believes anything of the sort. What Bryan says doesn't seem to these congenial Baptists and Methodists to be argument; it seems to be a mere graceful statement of the obvious.

Meanwhile, reinforcements continue to come in, some of them from unexpected sources. I had the honor of being present yesterday when Col. Patrick Callahan, of Louisville, marched up at the head of his cohort of 250,000,000 Catholic Fundamentalists. The two colonels embraced, exchanged a few military and legal pleasantries and then retired up a steep stairway to the office of the Hicks brothers to discuss strategy. Colonel Callahan's followers were present, of course, only by a legal fiction; the town of Dayton would not hold so large an army. In the actual flesh there were only the colonel himself and his aide-de-camp. Nevertheless, the 250,000,000 were put down as present and recorded as voting.

Later on I had the misfortune to fall into a dispute with Colonel Callahan on a point of canon law. It was my contention that the position of the Roman Church, on matters of doctrine, is not ordinarily stated by laymen—that such matters are usually left to high ecclesiastical authorities, headed by the Bishop of Rome. I also contended, perhaps somewhat fatuously, that there seemed to be a considerable difference of opinion regarding organic evolution among these authorities—that it was possible to find in their writings both ingenious arguments for it and violent protests against it. All these objections Colonel Callahan waved away with a genial gesture. He was here, he said, to do what he could for the authority of the Sacred Scriptures and the aiding and comforting of his old friend, Bryan, and it was all one to him whether atheists yelled or not. Then he began to talk about prohibition, which he favors, and the germ theory of diseases, which he regards as bilge.

A somewhat more plausible volunteer has turned up in the person of Pastor T. T. Martin, of Blue Mountain, Miss. He has hired a room and stocked it with pamphlets bearing such titles as *Evolution a Menace, Hell and the High Schools* and *God or Gorilla,* and addresses connoisseurs of scientific fallacy every night on a lot behind the Courthouse. Pastor Martin, a handsome and amiable old gentleman with a great mop of snow-white hair, was a professor of science in a Baptist college for years, and has given profound study to the biological sections of the Old Testament.

He told me today that he regarded the food regulations in Leviticus as so sagacious that their framing must have been a sort of feat even for divinity. The flesh of the domestic hog, he said, is a rank poison as ordinarily prepared for the table, though it is probably harmless when smoked and salted, as in bacon. He said that his investigations had shown that seven and a half out of every thirteen cows are quite free of tuberculosis, but that twelve out of every thirteen hogs have it in an advanced and highly communicable form. The Jews, protected by their piety against devouring pork, are immune to the disease. In all history, he said, there is authentic record of but one Jew who died of tuberculosis.

The presence of Pastor Martin and Colonel Callahan has given renewed confidence to the prosecution. The former offers proof that men of science are, after all, not unanimously atheists, and the latter that there is no division between Christians in the face of the common enemy. But though such encouragements help, they are certainly not necessary. All they really supply is another layer of icing on the cake. Dayton will give Scopes a rigidly fair and impartial trial. All his Constitutional rights will be jealously safeguarded. The question whether he voted for or against Coolidge will not be permitted to intrude itself into the deliberations of the jury, or the gallant effort of Colonel Bryan to get at and establish the truth. He will be treated very politely. Dayton, indeed, is proud of him, as Sauk Center, Minn., is proud of Sinclair Lewis and Whittingham, Vt., of Brigham Young. But it is lucky for Scopes that sticking pins into Genesis is still only a misdemeanor in Tennessee, punishable by a simple fine, with no alternative of the knout, the stone pile or exile to the Dry Tortugas.

[*Baltimore Evening Sun,* July 10, 1925]

MENCKEN LIKENS TRIAL TO A RELIGIOUS ORGY, WITH DEFENDANT A BEELZEBUB

Chattanooga, Tenn., July 11.—Life down here in the Cumberland mountains realizes almost perfectly the ideal of those righteous and devoted men, Dr. Howard A. Kelly, the Rev. Dr. W. W. Davis, the Hon. Richard H.

Edmonds, and the Hon. Henry S. Dulaney. That is to say, evangelical Christianity is one hundred per cent triumphant. There is, of course, a certain subterranean heresy, but it is so cowed that it is almost inarticulate, and at its worst it would pass for the strictest orthodoxy in such Sodoms of infidelity as Baltimore. It may seem fabulous, but it is a sober fact that a sound Episcopalian or even a Northern Methodist would be regarded as virtually an atheist in Dayton. Here the only genuine conflict is between true believers. Of a given text in Holy Writ one faction may say this thing and another that, but both agree unreservedly that the text itself is impeccable, and neither in the midst of the most violent disputation would venture to accuse the other of doubt.

To call a man a doubter in these parts is equal to accusing him of cannibalism. Even the infidel Scopes himself is not charged with any such infamy. What they say of him, at worst, is that he permitted himself to be used as a cat's paw by scoundrels eager to destroy the anti-evolution law for their own dark and hellish ends. There is, it appears, a conspiracy of scientists afoot. Their purpose is to break down religion, propagate immorality, and so reduce mankind to the level of the brutes. They are the sworn and sinister agents of Beelzebub, who yearns to conquer the world, and has his eye especially upon Tennessee. Scopes is thus an agent of Beelzebub once removed, but that is as far as any fair man goes in condemning him. He is young and yet full of folly. When the secular arm has done execution upon him, the pastors will tackle him and he will be saved.

The selection of a jury to try him, which went on all yesterday afternoon in the atmosphere of a blast furnace, showed to what extreme lengths the salvation of the local primates has been pushed. It was obvious after a few rounds that the jury would be unanimously hot for Genesis. The most that Mr. Darrow could hope for was to sneak in a few men bold enough to declare publicly that they would have to hear the evidence against Scopes before condemning him. The slightest sign of anything further brought forth a peremptory challenge from the State. Once a man was challenged without examination for simply admitting that he did not belong formally to any church. Another time a panel man who confessed that he was prejudiced against evolution got a hearty round of applause from the crowd.

The whole process quickly took on an air of strange unreality, at least to a stranger from heathen parts. The desire of the judge to be fair to the defense, and even polite and helpful, was obvious enough—in fact, he more than once stretched the local rules of procedure in order to give Darrow a hand. But it was equally obvious that the whole thing was resolving itself into the trial of a man by his sworn enemies. A local pastor led off with a prayer calling on God to put down heresy; the judge himself charged the grand jury to protect the schools against subversive ideas. And when the candidates for the petit jury came up Darrow had to pass Fundamentalist after Fundamentalist into the box—some of them glaring at him as if they expected him to go off with a sulphurous bang every time he mopped his bald head.

In brief this is a strictly Christian community, and such is its notion of fairness, justice and due process of law. Try to picture a town made up wholly of Dr. Crabbes and Dr. Kellys, and you will have a reasonably accurate image of it. Its people are simply unable to imagine a man who rejects the literal authority of the Bible. The most they can conjure up, straining until they are red in the face, is a man who is in error about the meaning of this or that text. Thus one accused of heresy among them is like one accused of boiling his grandmother to make soap in Maryland. He must resign himself to being tried by a jury wholly innocent of any suspicion of the crime he is charged with and unanimously convinced that it is infamous. Such a jury, in the legal sense, may be fair. That is, it may be willing to hear the evidence against him before bumping him off. But it would certainly be spitting into the eye of reason to call it impartial.

The trial, indeed, takes on, for all its legal forms, something of the air of a religious orgy. The applause of the crowd I have already mentioned. Judge Raulston rapped it down and threatened to clear the room if it was repeated, but he was quite unable to still its echoes under his very windows. The courthouse is surrounded by a large lawn, and it is peppered day and night with evangelists. One and all they are Fundamentalists and their yells and bawlings fill the air with orthodoxy. I have listened to twenty of them and had private discourse with a dozen, and I have yet to find one who doubted so much as the typographical errors in Holy Writ. They dispute raucously and far into the night, but they begin and end on the common ground of complete faith. One of these holy men wears a sign on his back announcing that he is the Bible champion of the world. He told me today that he had studied the Bible four hours a day for thirty-three years, and that he had devised a plan of salvation that would save the worst sinner ever heard of, even a scientist, a theater actor or a pirate on the high seas, in forty days. This gentleman denounced the hard-shell Baptists as swindlers. He admitted freely that their sorcerers were powerful preachers and could save any ordinary man from sin, but he said that they were impotent against iniquity. The distinction is unknown to city theologians, but is as real down here as that between sanctification and salvation. The local experts, in fact, debate it daily. The Bible champion, just as I left him, was challenged by one such professor, and the two were still hard at it an hour later.

Most of the participants in such recondite combats, of course, are yokels from the hills, where no sound is heard after sundown save the roar of the catamount and the wailing of departed spirits, and a man thus has time to ponder the divine mysteries. But it is an amazing thing that the more polished classes also participate actively. The professor who challenged the Bible champion was indistinguishable, to the eye, from a bond salesman or city bootlegger. He had on a natty palm beach suit and a fashionable soft collar and he used excellent English. Obviously, he was one who had been through the local high school and perhaps a country college. Yet he was so far uncontaminated by infidelity that he stood in the hot sun for a whole hour debating a point that even bishops might be excused for dodging, winter as well as summer.

The Bible champion is matched and rivaled by whole herds of other metaphysicians, and all of them attract good houses and have to defend themselves against constant attack. The Seventh Day Adventists, the Campbellites, the Holy Rollers and a dozen other occult sects have field agents on the ground. They follow the traveling judges through all this country. Everywhere they go, I am told, they find the natives ready to hear them and dispute with them. They find highly accomplished theologians in every village, but even in the county towns they never encounter a genuine skeptic. If a man has doubts in this immensely pious country, he keeps them to himself.

Dr. Kelly should come down here and see his dreams made real. He will find a people who not only accept the Bible as an infallible handbook of history, geology, biology and celestial physics, but who also practise its moral precepts—at all events, up to the limit of human capacity. It would be hard to imagine a more moral town than Dayton. If it has any bootleggers, no visitor has heard of them. Ten minutes after I arrived a leading citizen offered me a drink made up half of white mule and half of coca cola, but he seems to have been simply indulging himself in a naughty gesture. No fancy woman has been seen in the town since the end of the McKinley administration. There is no gambling. There is no place to dance. The relatively wicked, when they would indulge themselves, go to Robinson's drug store and debate theology.

In a word, the new Jerusalem, the ideal of all soul savers and sin exterminators. Nine churches are scarcely enough for the 1,800 inhabitants: many of them go into the hills to shout and roll. A clergyman has the rank and authority of a major-general of artillery. A Sunday-school superintendent is believed to have the gift of prophecy. But what of life here? Is it more agreeable than in Babylon? I regret that I must have to report that it is not. The incessant clashing of theologians grows monotonous in a day and intolerable the day following. One longs for a merry laugh, a burst of happy music, the gurgle of a decent jug. Try a meal in the hotel; it is tasteless and swims in grease. Go to the drug store and call for refreshment: the boy will hand you almost automatically a beaker of coca-cola. Look at the magazine counter: a pile of *Saturday Evening Post*s two feet high. Examine the books: melodrama and cheap amour. Talk to a town magnifico; he knows nothing that is not in Genesis.

I propose that Dr. Kelly be sent here for sixty days, preferably in the heat of summer. He will return to Baltimore yelling for a carboy of Pilsner and eager to master the saxophone. His soul perhaps will be lost, but he will be a merry and a happy man.

[*Baltimore Evening Sun,* July 11, 1925]

YEARNING MOUNTAINEERS' SOULS NEED RECONVERSION NIGHTLY, MENCKEN FINDS

Dayton, Tenn., July 13.—There is a Unitarian clergyman here from New York, trying desperately to horn into the trial and execution of the infidel Scopes. He will fail. If Darrow ventured to put him on the stand the whole audience, led by the jury, would leap out of the courthouse windows, and take to the hills. Darrow himself, indeed, is as much as they can bear. The whisper that he is an atheist has been stilled by the bucolic make-up and by the public report that he has the gift of prophecy and can reconcile Genesis and evolution. Even so, there is ample space about him when he navigates the streets. The other day a newspaper woman was warned by her landlady to keep out of the courtroom when he was on his legs. All the local sorcerers predict that a bolt from heaven will fetch him in the end. The night he arrived there was a violent storm, the town water turned brown, and horned cattle in the lowlands were afloat for hours. A woman back in the mountains gave birth to a child with hair four inches long, curiously bobbed in scallops.

The Book of Revelation has all the authority, in these theological uplands, of military orders in time of war. The people turn to it for light upon all their problems, spiritual and secular. If a text were found in it denouncing the Anti-Evolution law, then the Anti-Evolution law would become infamous overnight. But so far the exegetes who roar and snuffle in the town have found no such text. Instead they have found only blazing ratifications and reinforcements of Genesis. Darwin is the devil with seven tails and nine horns. Scopes, though he is disguised by flannel pantaloons and a Beta Theta Pi haircut, is the harlot of Babylon. Darrow is Beelzebub in person and Malone is the Crown Prince Friedrich Wilhelm.

I have hitherto hinted an Episcopalian down here in the coca-cola belt is regarded as an atheist. It sounds like one of the lies that journalists tell, but it is really an understatement of the facts. Even a Methodist, by Rhea county standards, is one a bit debauched by pride of intellect. It is the four Methodists on the jury who are expected to hold out for giving Scopes Christian burial after he is hanged. They all made it plain, when they were examined, that they were free-thinking and independent men, and not to be run amuck by the superstitions of the lowly. One actually confessed that he seldom read the Bible, though he hastened to add that he was familiar with its principles. The fellow had on a boiled shirt and a polka dot necktie. He sits somewhat apart. When Darrow withers to a cinder under the celestial blowpipe, this dubious Wesleyan, too, will lose a few hairs.

Even the Baptists no longer brew a medicine that is strong enough for the mountaineers. The sacrament of baptism by total immersion is over too quickly for them, and what follows offers nothing that they can get their teeth into. What they crave is a continuous experience of the divine power, an endless series of evidence that the true believer is a marked man, ever under the eye of God. It is not enough to go to a revival once a year or twice a year; there must be a revival every night. And it is not enough to accept the truth as a mere statement of indisputable and awful fact: it must be embraced ecstatically and orgiastically, to the accompaniment of loud shouts, dreadful heavings and gurglings, and dancing with arms and legs.

This craving is satisfied brilliantly by the gaudy practises of the Holy Rollers, and so the mountaineers are gradually gravitating toward the Holy Roller communion, or, as they prefer to call it, the Church of God. Gradually, perhaps, is not the word. They are actually going in by whole villages and townships. At the last count of noses there were twenty thousand Holy Rollers in these hills. The next census, I have no doubt, will show many more. The cities of the lowlands, of course, still resist, and so do most of the county towns, including even Dayton, but once one steps off the State roads the howl of holiness is heard in the woods, and the yokels carry on an almost continuous orgy.

A foreigner in store cloth going out from Dayton must approach the sacred grove somewhat discreetly. It is not that the Holy Rollers, discovering him, would harm him; it is simply that they would shut down their boiling of the devil and flee into the forests. We left Dayton an hour after nightfall and parked our car in a wood a mile or so beyond the little hill village of Morgantown. Far off in a glade a flickering light was visible and out of the silence came a faint rumble of exhortation. We could scarcely distinguish the figure of the preacher; it was like looking down the tube of a dark field microscope. We got out of the car and sneaked along the edge of a mountain cornfield.

Presently we were near enough to see what was going on. From the great limb of a mighty oak hung a couple of crude torches of the sort that car inspectors thrust under Pullman cars when a train pulls in at night. In their light was a preacher, and for a while we could see no one else. He was an immensely tall and thin mountaineer in blue jeans, his collarless shirt open at the neck and his hair a tousled mop. As he preached he paced up and down under the smoking flambeaux and at each turn he thrust his arms into the air and yelled, "Glory to God!" We crept nearer in the shadow of the cornfield and began to hear more of his discourse. He was preaching on the day of judgment. The high kings of the earth, he roared, would all fall down and die; only the sanctified would stand up to receive the Lord God of Hosts. One of these kings he mentioned by name—the king of what he called Greece-y. The King of Greece-y, he said, was doomed to hell.

We went forward a few more yards and began to see the audience. It was seated on benches ranged round the preacher in a circle. Behind him sat a row of elders, men and women. In front were the younger folk. We kept on cautiously, and individuals rose out of the ghostly gloom. A young mother sat suckling her baby, rocking as the preacher paced up and down. Two scared little girls hugged each other, their pigtails down their backs. An immensely huge mountain woman, in a gingham dress cut in one piece, rolled on her heels at every "Glory to God." To one side, but half visible, was what appeared to be a bed. We found out afterward that two babies were asleep upon it.

The preacher stopped at last and there arose out of the darkness a woman with her hair pulled back into a little tight knot. She began so quietly that we couldn't hear what she said, but soon her voice rose resonantly and we could follow her. She was denouncing the reading of books. Some wandering book agent, it appeared, had come to her cabin and tried to sell her a specimen of his wares. She refused to touch it. Why, indeed, read a book? If what was in it was true then everything in it was already in the Bible. If it was false then reading it would imperil the soul. Her syllogism complete, she sat down.

There followed a hymn, led by a somewhat fat brother wearing silver-rimmed country spectacles. It droned on for half a dozen stanzas, and then the first speaker resumed the floor. He argued that the gift of tongues was real and that education was a snare. Once his children could read the Bible, he said, they had enough. Beyond lay only infidelity and damnation. Sin stalked the cities. Dayton itself was a Sodom. Even Morgantown had begun to forget God. He sat down, and the female aurochs in gingham got up.

She began quietly, but was soon leaping and roaring, and it was hard to follow her. Under cover of the turmoil we sneaked a bit closer. A couple of other discourses followed, and there were two or three hymns. Suddenly a change of mood began to make itself felt. The last hymn ran longer than the others and dropped gradually into a monotonous, unintelligible chant. The leader beat time with his book. The faithful broke out with exultations. When the singing ended there was a brief palaver that we could not hear and two of the men moved a bench into the circle of light directly under the flambeaux. Then a half-grown girl emerged from the darkness and threw herself upon it. We noticed with astonishment that she had bobbed hair. "This sister," said the leader, "has asked for prayers." We moved a bit closer. We could now see faces plainly and hear every word.

What followed quickly reached such heights of barbaric grotesquerie that it was hard to believe it real. At a signal all the faithful crowded up the bench and began to pray—not in unison but each for himself. At another they all fell on their knees, their arms over the penitent. The leader kneeled, facing us, his head alternately thrown back dramatically or buried in his hands. Words spouted from his lips like bullets from a machine gun— appeals to God to pull the penitent back out of hell, defiances of the powers and principalities of the air, a vast impassioned jargon of apocalyptic texts. Suddenly he rose to his feet, threw back his head and began to speak in tongues—blub-blub-blub, gurgle-gurgle-gurgle. His voice rose to a higher register. The climax was a shrill, inarticulate squawk, like that of a man throttled. He fell headlong across the pyramid of supplicants.

A comic scene? Somehow, no. The poor half-wits were too horribly in earnest. It was like peeping through a knothole at the writhings of a people in pain. From the squirming and jabbering mass a young woman gradually detached herself—a woman not uncomely, with a pathetic home-made cap on her head. Her head jerked back, the veins of her neck swelled, and her fists went to her throat as if she were fighting for breath. She bent backward until she was like half of a hoop. Then she suddenly snapped forward. We caught a flash of the whites of her eyes. Presently her whole body began to be convulsed—great convulsions that began at the shoulders and ended at the hips. She would leap to her feet, thrust her arms in air and then hurl herself upon the heap. Her praying flattened out into a mere delirious caterwauling, like that of a tomcat on a petting party.

I describe the thing as a strict behaviorist. The lady's subjective sensations I leave to infidel pathologists. Whatever they were they were obviously contagious, for soon another damsel joined her, and then another and then a fourth. The last one had an extraordinary bad attack. She began with mild enough jerks of the head, but in a moment she was bounding all over the place, exactly like a chicken with its head cut off. Every time her head came up a stream of yells and barkings would issue out of it. Once she collided with a dark, undersized brother, hitherto silent and stolid. Contact with her set him off as if he had been kicked by a mule. He leaped into the air, threw back his head and began to gargle as if with a mouthful of BB shot. Then he loosened one tremendous stentorian sentence in the tongues and collapsed.

By this time the performers were quite oblivious to the profane universe. We left our hiding and came up to the little circle of light. We slipped into the vacant seats on one of the rickety benches. The heap of mourners was directly before us. They bounced into us as they cavorted. The smell that they radiated, sweating there in that obscene heap, half suffocated us. Not all of them, of course, did the thing in the grand manner. Some merely moaned and rolled their eyes. The female ox in gingham flung her great bulk on the ground and jabbered an unintelligible prayer. One of the men, in the intervals between fits, put on spectacles and read his Bible.

Beside me on the bench sat the young mother and her baby. She suckled it through the whole orgy, obviously fascinated by what was going on, but never venturing to take any hand in it. On the bed just outside the light two other babies slept peacefully. In the shadows, suddenly appearing and as suddenly going away, were vague figures, whether believers or scoffers I do not know. They seemed to come and go in couples. Now and then a couple at the ringside would step back and then vanish into the black night. After a while some came back. There was whispering outside the circle of vision. A couple of Fords lurched up in the wood road, cutting holes in the darkness with their lights. Once someone out of sight loosed a bray of laughter.

All this went on for an hour or so. The original penitent, by this time, was buried three deep beneath the heap. One caught a glimpse, now and then, of her yellow bobbed hair, but then she would vanish again. How she breathed down there I don't know; it was hard enough ten feet away, with a strong five-cent cigar to help. When the praying brothers would rise up for a bout with the tongues their faces were streaming with perspiration. The fat harridan in gingham sweated like a longshoreman. Her hair got loose and fell down over her face. She fanned herself with her skirt. A powerful old gal she was, equal in her day to obstetrics and a week's washing on the same morning, but this was worse than a week's washing. Finally, she fell into a heap, breathing in great, convulsive gasps.

We tired of it after a while and groped our way back to our automobile. When we got to Dayton, after 11 o'clock—an immensely late hour in these parts—the whole town was still gathered on the courthouse lawn, hanging upon the disputes of theologians. The Bible champion of the world had a crowd. The Seventh Day Adventist missionaries had a crowd. A volunteer from faraway Portland, Ore., made up exactly like Andy Gump, had another and larger crowd. Dayton was enjoying itself. All the usual rules were suspended and the curfew bell was locked up. The prophet Bryan, exhausted by his day's work for Revelation, was snoring in his bed up the road, but enough volunteers were still on watch to keep the battlements manned.

Such is human existence among the Fundamentalists, where children are brought up on Genesis and sin is unknown. If I have made the tale too long, then blame the spirit of garrulity that is in the local air. Even newspaper reporters, down here, get some echo of the call. Divine inspiration is as common as the hookworm. I have done my best to show you what the great heritage of mankind comes to in regions where the Bible is the beginning and end of wisdom, and the mountebank Bryan, parading the streets in his seersucker coat, is pointed out to sucklings as the greatest man since Abraham.

[*Baltimore Evening Sun,* July 13, 1925]

DARROW'S ELOQUENT APPEAL WASTED ON EARS THAT HEED ONLY BRYAN, SAYS MENCKEN

Dayton, Tenn., July 14.—The net effect of Clarence Darrow's great speech yesterday seems to be precisely the same as if he had bawled it up a rainspout in the interior of Afghanistan. That is, locally, upon the process against the infidel Scopes, upon the so-called minds of these Fundamentalists of upland Tennessee. You have but a dim notion of it who have only read it. It was not designed for reading, but for hearing. The clanging of it was as important as the logic. It rose like a wind and ended like a flourish of bugles. The very judge on the bench, toward the end of it, began to look uneasy. But the morons in the audience, when it was over, simply hissed it.

During the whole time of its delivery the old mountebank, Bryan, sat tight-lipped and unmoved. There is, of course, no reason why it should have shaken him. He has those hillbillies locked up in his pen and he knows it. His brand is on them. He is at home among them. Since his earliest days, indeed, his chief strength has been among the folk of remote hills and forlorn and lonely farms. Now with his political aspirations all gone to pot, he turns to them for religious consolations. They understand his peculiar imbecilities. His nonsense is their ideal of sense. When he deluges them with his theological bilge they rejoice like pilgrims disporting in the river Jordan.

The town whisper is that the local attorney-general, Stewart, is not a Fundamentalist, and hence has no stomach for his job. It seems not improbable. He is a man of evident education, and his argument yesterday was confined very strictly to the constitutional points—the argument of a competent and conscientious lawyer, and to me, at least very persuasive.

But Stewart, after all, is a foreigner here, almost as much so as Darrow or Hays or Malone. He is doing his job and that is all. The real animus of the prosecution centers in Bryan. He is the plaintiff and prosecutor. The local lawyers are simply bottle-holders for him. He will win the case, not by academic appeals to law and precedent, but by direct and powerful appeals to the immemorial fears and superstitions of man. It is no wonder that he is hot against Scopes. Five years of Scopes and even these mountaineers would begin to laugh at Bryan. Ten years and they would ride him out of town on a rail, with one Baptist parson in front of him and another behind.

But there will be no ten years of Scopes, nor five years, nor even one year.

Such brash young fellows, debauched by the enlightenment, must be disposed of before they become dangerous, and Bryan is here, with his tight lips and hard eyes, to see that this one is disposed of. The talk of the lawyers, even the magnificent talk of Darrow, is so much idle wind music. The case will not be decided by logic, nor even by eloquence. It will be decided by counting noses—and for every nose in these hills that has ever thrust itself into any book save the Bible there are a hundred adorned with the brass ring of Bryan. These are his people. They understand him when he speaks in tongues. The same dark face that is in his own eyes is in theirs, too. They feel with him, and they relish him.

I sincerely hope that the nobility and gentry of the lowlands will not make the colossal mistake of viewing this trial of Scopes as a trivial farce. Full of rustic japes and in bad taste, it is, to be sure, somewhat comic on the surface. One laughs to see lawyers sweat. The jury, marched down Broadway, would set New York by the ears. But all of that is only skin deep.

Deeper down there are the beginnings of a struggle that may go on to melodrama of the first caliber, and when the curtain falls at least all the laughter may be coming from the yokels. You probably laughed at the prohibitionists, say, back in 1914. Well, don't make the same error twice.

As I have said, Bryan understands these peasants, and they understand him. He is a bit mangey and flea-bitten, but no means ready for his harp. He may last five years, ten years or even longer. What he may accomplish in that time, seen here at close range, looms up immensely larger than it appears to a city man five hundred miles away. The fellow is full of such bitter, implacable hatreds that they radiate from him like heat from a stove. He hates the learning that he cannot grasp. He hates those who sneer at him. He hates, in general, all who stand apart from his own pathetic commonness. And the yokels hate with him, some of them almost as bitterly as he does himself. They are willing and eager to follow him—and he has already given them a taste of blood.

Darrow's peroration yesterday was interrupted by Judge Raulston, but the force of it got into the air nevertheless. This year it is a misdemeanor for a country school-teacher to flout the archaic nonsense of Genesis. Next year it will be a felony. The year after the net will be spread wider. Pedagogues, after all, are small game; there are larger birds to snare—larger and juicier. Bryan has his fishy eye on them. He will fetch them if his mind lasts, and the lamp holds out to burn. No man with a mouth like that ever lets go. Nor ever lacks followers.

Tennessee is bearing the brunt of the first attack simply because the civilized minority, down here, is extraordinarily pusillanimous.

I have met no educated man who is not ashamed of the ridicule that has fallen upon the State, and I have met none, save only Judge Neal, who had the courage to speak out while it was yet time. No Tennessee counsel of any importance came into the case until yesterday and then they came in stepping very softly as if taking a brief for sense were a dangerous matter. When Bryan did his first rampaging here all these men were silent.

They had known for years what was going on in the hills. They knew what the country preachers were preaching—what degraded nonsense was being rammed and hammered into yokel skulls. But they were afraid to go out against the imposture while it was in the making, and when any outsider denounced it they fell upon him violently as an enemy of Tennessee.

Now Tennessee is paying for that poltroonery. The State is smiling and beautiful, and of late it has begun to be rich. I know of no American city that is set in more lovely scenery than Chattanooga, or that has more charming homes. The civilized minority is as large here, I believe, as anywhere else.

It has made a city of splendid material comforts and kept it in order. But it has neglected in the past the unpleasant business of following what was going on in the crossroads Little Bethels.

The Baptist preachers ranted unchallenged.

Their buffooneries were mistaken for humor. Now the clowns turn out to be armed, and have begun to shoot.

In his argument yesterday Judge Neal had to admit pathetically that it was hopeless to fight for a repeal of the anti-evolution law. The Legislature of Tennessee, like the Legislature of every other American state, is made up of cheap job-seekers and ignoramuses.

The Governor of the State is a politician ten times cheaper and trashier. It is vain to look for relief from such men. If the State is to be saved at all, it must be saved by the courts. For one, I have little hope of relief in that direction, despite Hays' logic and Darrow's eloquence. Constitutions, in America, no longer mean what they say. To mention the Bill of Rights is to be damned as a Red.

The rabble is in the saddle, and down here it makes its first campaign under a general beside whom Wat Tyler seems like a wart beside the Matterhorn.

[*Baltimore Evening Sun,* July 14, 1925]

LAW AND FREEDOM, MENCKEN DISCOVERS, YIELD PLACE TO HOLY WRIT IN RHEA COUNTY

Dayton, Tenn., July 15.—The cops have come up from Chattanooga to help save Dayton from the devil. Darrow, Malone and Hays, of course, are immune to constabulary process, despite their obscene attack upon prayer. But all other atheists and anarchists now have public notice they must shut up forthwith and stay shut so long as they pollute this bright, shining buckle of the Bible belt with their presence. Only one avowed infidel has ventured to make a public address. The Chattanooga police nabbed him instantly, and he is now under surveillance in a hotel. Let him but drop one of his impious tracts from his window and he will be transferred to the town hoosegow.

The Constitution of Tennessee, as everyone knows, puts free speech among the most sacred rights of the citizen. More, I am informed by eminent Chattanooga counsel that there is no State law denying it—that is, for persons not pedagogues. But the cops of Chattanooga, like their brethren elsewhere, do not let constitutions stand in the way of their exercise of their lawful duty. The captain in charge of the squad now on watch told me frankly yesterday that he was not going to let any infidels discharge their damnable nonsense upon the town. I asked him what charge he would lay against them if they flouted him. He said he would jail them for disturbing the peace.

"But suppose," I asked him, "a prisoner is actually not disturbing the peace. Suppose he is simply saying his say in a quiet and orderly manner."

"I'll arrest him anyhow," said the cop.

"Even if no one complains of him?"

"I'll complain myself."

"Under what law precisely?"

"We don't need no law for them kind of people."

It sounded like New York in the old days, before Mayor Gaynor took the constitution out of cold storage and began to belabor the gendarmerie with it. The captain admitted freely that speaking in the streets was not disturbing the peace so long as the speaker stuck to orthodox Christian doctrine as it is understood by the local exegetes.

A preacher of any sect that admits the literal authenticity of Genesis is free to gather a crowd at any time and talk all he wants. More, he may engage in a disputation with any other expert. I have heard at least a hundred such discussions, and some of them have been very acrimonious. But the instant a speaker utters a word against divine revelation he begins to disturb the peace and is liable to immediate arrest and confinement in the calaboose beside the railroad tracks.

Such is criminal law in Rhea county as interpreted by the uniformed and freely sweating agents. As I have said, there are legal authorities in Chattanooga who dissent sharply, and even argue that the cops are a set of numskulls and ought to be locked up as public nuisances. But one need not live a long, incandescent week in the Bible belt to know that jurisprudence becomes a new science as one crosses the border. Here the ordinary statutes are reinforced by Holy Writ, and whenever there is a conflict Holy Writ takes precedence.

Judge Raulston himself has decided, in effect, that in a trial for heresy it is perfectly fair and proper to begin proceedings with a prayer for the confutation and salvation of the defendant. On lower levels, and especially in the depths where policemen do their thinking, the doctrine is even more frankly stated. Before laying Christians by the heels the cops must formulate definite charges against them. They must be accused of something specifically unlawful and there must be witnesses to the act. But infidels are *ferae naturae,* and any cop is free to bag at sight and to hold them in durance at his pleasure.

To the same category, it appears, belong political and economic radicals. News came the other day to Pastor T. T. Martin, who is holding a continuous anti-evolution convention in the town, that a party of I. W. W.'s, their pockets full of Russian gold, had started out from Cincinnati to assassinate him. A bit later came word they would bump off Bryan after they had finished Martin, and then set fire to the town churches. Martin first warned Bryan and then complained to the police. The latter were instantly agog. Guards were posted at strategic centers and a watch was kept upon all strangers of a sinister appearance. But the I. W. W.'s were not caught. Yesterday Pastor Martin told me that he had news that they had gone back to Cincinnati to perfect the plot. He posts audiences at every meeting. If the Reds return they will be scotched.

Arthur Garfield Hays, who is not only one of the counsel for the infidel Scopes but also agent and attorney of the notorious American Civil Liberties Union in New York, is planning to hold a free speech meeting on the Courthouse lawn and so make a test of the law against disturbing the peace as it is interpreted by the *Polizei.* Hays will be well advertised if he carries out this subversive intention. It is hot enough in the courtroom in the glare of a thousand fundamentalist eyes; in the town jail he would sweat to death.

Rhea county is very hospitable and, judged by Bible belt standards, very tolerant. The Dayton Babbitts gave a banquet to Darrow, despite the danger from lightning, meteors and earthquakes. Even Malone is treated politely, though the very horned cattle in the fields know that he is a Catholic and in constant communication with the Pope. But liberty is one thing and license is quite another. Within the bounds of Genesis the utmost play of opinion is permitted and even encouraged. An evangelist with a new scheme for getting into Heaven can get a crowd in two minutes. But once a speaker admits a doubt, however cautiously, he is handed over to the secular arm.

Two Unitarian clergymen are prowling around the town looking for a chance to discharge their "hellish heresies." One of them is Potter, of New

York; the other is Birckhead, of Kansas City. So far they have not made any progress. Potter induced one of the local Methodist parsons to give him a hearing, but the congregation protested and the next day the parson had to resign his charge. The Methodists, as I have previously reported, are regarded almost as infidels in Rhea county. Their doctrines, which seem somewhat severe in Baltimore, especially to persons who love a merry life, are here viewed as loose to the point of indecency. The four Methodists on the jury are suspected of being against hanging Scopes, at least without a fair trial. The State tried to get rid of one of them even after he had been passed; his neighbors had come in from his village with news that he had a banjo concealed in his house and was known to read the *Literary Digest*.

The other Unitarian clergyman, Dr. Birckhead, is not actually domiciled in the town, but is encamped, with his wife and child, on the road outside. He is on an automobile tour and stopped off here to see if a chance offered to spread his "poisons." So far he has found none.

Yesterday afternoon a Jewish rabbi from Nashville also showed up, Marks by name. He offered to read and expound Genesis in Hebrew, but found no takers. The Holy Rollers hereabout, when they are seized by the gift of tongues, avoid Hebrew, apparently as a result of Ku Klux influence. Their favorite among all the sacred dialects is Hittite. It sounds to the infidel like a series of college yells.

Judge Raulston's decision yesterday afternoon in the matter of Hays' motion was a masterpiece of unconscious humor. The press stand, in fact, thought he was trying to be jocose deliberately and let off a guffaw that might have gone far if the roar of applause had not choked it off. Hays presented a petition in the name of the two Unitarians, the rabbi and several other theological "reds," praying that in selecting clergymen to open the court with prayer hereafter he choose Fundamentalists and anti-Fundamentalists alternately. The petition was couched in terms that greatly shocked and enraged the prosecution. When the judge announced that he would leave the nomination of chaplains to the Pastors' Association of the town there was the gust of mirth aforesaid, followed by howls of approval. The Pastors' Association of Dayton is composed of Fundamentalists so powerfully orthodox that beside them such a fellow as Dr. John Roach Straton would seem an Ingersoll.

The witnesses of the defense, all of them heretics, began to reach town yesterday and are all quartered at what is called the Mansion, an ancient and empty house outside the town limits, now crudely furnished with iron cots, spittoons, playing cards and the other camp equipment of scientists. Few, if any, of these witnesses will ever get a chance to outrage the jury with their blasphemies, but they are of much interest to the townspeople. The common belief is that they will be blown up with one mighty blast when the verdict of the twelve men, tried and true, is brought in, and Darrow, Malone, Hays and Neal with them. The country people avoid the Mansion. It is foolish to take unnecessary chances. Going into the courtroom, with Darrow standing there shamelessly and openly challenging the wrath of God, is risk enough.

The case promises to drag into next week. The prosecution is fighting desperately and taking every advantage of its superior knowledge of the quirks of local procedure. The defense is heating up and there are few exchanges of courtroom amenities. There will be a lot of oratory before it is all over and some loud and raucous bawling otherwise, and maybe more than one challenge to step outside. The cards seem to be stacked against poor Scopes, but there may be a joker in the pack. Four of the jurymen, as everyone knows, are Methodists, and a Methodist down here belongs to the extreme wing of liberals. Beyond him lie only the justly and incurably damned.

What if one of those Methodists, sweating under the dreadful pressure of Fundamentalist influence, jumps into the air, cracks his heels together and gives a defiant yell? What if the jury is hung? It will be a good joke on the Fundamentalists if it happens, and an even better joke on the defense.

[*Baltimore Evening Sun,* July 15, 1925]

MENCKEN DECLARES STRICTLY FAIR TRIAL IS BEYOND KEN OF TENNESSEE FUNDAMENTALISTS

Dayton, Tenn., July 16.—Two things ought to be understood clearly by heathen Northerners who follow the great cause of the State of Tennessee against the infidel Scopes. One is that the old mountebank, Bryan, is no longer thought of as a mere politician and job-seeker in these Godly regions, but has become converted into a great sacerdotal figure, half man and half archangel—in brief, a sort of Fundamentalist pope. The other is that the Fundamentalist mind, running in a single rut for fifty years, is now quite unable to comprehend dissent from its basic superstitions, or to grant any common honesty, or even any decency, to those who reject them.

The latter fact explains some of the most astonishing singularities of the present trial—that is, singularities to one accustomed to more austere procedures. In the average Northern jurisdiction much of what is going on here would be almost unthinkable. Try to imagine a trial going on in a town in which anyone is free to denounce the defendant's case publicly and no one is free to argue for it in the same way—a trial in a courthouse placarded with handbills set up by his opponents—a trial before a jury of men who have been roweled and hammered by those opponents for years, and have never heard a clear and fair statement of his answer.

But this is not all. It seems impossible, but it is nevertheless a fact that public opinion in Dayton sees no impropriety in the fact that the case was opened with prayer by a clergyman known by everyone to be against Scopes and by no means shy about making the fact clear. Nor by the fact that Bryan, the actual complainant, has been preparing the ground for the prosecution for months. Nor by the fact that, though he is one of the attorneys of record in the case, he is also present in the character of a public evangelist and that throngs go to hear him whenever he speaks, including even the sitting judge.

I do not allege here that there is any disposition to resort to lynch law. On the contrary, I believe that there is every intent to give Scopes a fair trial, as a fair trial is understood among Fundamentalists. All I desire to show is that all the primary assumptions are immovably against him—that it is a sheer impossibility for nine-tenths of those he faces to see any merit whatever in his position. He is not simply one who has committed a misdemeanor against the peace and dignity of the State, he is also the agent of a heresy almost too hellish to be stated by reputable men. Such reputable men recognize their lawful duty to treat him humanely and even politely, but they also recognize their superior duty to make it plain that they are against his heresy and believe absolutely in the wisdom and virtue of his prosecutors.

In view of the fact that everyone here looks for the jury to bring in a verdict of guilty, it might be expected that the prosecution would show a considerable amiability and allow the defense a rather free plan. Instead, it is contesting every point very vigorously and taking every advantage of its greatly superior familiarity with local procedure. There is, in fact, a considerable heat in the trial. Bryan and the local lawyers for the State sit glaring at the defense all day and even the attorney-general, A. T. Stewart, who is supposed to have secret doubts about Fundamentalism, has shown such pugnacity that it has already brought him to forced apologies.

The high point of yesterday's proceedings was reached with the appearance of Dr. Maynard M. Metcalf, of the Johns Hopkins. The doctor is a somewhat chubby man of bland mien, and during the first part of his testimony, with the jury present, the prosecution apparently viewed him with great equanimity. But the instant he was asked a question bearing directly upon the case at bar there was a flurry in the Bryan pen and Stewart was on his feet with protests. Another question followed, with more and hotter protests. The judge then excluded the jury and the show began.

What ensued was, on the surface, a harmless enough dialogue between Dr. Metcalf and Darrow, but underneath there was very tense drama. At the first question Bryan came out from behind the State's table and planted himself directly in front of Dr. Metcalf, and not ten feet away. The two McKenzies followed, with young Sue Hicks at their heels.

Then began one of the clearest, most succinct and withal most eloquent presentations of the case for the evolutionists that I have ever heard. The doctor was never at a loss for a word, and his ideas flowed freely and smoothly. Darrow steered him magnificently. A word or two and he was howling down the wind. Another and he hauled up to discharge a broadside. There was no cocksureness in him. Instead he was rather cautious and deprecatory and sometimes he halted and confessed his ignorance. But what he got over before he finished was a superb counterblast to the Fundamentalist buncombe. The jury, at least in theory, heard nothing of it, but it went whooping into the radio and it went banging into the face of Bryan.

Bryan sat silent throughout the whole scene, his gaze fixed immovably on the witness. Now and then his face darkened and his eyes flashed, but he never uttered a sound. It was, to him, a string of blasphemies out of the devil's mass—a dreadful series of assaults upon the only true religion. The old gladiator faced his real enemy at last. Here was a sworn agent and attorney of the science he hates and fears—a well-fed, well-mannered spokesman of the knowledge he abominates. Somehow he reminded me pathetically of the old Holy Roller I heard last week—the mountain pastor who damned education as a mocking and a corruption. Bryan, too, is afraid of it, for wherever it spreads his trade begins to fall off, and wherever it flourishes he is only a poor clown.

But not to these Fundamentalists of the hills. Not to yokels he now turns to for consolation in his old age, with the scars of defeat and disaster all over him. To these simple folk, as I have said, he is a prophet of the imperial line— a lineal successor to Moses and Abraham. The barbaric cosmogony that he believes in seems as reasonable to them as it does to him. They share his peasant-like suspicion of all book learning that a plow hand cannot grasp. They believe with him that men who know too much should be seized by the secular arm and put down by force. They dream as he does of a world unanimously sure of Heaven and unanimously idiotic on this earth.

This old buzzard, having failed to raise the mob against its rulers, now prepares to raise it against its teachers. He can never be the peasants' President, but there is still a chance to be the peasants' Pope. He leads a new crusade, his bald head glistening, his face streaming with sweat, his chest heaving beneath his rumpled alpaca coat. One somehow pities him, despite his so palpable imbecilities. It is a tragedy, indeed, to begin life as a hero and to end it as a buffoon. But let no one, laughing at him, underestimate the magic that lies in his black, malignant eye, his frayed but still eloquent voice. He can shake and inflame these poor ignoramuses as no other man among us can shake and inflame them, and he is desperately eager to order the charge.

In Tennessee he is drilling his army. The big battles, he believes, will be fought elsewhere.

[*Baltimore Evening Sun,* July 16, 1925]

MALONE THE VICTOR, EVEN THOUGH COURT SIDES WITH OPPONENTS, SAYS MENCKEN

Dayton, Tenn., July 17.—Though the court decided against him this morning, and the testimony of the experts summoned for the defense will be banned out of the trial of the infidel Scopes, it was Dudley Field Malone who won yesterday's great battle of rhetoricians. When he got upon his legs it was the universal assumption in the courtroom that Judge Raulston's mind was already made up, and that nothing that any lawyer for the defense could say would shake him. But Malone unquestionably shook him. He was, at the end, in plain doubt, and he showed it by his questions. It took a night's repose to restore him to normalcy. The prosecution won, but it came within an inch of losing.

Malone was put up to follow and dispose of Bryan, and he achieved the business magnificently. I doubt that any louder speech has ever been heard in a court of law since the days of Gog and Magog. It roared out of the open windows like the sound of artillery practise, and alarmed the moonshiners and catamounts on distant peaks. Trains thundering by on the nearby rail-road sounded faint and far away and when, toward the end, a table covered with standing and gaping journalists gave way with a crash, the noise seemed, by contrast, to be no more than a *pizzicato* chord upon a viola da gamba. The yokels outside stuffed their Bibles into the loud-speaker horns and yielded themselves joyously to the impact of the original. In brief, Malone was in good voice. It was a great day for Ireland. And for the defense. For Malone not only out-yelled Bryan, he also plainly out-gen-eraled and out-argued him. His speech, indeed, was one of the best presen-tations of the case against the Fundamentalist rubbish that I have ever heard.

It was simple in structure, it was clear in reasoning, and at its high points it was overwhelmingly eloquent. It was not long, but it covered the whole ground and it let off many a gaudy skyrocket, and so it conquered even the Fundamentalists. At its end they gave it a tremendous cheer—a cheer at least four times as hearty as that given to Bryan. For these rustics delight in speechifying, and know when it is good. The devil's logic cannot fetch them, but they are not above taking a voluptuous pleasure in his lascivious phrases.

The whole speech was addressed to Bryan, and he sat through it in his usual posture, with his palm-leaf fan flapping energetically and his hard, cruel mouth shut tight. The old boy grows more and more pathetic. He has aged greatly during the past few years and begins to look elderly and enfeebled. All that remains of his old fire is now in his black eyes. They glitter like dark gems, and in their glitter there is immense and yet futile malignancy. That is all that is left of the Peerless Leader of thirty years ago. Once he had one leg in the White House and the nation trembled under his roars. Now he is a tin-pot pope in the coca-cola belt and a brother to the forlorn pastors who belabor half-wits in galvanized iron tabernacles behind the railroad yards. His own speech was a grotesque performance and downright touching in its imbecility. Its climax came when he launched into a furious denunciation of the doctrine that man is a mammal. It seemed a sheer impossibility that any literate man should stand up in public and discharge any such nonsense. Yet the poor old fellow did it. Darrow stared incredulous. Malone sat with his mouth wide open. Hays indulged himself one of his sardonic chuckles. Stewart and Bryan *fils* looked extremely uneasy, but the old mountebank ranted on. To call a man a mammal, it appeared, was to flout the revelation of God. The certain effect of the doctrine would be to destroy morality and promote infidelity. The defense let it pass. The lily needed no gilding.

There followed some ranting about the Leopold-Loeb case, culminating in the argument that learning was corrupting—that the colleges by setting science above Genesis were turning their students into murderers. Bryan alleged that Darrow had admitted the fact in his closing speech at the Leopold-Loeb trial, and stopped to search for the passage in a printed copy of the speech. Darrow denied making any such statement, and presently began reading what he actually had said on the subject. Bryan then proceeded to denounce Nietzsche, whom he described as an admirer and follower of Darwin. Darrow challenged the fact and offered to expound what Nietzsche really taught. Bryan waved him off.

The effect of the whole harangue was extremely depressing. It quickly ceased to be an argument addressed to the court—Bryan, in fact, constantly said "My friends" instead of "Your Honor"—and became a sermon at the camp-meeting. All the familiar contentions of the Dayton divines appeared in it—that learning is dangerous, that nothing is true that is not in the Bible, that a yokel who goes to church regularly knows more than any scientist ever heard of. The thing went to fantastic lengths. It became a farrago of puerilities without coherence or sense. I don't think the old man did himself justice. He was in poor voice and his mind seemed to wander. There was far too much hatred in him for him to be persuasive.

The crowd, of course, was with him. It has been fed upon just such balderdash for years. Its pastors assault it twice a week with precisely the same nonsense. It is chronically in the position of a populace protected by an espionage act in time of war. That is to say, it is forbidden to laugh at the arguments of one side and forbidden to hear the case of the other side. Bryan has been roving around in the tall grass for years and he knows the bucolic mind. He knows how to reach and inflame its basic delusions and superstitions. He has taken them into his own stock and adorned them with fresh absurdities. Today he may well stand as the archetype of the

American rustic. His theology is simply the elemental magic that is preached in a hundred thousand rural churches fifty-two times a year.

These Tennessee mountaineers are not more stupid than the city proletariat; they are only less informed. If Darrow, Malone and Hays could make a month's stumping tour in Rhea county I believe that fully a fourth of the population would repudiate Fundamentalism, and that not a few of the clergy now in practise would be restored to their old jobs on the railroad. Malone's speech yesterday probably shook a great many true believers; another like it would fetch more than one of them. But the chances are heavily against them ever hearing a second. Once this trial is over, the darkness will close in again, and it will take long years of diligent and thankless effort to dispel it—if, indeed, it is ever dispelled at all.

With a few brilliant exceptions—Dr. Neal is an example—the more civilized Tennesseans show few signs of being equal to the job. I suspect that politics is what keeps them silent and makes their State ridiculous. Most of them seem to be candidates for office, and a candidate for office, if he would get the votes of fundamentalists, must bawl for Genesis before he begins to bawl for anything else. A typical Tennessee politician is the Governor, Austin Peay. He signed the anti-evolution bill with loud hosannas, and he is now making every effort to turn the excitement of the Scopes trial to his private political uses. The local papers print a telegram that he has sent to Attorney-General A. T. Stewart whooping for prayer. In the North a Governor who indulged in such monkeyshines would be rebuked for trying to influence the conduct of a case in court. And he would be derided as a cheap mountebank. But not here.

I described Stewart the other day as a man of apparent education and sense and palpably superior to the village lawyers who sit with him at the trial table. I still believe that I described him accurately. Yet even Stewart toward the close of yesterday's session gave an exhibition that would be almost unimaginable in the North. He began his reply to Malone with an intelligent and forceful legal argument, with plenty of evidence of hard study in it. But presently he slid into a violent theological harangue, full of extravagant nonsense. He described the case as a combat between light and darkness and almost descended to the depths of Bryan. Hays challenged him with a question. Didn't he admit, after all, that the defense had a tolerable case; that it ought to be given a chance to present its evidence? I transcribe his reply literally:

"That which strikes at the very foundations of Christianity is not entitled to a chance."

Hays, plainly astounded by this bald statement of the Fundamentalist view of due process, pressed the point. Assuming that the defense would present, not opinion but only unadorned fact, would Stewart still object to its admission? He replied.

"Personally, yes."

"But as a lawyer and Attorney-General?" insisted Hays.

"As a lawyer and Attorney-General," said Stewart, "I am the same man."

Such is justice where Genesis is the first and greatest of law books and heresy is still a crime.

[*Baltimore Evening Sun,* July 17, 1925]

BATTLE NOW OVER, MENCKEN SEES; GENESIS TRIUMPHANT AND READY FOR NEW JOUSTS

Dayton, Tenn., July 18.—All that remains of the great cause of the State of Tennessee against the infidel Scopes is the formal business of bumping off the defendant. There may be some legal jousting on Monday and some gaudy oratory on Tuesday, but the main battle is over, with Genesis completely triumphant. Judge Raulston finished the benign business yesterday morning by leaping with soft judicial hosannas into the arms of the prosecution. The sole commentary of the sardonic Darrow consisted of bringing down a metaphorical custard pie upon the occiput of the learned jurist.

"I hope," said the latter nervously, "that counsel intends no reflection upon this court."

Darrow hunched his shoulders and looked out of the window dreamily.

"Your honor," he said, "is, of course, entitled to hope."

No doubt the case will be long and fondly remembered by connoisseurs of judicial delicatessen—that is, as the performances of Weber and Fields are remembered by students of dramatic science.[4] In immediate retrospect, it grows more fantastic and exhilarating. Scopes has had precisely the same fair trial that the Hon. John Philip Hill, accused of bootlegging on the oath of Howard A. Kelly, would have before the Rev. Dr. George

W. Crabbe. He is a fellow not without humor; I find him full of smiles today. On some near tomorrow the Sheriff will collect a month's wages from him, but he has certainly had a lot of fun.

More interesting than the hollow buffoonery that remains will be the effect upon the people of Tennessee, the actual prisoners at the bar. That the more civilized of them are in a highly feverish condition of mind must be patent to every visitor. The guffaws that roll in from all sides give them great pain. They are full of bitter protests and valiant projects. They prepare, it appears, to organize, hoist the black flag and offer the Fundamentalists of the dung-hills a battle to the death. They will not cease until the last Baptist preacher is in flight over the mountains, and the ordinary intellectual decencies of Christendom are triumphantly restored.

With the best will in the world I find it impossible to accept this tall talk with anything resembling confidence. The intelligentsia of Tennessee had their chance and let it get away from them. When the old mountebank, Bryan, first invaded the State with his balderdash they were unanimously silent. When he began to round up converts in the back country they offered him no challenge. When the Legislature passed the anti-evolution bill and the Governor signed it, they contented themselves with murmuring *pianissimo*. And when the battle was joined at last and the time came for rough stuff only one Tennesseean of any consequence volunteered.

That lone volunteer was Dr. John Neal, now of counsel for the defense, a good lawyer and an honest man. His services to Darrow, Malone and Hays have been very valuable and they come out of the case with high respect for him. But how does Tennessee regard him? My impression is that Tennessee vastly underestimates him. I hear trivial and absurd criticism of him on all sides and scarcely a word of praise for his courage and public spirit. The test of the State is to be found in its attitude toward such men. It will come out of the night of Fundamentalism when they are properly appreciated and honored, and not before. When that time comes I'll begin to believe that the educated minority here is genuinely ashamed of the Bryan obscenity and that it is prepared to combat other such disgraces hereafter resolutely in the open and regardless of the bellowing of the mob.

The Scopes trial, from the start, has been carried on in a manner exactly fitted to the anti-evolution law and the simian imbecility under it. There hasn't been the slightest pretense to decorum. The rustic judge, a candidate for re-election, has postured before the yokels like a clown in a ten-cent side show, and almost every word he has uttered has been an undisguised appeal to their prejudices and superstitions. The chief prosecuting attorney, beginning like a competent lawyer and a man of self-respect, ended like a convert at a Billy Sunday revival. It fell to him, finally, to make a clear and astounding statement of theory of justice prevailing under Fundamentalism. What he said, in brief, was that a man accused of infidelity had no rights whatever under Tennessee law.

This is probably not true yet, but it will become true inevitably if the Bryan murrain is not arrested. The Bryan of to-day is not to be mistaken for the political rabble-rouser of two decades ago. That earlier Bryan may have been grossly in error, but he at least kept his errors within the bounds of reason: it was still possible to follow him without yielding up all intelligence. The Bryan of to-day, old, disappointed and embittered, is a far different bird. He realizes at last the glories of this world are not for him, and he takes refuge, peasant-like, in religious hallucinations. They depart from sense altogether. They are not merely silly; they are downright idiotic. And, being idiotic, they appeal with irresistible force to the poor half-wits upon whom the old charlatan now preys.

When I heard him, in open court, denounce the notion that man is a mammal I was genuinely staggered and so was every other stranger in the courtroom. People looked at one another in blank amazement. But the native Fundamentalists, it quickly appeared, saw nothing absurd in his words. The attorneys for the prosecution smiled approval, the crowd applauded, the very judge on the bench beamed his acquiescence. And the same thing happened when he denounced all education as corrupting and began arguing incredibly that a farmer who read the Bible knew more than any scientist in the world. Such dreadful bilge, heard of far away, may seem only ridiculous. But it takes on a different smack, I assure you, when one hears it discharged formally in a court of law and sees it accepted as wisdom by judge and jury.

Darrow has lost this case. It was lost long before he came to Dayton. But it seems to me that he has nevertheless performed a great public service by fighting it to a finish and in a perfectly serious way. Let no one mistake it for comedy, farcical though it may be in all its details. It serves notice on the country that Neandertal man is organizing in these forlorn backwaters of the land, led by a fanatic, devoid of sense and devoid of conscience. Tennessee, challenging him too timorously and too late, now sees its courts converted into camp-meetings and its Bill of Rights made a mock of by its sworn officers of the law. There are other States that had better look to their arsenals before the Hun is at their gates.

[*Baltimore Evening Sun,* July 18, 1925]

TENNESSEE IN THE FRYING PAN

I

That the rising town of Dayton, when it put the infidel Scopes on trial, bit off far more than it has been able to chew—this melancholy fact must now be evident to everyone. The village Aristides Sophocles Goldsboroughs believed that the trial would bring in a lot of money, and produce a vast mass of free and profitable advertising. They were wrong on both counts, as boomers usually are. Very little money was actually spent by the visitors: the adjacent yokels brought their own lunches and went home to sleep, and the city men from afar rushed down to Chattanooga whenever there was a lull. As for the advertising that went out over the leased wires, I greatly fear that it has quite ruined the town. When people recall it here-after they will think of it as they think of Herrin, Ill., and Homestead, Pa.[5] It will be a joke town at best, and infamous at worst.

The natives reacted to this advertising very badly. The preliminary publicity, I believe, had somehow disarmed and deceived them. It was mainly amiable spoofing; they took it philosophically, assured by the local Aristideses that it was good for trade. But when the main guard of Eastern and Northern journalists swarmed down, and their dispatches began to show the country and the world exactly how the obscene buffoonery appeared to realistic city men, then the yokels began to sweat coldly, and in a few days they were full of terror and indignation. Some of the bolder spirits, indeed, talked gaudily of direct action against the authors of the "libels." But the history of the Ku Klux and the American Legion offers overwhelmingly evidence that 100 per cent Americans never fight when the enemy is in strength, and able to make a defense, so the visitors suffered nothing worse than black, black looks. When the last of them departs Day-tonians will disinfect the town with sulphur candles, and the local pastors will exorcise the devils that they left behind them.

II

Dayton, of course, is only a ninth-rate country town, and so its agonies are of relatively little interest to the world. Its pastors, I daresay, will be able to console it, and if they fail there is always the old mountebank, Bryan, to give a hand. Faith cannot only move mountains; it can also soothe the distressed spirits of mountaineers. The Daytonians, unshaken by Darrow's ribaldries, still believe. They believe that they are not mammals. They believe, on Bryan's word, that they know more than all the men of science of Christendom. They believe, on the authority of Genesis, that the earth is flat and that witches still infest it. They believe, finally and especially, that all who doubt these great facts of revelation will go to hell. So they are consoled.

But what of the rest of the people of Tennessee? I greatly fear that they will not attain to consolation so easily. They are an extremely agreeable folk, and many of them are highly intelligent. I met men and women—particularly women—in Chattanooga who showed every sign of the highest culture. They led civilized lives, despite Prohibition, and they were interested in civilized ideas, despite the fog of Fundamentalism in which they moved. I met members of the State judiciary who were as heartily ashamed of the bucolic ass, Raulston, as an Osler would be of a chiropractor. I add the educated clergy: Episcopalians, Unitarians, Jews and so on—enlightened men, tossing pathetically under the imbecilities of their evangelical colleagues. Chattanooga, as I found it, was charming, but immensely unhappy.

What its people ask for—many of them in plain terms—is suspended judgment, sympathy, Christian charity, and I believe that they deserve all these things. Dayton may be typical of Tennessee, but it is surely not *all* of Tennessee. The civilized minority in the State is probably as large as in any other Southern State. What ails it is simply the fact it has been, in the past, too cautious and politic—that it has been too reluctant to offend the Fundamentalist majority. To that reluctance something else has been added: an uncritical and somewhat childish local patriotism. The Tennesseans have tolerated their imbeciles for fear that attacking them would bring down the derision of the rest of the country. Now they have the derision, and to excess—and the attack is ten times as difficult as it ever was before.

III

How they are to fight their way out of their wallow I do not know. They begin the battle with the enemy in command of every height and every gun; worse, there is a great deal of irresolution in their own ranks. The newspapers of the State, with few exceptions, are very feeble. One of the best of them, the Chattanooga *News*, set up an eloquent whooping for Bryan the moment he got to Dayton. Before that it had been against the anti-evolution law. But with the actual battle joined, it began to wobble, and presently it was printing articles arguing that Fundamentalism, after all, made men happy—that a Tennesseean gained something valuable by being an ignoramus—in other words, that a hog in a barnyard was to be envied by an Aristotle. The *News* was far better than most: it gave space, too, to the other side, and at considerable risk. But its weight, for two weeks, was thrown heavily to Bryan and his balderdash.

The pusillanimous attitude of the bar of the State I described in my dispatches from Dayton. It was not until the trial was two days old that any Tennessee lawyers of influence and dignity went to the aid of Dr. John R. Neal—and even then all of the volunteers enlisted only on condition that their names be kept out of the newspapers. I should except one F. B. McElwee. He sat at the trial table and rendered valuable services. The rest lurked in the background. It was an astounding situation to a Marylander, but it seemed to be regarded as quite natural in Tennessee.

The prevailing attitude toward Neal himself was also very amazing. He is an able lawyer and a man of repute, and in any Northern State his courage would get the praise it deserves. But in Tennessee even the intelligentsia seem to feel that he has done something discreditable by sitting at the trial table with Darrow, Hays and Malone. The State buzzes with trivial, idiotic gossip about him—that he dresses shabbily, that he has political aspirations, and so on. What if he does and has? He has carried himself, in this case, in a way that does higher credit to his native State. But his native State, instead of being proud of him, simply snarls at him behind his back.

IV

So with every other man concerned with the defense—most of them, alackaday, foreigners. For example, Rappleyea, the Dayton engineer who was first to go to the aid of Scopes. I was told solemnly in Dayton, not once but twenty times, that Rappleyea was (*a*) a Bowery boy from New York, and (*b*) an incompetent and ignorant engineer. I went to some trouble to unearth the facts. They were (*a*) that he was actually a member of one of the oldest Huguenot families in America, and (*b*) that his professional skill and general culture were such that the visiting scientists sought him out and found pleasure in his company.

Such is the punishment that falls upon a civilized man cast among Fundamentalists. As I have said, the worst of it is that even the native intelligentsia help to pull the rope. In consequence all the brighter young men of the State—and it produces plenty of them—tend to leave it. If they remain, they must be prepared to succumb to the prevailing blather or resign themselves to being more or less infamous. With the anti-evolution law enforced, the State university will rapidly go to pot; no intelligent youth will waste his time upon its courses if he can help it. And so, with the young men lost, the struggle against darkness will become almost hopeless.

As I have said, the State still produces plenty of likely young bucks—if only it could hold them! There is good blood everywhere, even in the mountains. During the dreadful buffooneries of Bryan and Raulston last week two typical specimens sat at the press table. One was Paul Y. Anderson, correspondent of the St. Louis *Post-Dispatch*, and the other was Joseph Wood Krutch, one of the editors of the *Nation*. I am very familiar with the work of both of them, and it is my professional judgment that it is of the first caliber. Anderson is one of the best newspaper reporters in America and Krutch is one of the best editorial writers.

Well, both were there as foreigners. Both were working for papers that could not exist in Tennessee. Both were viewed by their fellow Tennesseeans not with pride, as credits to the State, but as traitors to the Tennessee *Kultur* and public enemies. Their crime was that they were intelligent men, doing their jobs intelligently.

[*Baltimore Evening Sun*, July 20, 1925]

BRYAN

I

It was plain to everyone, when Bryan came to Dayton, that his great days were behind him—that he was now definitely an old man, and headed at last for silence. There was a vague, unpleasant manginess about his appearance; he somehow seemed dirty, though a close glance showed him carefully shaved, and clad in immaculate linen. All the hair was gone from the dome of his head, and it had begun to fall out, too, behind his ears, like that of the late Samuel Gompers. The old resonance had departed from his voice: what was once a bugle blast had become reedy and quavering. Who knows that, like Demosthenes, he had a lisp? In his prime, under the magic of his eloquence, no one noticed it. But when he spoke at Dayton it was always audible.

When I first encountered him, on the sidewalk in front of the Hicks brothers law office, the trial was yet to begin, and so he was still expansive and amiable. I had printed in the *Nation*, a week or so before, an article arguing that the anti-evolution law, whatever its unwisdom, was at least constitutional—that policing school-teachers was certainly not putting down free speech. The old boy professed to be delighted with the argument, and gave the gaping bystanders to understand that I was a talented publicist. In turn I admired the curious shirt he wore—sleeveless and with the neck cut very low. We parted in the manner of two Spanish ambassadors.

But that was the last touch of affability that I was destined to see in Bryan. The next day the battle joined and his face became hard. By the end of the first week he was simply a walking malignancy. Hour by hour he grew more bitter. What the Christian Scientists call malicious animal magnetism seemed to radiate from him like heat from a stove. From my place in the courtroom, standing upon a table, I looked directly down upon him, sweating horribly and pumping his palm-leaf fan. His eyes fascinated me: I watched them all day long. They were blazing points of hatred. They glittered like occult and sinister gems. Now and then they wandered to me, and I got my share. It was like coming under fire.

II

What was behind that consuming hatred? At first I thought that it was mere evangelical passion. Evangelical Christianity, as everyone knows, is founded upon hate, as the Christianity of Christ was founded upon love. But even evangelical Christians occasionally loose their belts and belch amicably; I have known some who, off duty, were very benignant. In that very courtroom, indeed, were some of them—for example, old Ben McKenzie, Nestor of the Dayton bar, who sat beside Bryan. Ben was full of good humor. He made jokes with Darrow. But Bryan only glared.

One day it dawned on me that Bryan, after all, was an evangelical Christian only by sort of afterthought—that his career in this world, and the glories thereof, had actually come to an end before he ever began whooping for Genesis. So I came to this conclusion: that what really moved him was a lust for revenge. The men of the cities had destroyed him and made a mock of him; now he would lead the yokels against them. Various facts clicked into the theory, and I hold it still. The hatred in the old man's burning eyes was not for the enemies of God; it was for the enemies of Bryan.

Thus he fought his last fight, eager only for blood. It quickly became frenzied and preposterous, and after that pathetic. All sense departed from him. He bit right and left, like a dog with rabies. He descended to demagogy so dreadful that his very associates blushed. His one yearning was to keep his yokels heated up—to lead his forlorn mob against the foe. That foe, alas, refused to be alarmed. It insisted upon seeing the battle as a comedy. Even Darrow, who knew better, occasionally yielded to the prevailing spirit. Finally, he lured poor Bryan into a folly almost incredible.

I allude to his astounding argument against the notion that man is a mammal. I am glad I heard it, for otherwise I'd never believe it. There stood the man who had been thrice a candidate for the Presidency of the Republic—and once, I believe, elected[6]—there he stood in the glare of the world, uttering stuff that a boy of eight would laugh at! The artful Darrow led him on: he repeated it, ranted for it, bellowed it in his cracked voice. A tragedy, indeed! He came into life a hero, a Galahad, in bright and shining armor. Now he was passing out a pathetic fool.

III

Worse, I believe that he somehow sensed the fact—that he realized his personal failure, whatever the success of the grotesque cause he spoke for. I had left Dayton before Darrow's cross-examination brought him to his final absurdity, but I heard his long speech against the admission of expert testimony, and I saw how it fell flat and how Bryan himself was conscious of the fact. When he sat down he was done for, and he knew it. The old magic had failed to work; there was applause but there was no exultant shouts. When, half an hour later, Dudley Field Malone delivered his terrific philippic, the very yokels gave him five times the clapper-clawing that they had given to Bryan.

This combat was the old leader's last, and it symbolized in more than one way his passing. Two women sat through it, the one old and crippled, the other young and in the full flush of beauty. The first was Mrs. Bryan; the second was Mrs. Malone. When Malone finished his speech the crowd stormed his wife with felicitations, and she glowed as only a woman can who has seen her man fight a hard fight and win gloriously. But no one congratulated Mrs. Bryan. She sat hunched in her chair near the judge, apparently very uneasy. I thought then that she was ill—she has been making the round of sanitariums for years, and was lately in the hands of a faith-healer—but now I think that some appalling prescience was upon her, and that she saw in Bryan's eyes a hint of the collapse that was so near.

He sank into his seat a wreck, and was presently forgotten in the blast of Malone's titanic rhetoric. His speech had been maundering, feeble and often downright idiotic. Presumably, he was speaking to a point of law, but it was quickly apparent that he knew no more law than the bailiff at the door. So he launched into mere violet garrulity. He dragged in snatches of ancient chautauqua addresses; he wandered up hill and down dale. Finally, Darrow lured him into that fabulous imbecility about man as a mammal. He sat down one of the most tragic asses in American history.

IV

It is the national custom to sentimentalize the dead, as it is to sentimentalize men about to be hanged. Perhaps I fall into that weakness here. The Bryan I shall remember is the Bryan of his last weeks on earth—broken,

furious and infinitely pathetic. It was impossible to meet his hatred with
hatred to match it. He was winning a battle that would make him forever
infamous wherever enlightened men remembered it and him. Even his old
enemy, Darrow, was gentle with him at the end. That cross-examination
might have been ten times as devastating. It was plain to everyone that the
old Berseker Bryan was gone—that all that remained of him was a pair of
glaring and horrible eyes.

But what of his life? Did he accomplish any useful thing? Was he, in his
day, of any dignity as a man, and of any value to his fellow-men? I doubt it.
Bryan, at his best, was simply a magnificent job-seeker. The issues that he
bawled about usually meant nothing to him. He was ready to abandon them
whenever he could make votes by doing so, and to take up new ones at a
moment's notice. For years he evaded Prohibition as dangerous; then he
embraced it as profitable. At the Democratic National Convention last year he
was on both sides, and distrusted by both. In his last great battle there was only
a baleful and ridiculous malignancy. If he was pathetic, he was also disgusting.

Bryan was a vulgar and common man, a cad undiluted. He was ignorant, bigoted, self-seeking, blatant and dishonest. His career brought him
into contact with the first men of his time; he preferred the company of
rustic ignoramuses. It was hard to believe, watching him at Dayton, that he
had traveled, that he had been received in civilized societies, that he had
been a high officer of state. He seemed only a poor clod like those around
him, deluded by a childish theology, full of an almost pathological hatred
of all learning, all human dignity, all beauty, all fine and noble things. He
was a peasant come home to the dung-pile. Imagine a gentleman, and you
have imagined eveything that he was not.

The job before democracy is to get rid of such canaille. If it fails, they
will devour it.

[*Baltimore Evening Sun,* July 27, 1925]

ROUND TWO

I

The translation of Bryan to a higher sphere was a body blow to the imbecility called Fundamentalism, and its effects are already visible. Not only has

the Georgia Legislature incontinently rejected the anti-evolution bill; there has been a marked improvement in the discussion of the whole subject throughout the South. While Bryan lived it was almost impossible, in most Southern States, to make any headway against him. His great talent for inflaming the mob, and his habit of doing it by lying about his opponents, made many Southern editors hesitate to tackle him. In a region where education is backward, and popular thinking is largely colored by disreputable politicians and evangelical pastors, such a fellow was dangerous.

But a dead man cannot bite, and so the Southern editors now show a new boldness. I speak, of course, of the general. A few daring spirits have been denouncing Bryan as a charlatan for a long while, and some of them have even carried their readers with them. I point, for example, to Julian Harris in Columbus, Ga., and to Charlton Wright in Columbia, S. C.—two highly civilized men, preaching sense and decency without fear. But the average Southern editor, it must be manifest, has been, in the past, of a different sort. What ails the South, primarily, is simply lack of courage. Its truculence is only protective coloration; it is really very timid. If there had been bolder editors in Tennessee there would have been no anti-evolution bill and no Scopes trial.

But, as I say, the removal of Bryan to Paradise gives heart to skittish spirits, for his heirs and assigns are all palpable fifth-raters, and hence not formidable. In South Carolina, for example, the cause falls to the Hon. Cole L. Blease, who is to Bryan what a wart is to the Great Smoky Mountains. In Tennessee itself he is succeeded by a junta of hedge lawyers, county school superintendents, snide politicians and rustic clergymen—in brief, by worms. It will be easy to make practise against them.

II

The circumstances of Bryan's death, indeed, have probably done great damage to Fundamentalism, for it is nothing if it is not a superstition, and the rustic pastors will have a hard time explaining to the faithful why the agent of God was struck down in the midst of the first battle. How is it that Darrow escaped and Bryan fell? There is, no doubt, a sound theological reason, but I shouldn't like to have to expound it, even to a country Bible class. In the end, perhaps, the true believers will have to take refuge from the torment of doubt in the theory that the hero was murdered, say by the Jesuits. Even so, there will be the obvious and disquieting inference that, in the first battle, the devil really won.

The theory I mention is already launched. I find it in the current issue of the *American Standard,* a leading Fundamentalist organ, edited by an eminent Baptist pastor. This journal, which is written in good English and attractively printed, voices the opinion of the more refined and thoughtful Fundamentalists. What it says today is said by scores of little denominational papers tomorrow. Its notion is that the Catholics, represented by Dudley Field Malone, and the Jews, represented by Darrow (!), concentrated such malicious animal magnetism upon poor Bryan that he withered and perished. The late martyr Harding, it appears, was disposed of in the same way: his crime was that he was a Freemason. Thus Fundamentalism borrows the magic of Christian Science, and idiot kisses idiot.

But something remains for the rev. clergy to explain, and that is Bryan's vulnerability. If he was actually divinely inspired, and doing battle for the True Faith, then how come that he did not throw off Malone's and Darrow's sorceries? He had ample warning. Dayton, during the Scopes trial, was full of whispers. At least a dozen times I was told of hellish conspiracies afoot. Every pastor in the town knew that demons filled the air. Why didn't they exorcise these dreadful shapes? One must assume that they prayed for the champion of light. In fact, they prayed openly, and in loud, ringing, confident tones. Then why did their prayers fail?

III

I do not propound such questions in an effort to be jocose; I offer them as characteristic specimens of Fundamentalist reasoning. The Fundamentalist prayer is not an inner experience; it is a means to objective ends. He prays precisely as more worldly Puritans complain to the police. He expects action, and is disappointed and dismayed if it does not follow. The mind of this Fundamentalist is extremely literal—indeed, the most literal mind ever encountered on this earth. He doubts nothing in the Bible, not even the typographical errors. He believes absolutely that Noah took two behemoths and two streptococci into the Ark, and he believes with equal faith that the righteous have angels to guard them.

Thus the dramatic death of Bryan is bound to give him great concern, and in the long run, I believe, it will do more to break down his cocksureness than ten thousand arguments. Try to imagine the debates that must be going on in Dayton itself, in Robinson's drug store and on the courthouse lawn. What is old Ben McKenzie's theory? How does the learned Judge Raulston, J., explain it? And the Hicks boys? And Pastor Stribling? I venture to guess that the miracle—for everything that happens, to a Fundamentalist, is a miracle—has materially cooled off enthusiasm for the Bryan Fundamentalist University. If Darrow could blast Bryan, then what is to prevent him blasting the university, and so setting fire to the town?

My belief is that the last will soon be heard of that great institution. It will engage the newspapers for a few weeks or months longer, and various enterprising souls will get a lot of free publicity by subscribing to its endowment, and then it will be quietly shelved. I doubt that anyone in Tennessee wants it—that is, anyone who has any notion what a university is.

The yokels of the hills may be bemused by it, as they are bemused by the scheme to put God into the Constitution. But the rest of the Tennesseeans are eager only to shove Fundamentalism into a cellar, and to get rid of the disgrace that it has brought upon the State.

IV

They will tackle it with more vigor than last time when it next takes to the warpath. They have learned a lesson. Already, indeed, they make plans for the repeal of the anti-evolution law—a long business, but certainly not hopeless. It was supported by the politicians of the State simply because those in favor of it were noisy and determined, and those against it were too proud to fight. These politicians will begin to wobble the moment it becomes clear that there are two sides engaged, and they will desert Genesis at the first sign that the enemy has artillery, and is eager to use it. They are, like politicians everywhere, men without conscience. One of the chief of them began life as legislative agent for the brewers. When Prohibition came in he became a violent Prohibitionist.

Their brethren elsewhere in the South are of the same sort; it is hard to find, in that whole region, a politician who is an honest man. The news from Georgia shows which way the wind is blowing. If it had seemed to them that Fundamentalism was prospering, the Georgia legislators would have rammed through the anti-evolution bill with a whoop. But the

whisper reached them that there were breakers ahead, and so they hesi-
tated, and the measure was lost. Those breakers were thrown up by a few
determined men, notably the Julian Harris aforesaid, son of Joel Chandler
Harris. What he has accomplished in Georgia, almost single-handed, will
not be lost upon the civilized minorities of the other Southern States.
Imbecility has raged down there simply because no has challenged it. Challenged, it will have hard going, there as elsewhere.

    With Bryan alive and on the warpath, inflaming the morons and
spreading his eloquent nonsense, the battle would have been ten times
harder. But Bryan was unique, and can have no successor. His baleful rhetoric died with him; in fact, it died a week before his corporeal frame. In a
very true sense Darrow killed him. When he emerged from that incredible
cross-examination, all that was most dangerous in his old following
deserted him. It was no longer possible for a man of any intelligence to
view him as anything save a pathetic has-been.

[Baltimore Evening Sun, August 10, 1925]

AFTERMATH

The Liberals, in their continuing discussion of the late trial of the infidel
Scopes at Dayton, Tenn., run true to form. That is to say, they show all their
habitual lack of humor and all their customary furtive weakness for the
delusions of *Homo neandertalensis.* I point to two of their most enlightened
organs: the eminent New York *World* and the gifted *New Republic.* The
World is displeased with Mr. Darrow because, in his appalling cross-examination of the mountebank Bryan, he did some violence to the theological
superstitions that millions of Americans cherish. The *New Republic*
denounces him because he addressed himself, not to "the people of Tennessee" but to the whole country, and because he should have permitted
"local lawyers" to assume "the most conspicuous position in the trial."[7]

    Once more, alas, I find myself unable to follow the best Liberal
thought. What the *World*'s contention amounts to, at bottom, is simply the
doctrine that a man engaged in combat with superstition should be very
polite to superstition. This, I fear, is nonsense. The way to deal with superstition is not to be polite to it, but to tackle it with all arms, and so rout it,
cripple it, and make it forever infamous and ridiculous. Is it, perchance,

cherished by persons who should know better? Then their folly should be brought out into the light of day, and exhibited there in all its hideousness until they flee from it, hiding their heads in shame.

True enough, even a superstitious man has certain inalienable rights. He has a right to harbor and indulge his imbecilities as long as he pleases, provided only he does not try to inflict them upon other men by force. He has a right to argue for them as eloquently as he can, in season and out of season. He has a right to teach them to his children. But certainly he has no right to be protected against the free criticism of those who do not hold them. He has no right to demand that they be treated as sacred. He has no right to preach them without challenge. Did Darrow, in the course of his dreadful bombardment of Bryan, drop a few shells, incidentally, into measurably cleaner camps? Then let the garrisons of those camps look to their defenses. They are free to shoot back. But they can't disarm their enemy.

II

The meaning of religious freedom, I fear, is sometimes greatly misapprehended. It is taken to be a sort of immunity, not merely from governmental control but also from public opinion. A dunderhead gets himself a long-tailed coat, rises behind the sacred desk and emits such bilge as would gag a Hottentot. Is it to pass unchallenged? If so, then what we have is not religious freedom at all, but the most intolerable and outrageous variety of religious despotism. Any fool, once he is admitted to holy orders, becomes infallible. Any half-wit, by the simple device of ascribing his delusions to revelation, takes on an authority that is denied to all the rest of us.

I do not know how many Americans entertain the ideas defended so ineptly by poor Bryan, but probably the number is very large. They are preached once a week in at least a hundred thousand rural churches, and they are heard too in the meaner quarters of the great cities. Nevertheless, though they are thus held to be sound by millions, these ideas remain mere rubbish. Not only are they not supported by the known facts; they are in direct contravention of the known facts. No man whose information is sound and whose mind functions normally can conceivably credit them. They are the products of ignorance and stupidity, either or both.

What should be a civilized man's attitude toward such superstitions? It seems to me that the only attitude possible to him is one of contempt. If he admits that they have any intellectual dignity whatever, he admits that he himself has none. If he pretends to a respect for those who believe in them, he pretends falsely, and sinks almost to their level. When he is challenged he must answer honestly, regardless of tender feelings. That is what Darrow did at Dayton, and the issue plainly justified the fact. Bryan went there in a hero's shining armor, bent deliberately upon a gross crime against sense. He came out a wrecked and preposterous charlatan, his tail between his legs. Few Americans have ever done so much for their country in a whole lifetime as Darrow did in two hours.

III

The caveat of the *New Republic* is so absurd that it scarcely deserves an answer. It is based upon a complete misunderstanding of the situation that the Scopes trial revealed. What good would it have done to have addressed an appeal to the people of Tennessee? They had already, by their lawful representatives, adopted the anti-evolution statute by an immense majority, and they were plainly determined to uphold it. The newspapers of the State, with one or two exceptions, were violently in favor of the prosecution, and applauded every effort of the rustic judge and district attorney to deprive the defense of its most elemental rights.

True enough, there was a minority of Tennesseeans on the other side—men and women who felt keenly the disgrace of their State, and were eager to put an end to it. But their time had passed; they had missed their chance. They should have stepped forward at the very beginning, long before Darrow got into the case. Instead, they hung back timorously, and so Bryan and the Baptist pastors ran amok. There was a brilliant exception: John R. Neal. There was another: F. B. McElwee. Both lawyers. But the rest of the lawyers of the State, when the issue was joined at last, actually helped the prosecution. Their bar associations kept up a continuous fusillade. They tried their best to prod the backwoods Dogberry, Raulston, into putting Darrow into jail.

There was but one way to meet this situation and Darrow adopted it. He appealed directly to the country and to the world. He had at these recreant Tennesseeans by exhibiting their shame to all men, near and far. He showed them cringing before the rustic theologians, and afraid of Bryan. He turned the State inside out, and showed what civilization can come to under Fundamentalism. The effects of that cruel exposure are now visible. Tennessee is still spluttering—and blushing. The uproar staggered its people. And they are doing some very painful thinking. Will they cling to Fundamentalism or will they restore civilization? I suspect that the quick decision of their neighbor, Georgia, will help them to choose. Darrow did more for them, in two weeks, than all their pastors and politicians had done since the Civil War.

IV

His conduct of the case, in fact, was adept and intelligent from beginning to end. It is hard, in retrospect, to imagine him improving it. He faced immense technical difficulties. In order to get out of the clutches of the village Dogberry and before judges of greater intelligence he had to work deliberately for the conviction of his client. In order to evade the puerile question of that client's guilt or innocence and so bring the underlying issues before the country, he had to set up a sham battle on the side lines. And in order to expose the gross ignorance and superstition of the real prosecutor, Bryan, he had to lure the old imposter upon the stand.

It seems to me that he accomplished all of these things with great skill. Scopes was duly convicted, and the constitutional questions involved in the law will now be heard by competent judges and decided without resort to prayer and moving pictures. The whole world has been made familiar with the issues, and the nature of the menace that Fundamentalism offers to civilization is now familiar to every schoolboy. And Bryan was duly scotched, and, if he had lived, would be standing before the country today as a comic figure, tattered and preposterous.

All this was accomplished, in infernal weather, by a man of sixty-eight, with the scars of battles all over him. He had, to be sure, highly competent help. At his table sat lawyers whose peculiar talents, in combination, were of the highest potency—the brilliant Hays, the eloquent Malone, the daring and patriotic Tennesseean, Neal. But it was Darrow who carried the main burden, and Darrow who shaped the final result. When he confronted Bryan at last, the whole combat came to its climax. On the one side was bigotry, ignorance, hatred, superstition, every sort of blackness that the human mind is capable of. On the other side was sense. And sense achieved a great victory.

[*Baltimore Evening Sun,* September 24, 1925]

WILLIAM JENNINGS BRYAN

Has it been marked by historians that the late William Jennings Bryan's last secular act on this earth was to catch flies? A curious detail, and not without its sardonic overtones. He was the most sedulous flycatcher in American history, and by long odds the most successful. His quarry, of course, was not *Musca domestica* but *Homo neandertalensis.* For forty years he tracked it with snare and blunderbuss, up and down the backways of the Republic. Wherever the flambeaux of Chautauqua smoked and guttered, and the bilge of Idealism ran in the veins, and Baptist pastors dammed the brooks with the saved, and men gathered who were weary and heavy laden, and their wives who were unyieldingly multiparous and full of Peruna—there the indefatigable Jennings set up his traps and spread his bait. He knew every forlorn country town in the South and West, and he could crowd the most remote of them to suffocation by simply winding his horn. The city proletariat, transiently flustered by him in 1896, quickly penetrated his buncombe and would have no more of him; the gallery jeered him at every Democratic national convention for twenty-five years. But out where the grass grows high, and the horned cattle dream away the lazy days, and men still fear the powers and principalities of the air—out there between the corn-rows he held his old puissance to the end. There was no need of beaters to drive in his game. The news that he was coming was enough. For miles the flivver dust would choke the roads. And when he rose at the end of the day to discharge his Message there would be such breathless attention, such a rapt and enchanted ecstasy, such a sweet rustle of amens as the world had not known since Johanan fell to Herod's headsman.

There was something peculiarly fitting in the fact that his last days were spent in a one-horse Tennessee village, and that death found him there. The man felt at home in such scenes. He liked people who sweated freely, and were not debauched by the refinements of the toilet. Making his progress up and down the Main street of little Dayton, surrounded by gaping primates from the upland valleys of the Cumberland Range, his coat laid aside, his bare arms and hairy chest shining damply, his bald head sprinkled with dust—so accoutred and on display he was obviously happy.

He liked getting up early in the morning, to the tune of cocks crowing on the dung-hill. He liked the heavy, greasy victuals of the farmhouse kitchen. He liked country lawyers, country pastors, all country people. I believe that this liking was sincere—perhaps the only sincere thing in the man. His nose showed no uneasiness when a hillman in faded overalls and hickory shirt accosted him on the street, and besought him for light upon some mystery of Holy Writ. The simian gabble of a country town was not gabble to him, but wisdom of an occult and superior sort. In the presence of city folks he was palpably uneasy. Their clothes, I suspect, annoyed him, and he was suspicious of their too delicate manners. He knew all the while that they were laughing at him—if not at his baroque theology, then at least at his alpaca pantaloons. But the yokels never laughed at him. To them he was not the huntsman but the prophet, and toward the end, as he gradually forsook mundane politics for purely ghostly concerns, they began to elevate him in their hierarchy. When he died he was the peer of Abraham. Another curious detail: his old enemy, Wilson, aspiring to the same white and shining robe, came down with a thump. But Bryan made the grade. His place in the Tennessee hagiocracy is secure. If the village barber saved any of his hair, then it is curing gall-stones down there to-day.

II

But what label will he bear in more urbane regions? One, I fear, of a far less flattering kind. Bryan lived too long, and descended too deeply into the mud, to be taken seriously hereafter by fully literate men, even of the kind who write school-books. There was a scattering of sweet words in his funeral notices, but it was no more than a response to conventional sentimentality. The best verdict the most romantic editorial writer could dredge up, save in the eloquent South, was to the general effect that his imbecilities were excused by his earnestness—that under his clowning, as under that of the juggler of Notre Dame, there was the zeal of a steadfast soul. But this was apology, not praise; precisely the same thing might be said of Mary Baker G. Eddy, the late Czar Nicholas, or Czolgosz.[8] The truth is that even Bryan's sincerity will probably yield to what is called, in other fields, definitive criticism. Was he sincere when he opposed imperialism in the Philippines, or when he fed it with deserving Democrats in Santo Domingo? Was he sincere when he tried to shove the Prohibitionists under the table, or when he seized their banner and began to lead them with loud whoops? Was he sincere when he bellowed against war, or when he dreamed of himself as a tin-soldier in uniform, with a grave reserved among the generals? Was he sincere when he denounced the late John W. Davis, or when he swallowed Davis? Was he sincere when he fawned over Champ Clark, or when he betrayed Clark? Was he sincere when he pleaded for tolerance in New York, or when he bawled for the fagot and the stake in Tennessee?

This talk of sincerity, I confess, fatigues me. If the fellow was sincere, then so was P. T. Barnum. The word is disgraced and degraded by such uses. He was, in fact, a charlatan, a mountebank, a zany without shame or dignity. What animated him from end to end of his grotesque career was simply ambition—the ambition of a common man to get his hand upon the collar of his superiors, or, failing that, to get his thumb into their eyes. He was born with a roaring voice, and it had the trick of inflaming half-wits. His whole career was devoted to raising these half-wits against their betters, that he himself might shine. His last battle will be grossly misunderstood if it is thought of as a mere exercise in fanaticism—that is, if Bryan the Fundamentalist Pope is mistaken for one of the bucolic Fundamentalists. There was much more in it than that, as everyone knows who saw him on the field. What moved him, at bottom, was simply hatred of the city men who had laughed at him so long, and brought him at last to so tatterdemalion an estate. He lusted for revenge upon them. He yearned to lead the anthropoid rabble against them, to set *Homo neandertalensis* upon them, to punish them for the execution they had done upon him by attacking the very vitals of their civilization. He went far beyond the bounds of any merely religious frenzy, however inordinate. When he began denouncing the notion that man is a mammal even some of the hinds at Dayton were agape. And when, brought upon Darrow's cruel hook, he writhed and tossed in a very fury of malignancy, bawling against the baldest elements of sense and decency like a man frantic—when he came to that tragic climax there were snickers among the hinds as well as hosannas.

Upon that hook, in truth, Bryan committed suicide, as a legend as well as in the body. He staggered from the rustic court ready to die, and he staggered from it ready to be forgotten, save as a character in a third-rate farce, witless and in execrable taste. The chances are that history will put the peak of democracy in his time; it has been on the downward curve among us since the campaign of 1896. He will be remembered, perhaps, as its supreme impostor, the *reductio ad absurdum* of its pretension. Bryan came very near being President of the United States. In 1896, it is possible, he was actually elected. He lived long enough to make patriots thank the inscrutable gods for Harding, even for Coolidge. Dulness has got into the White House, and the smell of cabbage boiling, but there is at least nothing to compare to the intolerable buffoonery that went on in Tennessee. The President of the United States doesn't believe that the earth is square, and that witches should be put to death, and that Jonah swallowed the whale. The Golden Text is not painted weekly on the White House wall, and there is no need to keep ambassadors waiting while Pastor Simpson, of Smithsville, prays for rain in the Blue Room. We have escaped something—by a narrow margin, but still safely.

III

That is, so far. The Fundamentalists continue at the wake, and sense gets a sort of reprieve. The legislature of Georgia, so the news comes, has shelved the anti-evolution bill, and turns its back upon the legislature of Tennessee. Elsewhere minorities prepare for battle—here and there with some assurance of success. But it is too early, it seems to me, to send the firemen home; the fire is still burning on many a far-flung hill, and it may begin to roar again at any moment. The evil that men do lives after them. Bryan, in his malice, started something that it will not be easy to stop. In ten thousand country towns his old heelers, the evangelical pastors, are propagating his gospel, and everywhere the yokels are ready for it. When he disappeared from the big cities, the cities made the capital error of assuming that he was done for. If they heard of him at all, it was only as a crimp for real-estate speculators— the heroic foe of the unearned increment hauling it in with both hands. He seemed preposterous, and hence harmless. But all the while he was busy among his old lieges, preparing for a *jacquerie* that should floor all his enemies at one blow. He did the job competently. He had vast skill at such enterprises. Heave an egg out of a Pullman window, and you will hit a Fundamentalist almost anywhere in the United States today. They swarm in the country towns, inflamed by their pastors, and with a saint, now, to venerate. They are thick in the mean streets behind the gas-works. They are everywhere that learning is too heavy a burden for mortal minds, even the vague, pathetic learning on tap in little red schoolhouses. They march with the Klan, with the Christian Endeavor Society, with the Junior Order of United American Mechanics, with the Epworth League, with all the rococo bands that poor and unhappy folk organize to bring some light of purpose into their lives. They have had a thrill, and they are ready for more.

Such is Bryan's legacy to his country. He couldn't be President, but he could at least help magnificently in the solemn business of shutting off the presidency from every intelligent and self-respecting man. The storm, perhaps, won't last long, as time goes in history. It may help, indeed, to break up the democratic delusion, now already showing weakness, and so hasten its own end. But while it lasts it will blow off some roofs and flood some sanctuaries.

[*American Mercury*, October 1925]

VII

RELIGION AND SCIENCE

COUSIN JOCKO

The late William Jennings Bryan, LL.D., always had one great advantage in controversy: he was never burdened with an understanding of his opponent's case. His talents, indeed, were always far more homiletical than dialectical; he was at his best, not in argument, but in denunciation. The fact made itself felt brilliantly during his last great combat with the evolutionists. Whenever he stated their doctrines he stated them inaccurately, and whenever he undertook to refute them he resorted to nonsense. His mind was of the sort that is simply unable to grasp scientific facts. They fevered him as flies fever a bull, and he got rid of them by lashing his tail.

Unfortunately, some of his scientific antagonists played into his hands by trying idiotically to perfume their own case. Of such sort were all the more fatuous reconcilers of science and religion, led by Prof. Henry Fairfield Osborn, Sc.D., D.Sc., LL.D., Ph.D. And of the same sort were the professors who hastened to assure the booboisie that Darwinism, after all, did not mean that men had descended from the monkey. These earnest gentlemen, I believe, went a great deal too far. They admitted too much, and so played into Bryan's hands. And by the same token they gave an air of dubiousness and uncertainty to the doctrines they ostensibly defended.

There is, in point of fact, no possibility of reconciling science and religion—that is, religion of the sort preached to the peasantry by Bryan. If the one is sound, then the other is bilge. He himself, for all his ignorance, was well aware of the fact. When the biblical narrative collided with a known fact he instantly rejected the known fact. I myself, with my own ears, heard him argue violently against the notion that man is a mammal. To maintain that such "religious" ideas can be reconciled with science is to maintain that the Volstead act can be reconciled with the Bill of Rights. The two things are not only different; they are squarely and eternally antagonistic.

The yokels that Bryan preyed upon, when they thought of the evolutionary hypothesis at all, thought of it as the doctrine that their own grandfathers were gorillas. They could not grasp the concept of great spaces of time; moreover, most of them had seen their grandfather—and so the plausibility of the notion made them shiver. Bryan took advantage of the fact. Discreetly disregarding their grandfathers, he based his case upon their grandmothers, thus appealing powerfully to their chivalry. They responded by whooping for Genesis, in which Eve, though she is depicted as a somewhat loose woman, is at least 100 per cent human.

The professors of scientific apologetics responded by attempting an elaborate and none too convincing explanation. It was no longer contended, they said, that man was descended directly from the monkey; all that was argued was that man and monkey, in some remote past, had a common ancestor. The remoteness of that past was sufficient to make the connection aseptic. It ran to hundreds of thousands, millions, perhaps, even billions, of years. Long before the civil war, even before the revolution, the separation was complete. It was rammed home, so to speak, by man's acquirement of a soul—no doubt in early biblical days.

This explanation, I believe, failed to fool the Fundamentalists, and I see no reason why it should fool anyone else. Its defect was that it simply begged the question. What difference did it make whether man was descended from a monkey, or from some remote ancestor of all the monkeys—a more primitive and hence obviously more unappetizing quadruped than any monkey ever heard of? All the scientists accomplished by their nonsense was to make the Fundamentalists even more skittish than they had been before. Some of the harder hearted of them had begun to be reconciled to the notion that their grandfathers had tails and lived in cages. But when they began to hear talk of remoter ancestors it made them think of skunks, rats, pigs and other such abhorrent creatures, and so they shivered again, and resumed their whooping for Bryan.

The truth is that the biological relationship between man and monkey, whatever the precise lines of descent, is quite as close as even the most frantic Fundamentalist ever accused scientists of believing, and that increasing knowledge tends to make it appear closer and closer. I turn, for example, to the latest authoritative work upon the subject, *The Morphology and Evolution of the Apes and Man,* by Dr. Charles F. Sonntag of University College, London, and point to page 255. There Dr. Sonntag announces the pleasing news that the blood of man and that of the higher apes is chemically almost identical.

This is an accurate and an extremely subtle test. In its more refined forms it is sufficiently delicate to differentiate one man and another. As between man and, say, the horse or the dog it is infallible. A horse's blood or a dog's blood can never be mistaken for the blood of a man. But when one comes to the higher apes the test begins to grow unreliable. The blood of a common organ grinder's monkey (*Cebus capichinus*) is easily differentiated from man's, but that of the baboons begins to show similarities, and that of the gibbons, chimpanzees, orangutans and gorillas is so nearly identical that one begins to sympathize with the shivering of the Fundamentalists.

Such proofs of extremely close relationship—and there are others—make all questions of descent seem academic. Whether man is a glorified grandson of the ape, or the ape is a degenerate man, or the two are descendents of a common ancestor—this problem, perhaps, will never be solved. Nor is it important. The important thing is that ape and man are biological cousins and as closely related as duck and canary bird. The anatomical and physiological differences between them are mainly trivial; the likenesses are innumerable and profound. Shave a gorilla and it would be almost impossible, at twenty paces, to distinguish him from a heavyweight champion of the world. Skin a chimpanzee, and it would take an autopsy to prove he was not a theologian.

Dr. Sonntag's investigations into the physical makeup of the primates have been admirably supplemented of late by elaborate studies of their mental powers. This work has been done chiefly by Dr. Wolfgang Köhler of the University of Berlin, who spent four years at Teneriffe, in Canary Islands, studying a collection of chimpanzees gathered there. But important additions to the knowledge thus gained have been made by Dr. Robert M. Yerkes of Yale, who worked at Quinta Palatino, Cuba, where Mme. Rosalia Abreu has an immense collection of all sorts of monkeys—the largest, indeed, in the world. Dr. Köhler's conclusions are printed in a book called *The Mentality of Apes*, and Dr. Yerkes' in three volumes: *The Mental Life of Monkeys and Apes, Chimpanzee Intelligence and Its Vocal Expression* and *Almost Human.*

What these investigations demonstrate, in brief, is that all the higher apes actually think, and that their thinking process differs very little, if at all, from that of the lower orders of man. A gorilla, true enough, cannot write poetry, and neither can it grasp such a concept as that of Americanization or that of relativity, but is fully equal to all of thinking that a subway guard, a bass drummer, or a chiropractor has to do, and if it could only speak English it could be made into a competent train conductor or congressman in thirty days.

In some ways, indeed, it is measurably more clever than many men. It cannot be fooled as easily; it does not waste so much time doing useless things. If it desires, for example, to get a banana hung out of reach, it proceeds to the business with a singleness of purpose and a fertility of resource that, in a traffic policeman, would seem almost pathological. There are no Fundamentalists among the primates. They believe nothing that is not demonstrable. When they confront a fact they recognize it instantly, and turn it to their use with admirable readiness. There are liars among them, but no idealists.

[*Chicago Sunday Tribune,* November 8, 1925]

FIDES ANTE INTELLECTUM

A SCIENTIFIC MAN AND THE BIBLE, by Howard A. Kelly. Philadelphia: *The Sunday-School Times Company.*

The author of this astounding book is emeritus professor of gynecological surgery at the Johns Hopkins, and one of the most celebrated surgeons now alive in the United States. This is what his own university says of him in an official document:

> His contribution to the development of genito-urinary surgery for women has been unparalleled. Step by step he unravelled the diseases of the bladder, ureter and kidney. . . . His methods of examination revolutionized gynecological diagnosis.

And much more to the same effect. In brief, a medical man of the first caliber: when he speaks of himself as a scientist, as he does very often in his book, he has every right to use the word. His life has been devoted to exact observation, and that observation has been made so competently and interpreted so logically that the result has been a series of immensely valuable improvements in the healing art and craft. And yet—and yet— But how am I to make you believe that such a man has actually written such a volume as this one? How am I to convince you that one of the four men who laid the foundations of the Johns Hopkins Medical School—the daily associate and peer of Osler, Welch and Halsted—is here on exhibition as a Fundamentalist of the most extreme wing, compared to whom Judge Raulston, of Dayton, Tenn., seems almost an atheist?

Yet it is so—and I go, for the depressing proof, behind the book and to the man himself. I have known Dr. Kelly for twenty years, and at different times have seen a great deal of him. Hours on end I have discussed his theological ideas with him, and heard his reasons for cherishing them. They seem to me now, as they seemed when I first heard them, to be completely insane—yet Kelly himself is surely not insane. Nor is there the remotest suspicion of insincerity about him. It would be of vast benefit to him professionally to throw over his great cargo of supernatural rubbish, and trim his course as his colleagues trim theirs. If he did so, the Johns Hopkins would be illuminated with Roman candles, star shells and incandescent bock beer signs, and the very cadavers in the deadhouse would have their backs slapped. But he will not budge. He believes that God created the world in six calendar days, and rested on the seventh. He believes that God caused forty-two little children to be devoured by she-bears because they made fun of Elijah's bald head. He believes that Jonah was three days and three nights in the belly of a whale (*Physeter macrocephalus*), and then came out alive. *Medicinae doctor* though he be, he believes that the hallucinations of John on the island of Patmos were real. An LL.D. of Aberdeen, he believes (Exodus 22:18) that witches exist and should be put to death. An honorary member of learned societies in Paris, Vienna, Rome, Berlin, Leipzig, Bucharest and Moscow, he believes in both the Virgin Birth (Matthew 1:18–25), and in the descent of Jesus from David through Joseph (Matthew 1:1–17). All this, and much more, he believes absolutely without reservation, as a Tennessee hind believes it. "I accept the *whole* Bible," he says, "as God's Word." And he adds something that even the hind balks at: he believes in the Second Coming—"at any moment"!

In his book Dr. Kelly offers powerful argument for his amazing credo, but I can only report that, in cold type as *viva voce,* it leaves me full of what the lawyers call reasonable doubt. His logic has a curious habit of going half way to a plausible conclusion, and then blowing up completely. For example, he starts off, in one place, by showing how the early criticism of the Gospel of John has broken down—and then proceeds gaily to the assumption that proving an error in criticism is identical with proving the complete authenticity of the thing criticized. Again, he denounces the effort to raise up doubts of the Mosaic authorship and divine inspiration of the Pentateuch—and then clinches his case by showing that the Bible itself "claims in all its parts" that it is "the very literal Word of God." But the record of a personal experience exhibits the workings of his mind even more beautifully. Early in manhood he had to give up his medical studies on account of ill-health, and went West to recuperate. In Colorado, during a blizzard, he was beset by snow blindness, and had to take to his bed. Suddenly there came upon him "an overwhelming sense of a great light in the room." How would any ordinary medical student interpret that great light? How would any ordinary ice-wagon driver, or chiropractor, or Methodist bishop, or even catfish interpret it? Obviously, he would refer it to the violent conjunctivitis from which he was suffering—in other words, to a purely physical cause. But not Kelly. After forty-four years of active medical practice he still believes that the glare was due to the presence of God! This divine visitation he speaks of very simply as "the chief event" of his life! It surely was—if it was real!

What I'd like to read is a scientific review, by a scientific psychologist—if any exists—of *A Scientific Man and the Bible.* By what route do otherwise sane men come to believe such palpable nonsense? How is it possible for a human brain to be divided into two insulated halves, one functioning normally, naturally and even brilliantly, and the other capable only of the ghastly balderdash which issues from the minds of Baptist evangelists? Such balderdash takes various forms, but it is at its worst when it is religious. Why should this be so? What is there in religion that completely flabbergasts the wits of those who believe in it? I see no logical necessity for that flabbergasting. Religion, after all, is nothing but an hypothesis framed to account for what is evidentially unaccounted for. In other fields such hypotheses are common, and yet they do no apparent damage to those who incline to them. But in the religious field they quickly rush the believer to the intellectual Bad Lands. He not only becomes anæsthetic to objective fact; he becomes a violent enemy of objective fact. It annoys and irritates him. He sweeps it away as something somehow evil.

This little book I commend to all persons interested in the mysteries of the so-called mind of man. It is a document full of fascination, especially to the infidel and damned. There is a frankness about it that is refreshing and commendable. The author does not apologize for his notions, nor does he try to bring them into grotesque and incredible harmony with scientific facts. He believes the Bible from cover to cover, fly-specks and all, and he says so (considering his station in life) with great courage.

[*American Mercury*, February 1926]

COUNTER-OFFENSIVE

IS IT GOD'S WORD? by Joseph Wheless. New York: *The Wheless Publishers.*

This is one of the soundest and most interesting books that I have read in months. The author, who is an associate editor of the *American Bar Association Journal,* was trained as a lawyer, but that training, somewhat surprisingly, seems to have left his logical powers unimpaired, and with them his capacity for differentiating between facts and mere appearances. There is no hint of the usual evasions and obfuscations of the advocate in his pages. His business is to examine calmly the authority and plausibility of Holy Writ, both as history and as revelation of the Omnipotent Will, and to that business he brings an immense and meticulous knowledge, an exact and unfailing judicial sense, and a skill at orderly exposition which is quite extraordinary. There is no vaporing of the orthodox exegetes that he is not familiar with, and none that he fails to refute, simply and devastatingly. Nine-tenths of his evidence he takes out of the mouths of his opponents. Patiently, mercilessly, irresistibly, he subjects it to logical analysis, and when he is done at last—his book runs to 462 pages of fine print—there is little left of the two Testaments save a farrago of palpable nonsense, swathed, to be sure, in very lovely poetry. He exposes all their gross and preposterous contradictions, their violations of common sense and common decency, their grotesque collisions with the known and indubitable facts, their petty tergiversations and fraudulences. He goes behind the mellifluous rhetoric of the King James Version to the harsh balderdash of the originals, and brings it out into the horrible light of day. He exposes the prophecies that have failed to come off. He exhibits the conflicts of romantic and unreliable witnesses, most of them with something to sell. He tracks down ideas to their barbaric sources. He concocts an almost endless series of logical dilemmas. And he does it all with good manners, never pausing to rant and nowhere going beyond the strict letter of the record.

Obviously, there is room and need for such a book, and it deserves to be widely read. For in the America of today, after a time of quiescence, the old conflict between religion and science has been resumed with great ferocity, and the partisans of the former, not content with denouncing all free inquiry as evil, have now undertaken to make it downright unlawful. Worse, they show signs of succeeding. And why? Chiefly, it seems to me, because the cause of their opponents has been badly handled—above all, because it has lacked vigorous *offensive* leadership. The defense, indeed, is largely an abject running away. We are assured with pious snuffling that there is actually no conflict, that the domains of science and religion do not overlap, that it is quite possible for a man to be a scientist (even a biologist!) and yet believe that Jonah swallowed the whale. No wonder the whoopers for Genesis take courage, and lay on with glad, if *sforzando* shouts. At one stroke they are lifted to parity with their opponents, nay, to superiority. The bilge they believe in becomes something sacrosanct; its manifest absurdities are not mentioned, and hence tend to pass unnoticed. But meanwhile they are quite free to belabor science with their whole armamentarium of imbecilities. Every crossroads Baptist preacher becomes an authority upon its errors, and is heard gravely. In brief, science exposes itself to be shot at, but agrees not to shoot back. It would be difficult to imagine any strategy more idiotic.

Or to imagine a Huxley adopting it. Huxley, in his day, followed a far different plan. When the Gladstones, Bishop Wilberforces and other such obscurantists denounced the new biology, he did not waste any time upon conciliatory politeness.[1] Instead, he made a bold and headlong attack upon Christian theology—an attack so vigorous and so skillful that the enemy was soon in ignominious flight. Huxley knew the first principle of war: he knew that a hearty offensive is worth a hundred defensives. How well he succeeded is shown by the fact that even today, with theology once more on the prowl and the very elements of science under heavy attack, some of the gaudiest of the ancient theological notions are not heard of. Huxley disposed of them complete!;; ..ven in Darkest Tennessee the yokels no longer give them credit. But if the Millikans and other such amiable bunglers continue to boss the scientific camp you may be sure that all these exploded myths and superstitions will be revived, and that the mob will once more embrace them. For it is the natural tendency of the ignorant to believe what is not true. In order to overcome that tendency it is not sufficient to exhibit the true; it is also necessary to expose and denounce the false. To admit that the false has any standing in court, that it ought to be handled gently because millions of morons cherish it and thousands of quacks make their livings propagating it—to admit this, as the more fatuous of the reconcilers of science and religion inevitably do, is to abandon a just cause to its enemies, cravenly and without excuse.

It is, of course, quite true that there is a region in which science and religion do not conflict. That is the region of the unknowable. No one knows Who created the visible universe, and it is infinitely improbable that anything properly describable as evidence on the point will ever be discovered. No one knows what motives or intentions, if any, lie behind what we call natural laws. No one knows why man has his present form. No one knows why sin and suffering were sent into the world—that is, why the fashioning of man was so badly botched. Naturally enough, all these problems have engaged the interest of humanity since the remotest days, and in every age, with every sort of evidence completely lacking, men of speculative mind have sought to frame plausible solutions. Some of them, more bold than the rest, have pretended that their solutions were revealed to them by God, and multitudes have believed them. But no man of science believes them. He does not say positively that they are wrong; he simply says that there is no proof that they are right. If he admitted, without proof, that they were right, he would not be a man of science. In his view all such theories and speculations stand upon a common level. In the most ambitious soarings of a Christian theologian he can find nothing that differs in any essential way from the obvious hocus-pocus of a medicine man in the jungle. Superficially, of course, the two stand far apart. The Christian theologian, confined like all the rest to the unknowable, has to be more careful than the medicine man, for in Christendom the unknowable covers a far less extensive field than in the jungle. Christian theology is thus, in a sense, more reasonable than voodooism. But it is not more reasonable because its professors know more than the voodoo-man about the unknowable; it is more reasonable simply because they are under a far more rigorous and enlightened scrutiny, and run a risk of being hauled up sharply every time they venture too near the borders of the known.

This business of hauling them up is one of the principal functions of science. Its prompt execution is the gauge of a high and progressive civilization. So long as theologians keep within their proper bounds, science has no quarrel with them, for it is no more able to prove that they are wrong than they themselves are able to prove that they are right. But human experience shows that they never keep within their proper bounds voluntarily; they are always bulging over the line, and making a great uproar over things that they know nothing about. Such an uproar is going on at the present moment. Hordes of theologians come marching down from the Southern mountains, declaring raucously that God created the universe during a certain single week of the year 4004 B.C.,[2] and demanding that all persons who presume to doubt it be handed over to the secular arm. Here, obviously, science cannot suffer them gladly, nor even patiently. Their proposition is a statement of scientific fact; it may be examined and tested like any other statement of scientific fact. So examined and tested, it turns out to be wholly without evidential support. All the known evidence, indeed, is against it, and overwhelmingly. No man who knows the facts—that is, no man with any claim to scientific equipment—is in any doubt about that. He disbelieves it as thoroughly as he believes that the earth moves round the sun. Disbelieving it, it is his professional duty, his first obligation of professional honor, to attack and refute those who uphold it. Above all, it is his duty to attack the false evidence upon which they base their case.

Thus an actual conflict is joined, and it is the height of absurdity for the Millikans and other such compromisers to seek to evade it with soft words. That conflict was not begun by science. It did not start with an invasion of the proper field of theological speculation by scientific raiders. It started with an invasion of the field of science by theological raiders. Now that it is on, it must be pressed vigorously from the scientific side, and without any flabby tenderness for theological susceptibilities. A defensive war is not enough; there must be a forthright onslaught upon the theological citadel, and every effort must be made to knock it down. For so long as it remains a stronghold, there will be no security for sound sense among us, and little for common decency. So long it may be used as a recruiting-station and rallying-point for the rabble, science will have to submit to incessant forays, and the same forays will be directed against every sort of rational religion. The latter danger is not unobserved by the more enlightened theologians. They are well aware that, facing the Fundamentalists, they must either destroy or be destroyed. It is to be hoped that the men of science will perceive the same plain fact, and so give over their vain effort to stay the enemy with weasel words.

I commend Mr. Wheless' book to all who are interested in the battle. I am reasonably familiar, for a layman, with the literature of Biblical criticism. It has amused me for many years to follow the combat between the so-called higher critics and the more orthodox theologians—a combat marked by immense emissions of red-hot gases and malicious animal magnetism on both sides. But in all the books I have read I know of none that marshals the case against the historical soundness and divine inspiration of Holy Writ more effectively than this one. It simply knocks the Fundamentalists' case to pieces, and with it the cases of many theologians who hold themselves far above such canaille. How any man, after reading it, can still believe that the two Testaments were dictated by Omnipotence is more than I am able, on this lovely Spring morning, to imagine.

[*American Mercury,* May 1926]

ANOTHER INQUISITION FAILS

Nothing could prove more dramatically the futility of trying to put down ideas by force than the failure of the anti-evolution campaign in the South. The Fundamentalists began with grand and lofty talk of driving the Darwinian heresy from the whole United States; they are ending by quarreling among themselves. Only two states have succumbed to their blather, and in only one, Mississippi, is their prohibition of elementary reason actually enforced. In the other, Tennessee, the obiter dictum of the Supreme court in the Scopes appeal is a plain invitation to pedagogues to violate the law as much as they please—that is, when there is no local sentiment in favor of it. It will be observed in such dreadful jungle towns as Dayton, but in Chattanooga, Memphis and Nashville, and maybe even in Knoxville, it will be quickly forgotten.

The anti-evolutionists may still bag a legislature or two in the Middle West, but it is not likely, nor is there any possibility that such occasional victories will ever have the effects that they hope for. For in the South they have been badly beaten, even when they seemed to win. Every uproar that they have raised has sent the youth of the adjacent wastes to reading the forbidden books, and, youthlike, to adopting and whooping up the forbidden ideas in them. In Tennessee the Scopes trial fell very far short of promoting the study of Genesis; instead, it turned Genesis into a joke, and produced a great flock of campus "atheist" societies. Even in Mississippi, I am informed by hardy explorers, such societies have begun to appear.

But Mississippi is a special case, and it may be that the Fundamentalists have really triumphed there. The state's great lack is decent newspapers. Its public journals are all of the crossroads type. What a free and intelligent press has accomplished in the adjoining states of Georgia and Alabama is thus impossible there, and the rural pastors go almost unchallenged. But soon or late, even in Mississippi, someone will set up a good paper, and when that happens Fundamentalism will fall upon evil days. For it can never withstand intelligence. One blast of common sense, and it begins to wither and die.

The time is now ripe in the South, indeed, for a vigorous counter-offensive, and I marvel that the young men of the enlightened minority do not undertake it. What is needed, in particular, is a series of tracts for distribution among the peasants of the hinterland and the villagers of the small towns. These poor creatures have been bombarded for a long while not only by the verbal discourses of their pastors but also by tons of anti-evolution literature, much of it very cunningly contrived. It states the case against the evolutionary hypothesis unfairly, but I am certainly not one to argue that it states it ineffectively. On the contrary, I believe that its authors, in the main, did a very good job.

One of them was the late Archangel Bryan. During the Scopes trial he handed me some of his compositions, printed in huge editions by opulent fellow Fundamentalists, and I read them with great interest. The basic argument in them was that the fact of evolution could not be proved experimentally—that no one had ever actually seen one species turn into another. Is there an answer to this? There is—and not one, but many. But so far as I know these answers have not been put into such form that ignorant rustics may be expected to understand them. What is needed is a literature couched in simple and familiar terms.

One excellent argument immediately suggests itself: I believe that even the most pious Mississippi peasant would have difficulty in resisting it. It is that the fact of evolution is proved every day in rural Mississippi by the case of the horsehair that, on being put into a bottle of water, turns into a snake. That this transformation really occurs is certainly not doubted by any Mississippi Fundamentalist; to question it would seem to him to be as insane as to question the existence of ghosts. Yet no one has ever thought to have at him with it. I believe that a short tract in words of one syllable, setting forth the horsehair argument and embellished with a few disarming quotations from holy writ, would do more execution in the Yazoo country than even a decent newspaper.

Many other similar arguments might be concocted by ingenious men, and after they had done their work of shaking the confidence of the rural Bible students it would be in order to follow them up with more apposite and intelligent documents. There is an immense mass of material in the literature of biology, and particularly in that of zoölogy. But as it stands it is without effect, for it is written in terms that no yokel may be expected to grasp. Very few country high-school teachers—and practically no country high-school superintendents at all—could read it without painful sweating. What is needed is its translation into the simple terminology of the camp-meeting and the barnyard.

The circulation of such literature in the Hookworm belt, to be sure, would be stoutly resisted by the resident clergy, and perhaps by the majority of local politicians, editors and other such dung-hill *hetaerae*. It would be alleged that the campaign was being paid for by the bolsheviki, the Mexican government or the pope, and no doubt the complaisant wowsers of the postoffice, on some pious pretext or other, would be induced to bar the tracts from the mails. But it would be easy to beat these wowsers in the courts, and, moreover, all other avenues of communication would remain open. So-called "art" magazines filled with portraits of naked chorus girls now flood all the Southern towns; documents bearing the portraits of such hairy fellows as Darwin and Huxley might very well follow the same route.

The effort to shut them out, in fact, would greatly promote their circulation, as it now promotes the circulation of the "art" magazines. Whenever a bucolic Savonarola denounced the invitation from his pulpit, two-thirds of his hearers would rush out to hunt for the forbidden goods, as they now rush out to neck, bootleg and smoke cigarets. And whenever a southern governor, with his eye on re-election, bellowed for the Federal army and navy to help him put down the traffic, there would be a great rush of orders.

What I here propose is nothing new. Practically all of the sound ideas that the human race cherishes today were put into circulation by just such means. So far as I know, there is no record in history of an idea of that sort getting a spontaneous and official welcome. The first men to argue that witchcraft was a delusion had to circulate their arguments anonymously, and even so they ran grave risks. Had newspapers existed none would have dared to print what they had to say. In the same way, the first men to argue against slavery had to do it discreetly and at long distance. Had they gone into Mississippi to state their case, they would have been denounced by the local journals as the evolutionists are denounced to-day, and no doubt some of them would have been lynched.

In this department the South is not peculiar. There is something in the human mind, at all times and everywhere, that resists the intrusion of new ideas, and the sounder they are the more violently it resists them. Who was it that discovered that two and two make four? Probably some Egyptian or Phoenician. Whoever he was, you may be sure that the clergy of the time damned him to hell for blasphemy, and that the politicians accused him of taking Greek or Babylonian gold. Mississippi is a bit archaic, but still thoroughly human. Its resistance to the idea of organic evolution is a bit belated, and hence seems amusing to the people of more enlightened places, but it doesn't differ a particle from the resistance of our own forefathers to the idea of bathing.

Such ideas are never propagated officially, but only by a process of bootlegging; the state is always against them, and tries to put them down. But when pertinacious men stand behind them, they always prevail. What the late confederacy needs to-day is a few such pertinacious men. It needs a Voltaire—maybe a whole herd of Voltaires—to bootleg the rudiments of the enlightenment into the peasants, and so rid them of their superstitions. Its difficulties are largely due to the fact that it depends too much upon help from outside. Ten resolute Tennesseeans, fighting to a finish, might have prevented the indelible disgrace of the Scopes trial. One bold and intelligent editor could almost save Mississippi.

[*Chicago Sunday Tribune*, April 3, 1927]

THE POWERS OF THE AIR

THE HISTORY OF WITCHCRAFT AND DEMONOLOGY, by Montague Summers. $5. 353 pp. New York: *Alfred A. Knopf.*

This tome is learned, honest and amusing. Its author, an English clergyman—his full name is the Rev. Alphonsus Joseph-Mary Augustus Montague, M.A.—wastes no time trying to reconcile religion and science, a folly that has brought so many American scientists, including the eminent Dr. Robert Andrews Millikan, to grief. He is in favor of religion, not of science, and with it, in the manner of a true believer, he goes the whole hog. Does Exodus 22:18 say flatly that witches exist, and that it is the duty of every righteous man to butcher them when found? Then Dr. Summers accepts the fact and the duty without evasion, and proceeds to elaborate on both. He can't imagine a Christian who refuses to believe in demoniacal possession, and no more can I. Marshaling an array of proofs that must shake even an atheistic archbishop, he demonstrates with fine eloquence and impeccable logic that the air is full of sinister spirits, and that it is their constant effort to enter into the bodies of men and women, and so convert good Christians, made in God's image, into witches, sorcerers, spiritualists, biologists and other such revolting shapes. The Bible is the rock of his argument, but he also makes frequent and very effective use of the revelations vouchsafed to Holy Church. There has never been a time in Christian history, he shows, when its chief experts and wiseacres did not believe in demons. The Roman rite, accepting their existence as indubitable, provides elaborate machinery for their scotching to this day. That machinery, to be sure, is not put into effect lightly. So long as the medical faculty is convinced that the patient is suffering from nothing worse than a leaping tapeworm or delirium tremens, and hope of his cure by chemical and mechanical means is thus held out, he is resigned to the secular arm. But once it becomes manifest that a fiend or goblin has got into him, the business becomes a matter for supernatural intervention, and the subsequent proceedings must be carried on by an ordained pastor, and according to a formula set forth in the *Rituale Romanum,* and in use since the pontificate of Peter I.

This formula is extremely complicated, and I suspect that using it must be somewhat fatiguing to the officiating clergyman. He must be himself a man of mature years, guiltless of anything even remotely approaching loose living, and, according to Mr. Summers, "a systematic student, and well versed in the latest trends and developments of psychological science." He is required to make himself quite sure, before he begins his exorcism, that the patient before him is actually possessed by a demon—that he is not confronting a mere case of insanity, or, worse still, imposture. Once convinced, he proceeds with the utmost heat and diligence, never relenting until the unclean spirit takes wing, and so returns to Hell. Mr. Summers gives the words of the exorcism, translated into English; they are so terrifying that I hesitate to reprint them in a magazine designed for reading aloud at the domestic hearth. The demon is denounced in words that sting and wither. Launched upon a merely human sinner, they would undoubtedly shake him up dreadfully. If, at the first attack, they fail to dislodge the demon, they are to be used again, and then again, and so on until the exorcism is completed. The patient, it appears, is apt to fall asleep while they are being intoned: making him do so is one of the Devil's favorite tricks. If it happens, then the exorcist must awaken him, and by any device that seems workable, including physical agitation of his person. Ordinarily, all this must be done in a church, but if the patient is too ill to leave his bed the exorcist may visit him in his own home. Idle spectators are forbidden, but the canon requires that a number of official witnesses, of known piety and sober mien, shall be present. There is no provision for failure. In case the demon proves recalcitrant to-day, he is to be tackled again to-morrow. No unnecessary conversation with him is permitted. If he speaks through the mouth of the patient, he is to be heard politely, but when he has had a sufficient say he is to be shut off. In particular, he is not to be permitted to indulge in ribaldries.

It is commonly believed that Protestantism questions the actuality of demoniacal possession, but this is not so. True enough, the Unitarians and Universalists have doubts about it, but so far as I am aware no other Protestant sect has ever formally repudiated it. There is a canon of the Church of England which forbids a priest to exorcise demons without the "license or direction (*mandatum*)" of his Bishop, but there is nothing to prevent a Bishop issuing such a *mandatum*. If Bishop Manning became convinced to-morrow that Heywood Broun or Sinclair Lewis or any other such antinomian was possessed, he could, I believe, give Dr. William N. Guthrie a *mandatum* to exorcise the invading gaseous organism. I do not allege that Dr. Manning would do it or that Dr. Guthrie would take advantage of the license; all I argue is that the transaction would lie within the confines of canon law. The Lutherans all believe in demoniacal possession, and hence, by a necessary inference, in witches; if they did not they would have to put Martin Luther down as a liar. As for the Methodists, the Baptists and other such proletarians of the Lord, it must be obvious that doubts among them are confined to a few advanced intellectuals, debauched by reading the epicurean poetry of Edgar A. Guest. The Baptists, at least in the South, even believe in ghosts, especially the colored brethren. The colored pastors have an elaborate ceremonial for exorcising all varieties of spirits, good or evil; an important part of it is the free-will offering just before the curative anathema is launched. In my own native republic, the Saorstát Maryland, I once made an attempt to ascertain the number of people, regardless of creed, who believed in ghosts and witches. After elaborate inquiries through prudent agents, I came to the conclusion that 92 per cent of the population believed in ghosts, and that 74 per cent also believed in witches. In the latter group was the then Governor of the State. He believed that rheumatism was caused by witchcraft, and wore a string around his middle to ward it off. The Marylanders are a gay and liberty-loving people, and drink, perhaps, somewhat more than is good for them, but atheism has never made much progress among them. At least one of the eminent professors in the Johns Hopkins Medical School has been publicly accused of believing in witches, and has never, so far as I know, denied it. He is a Fundamentalist, and accepts the Bible from cover to cover. He is too honest a man to cherish any mental reservations about Exodus 22:18.

Dr. Summers is equally honest, and I think he deserves all praise for being so. Most ecclesiastics, when they write upon such subjects, try to evade the clear issue. They seem to be convinced—on what ground I don't know—that the old belief in demons is now dying out in the world, and to be afraid that they will be laughed at if they confess to it. All I can say is that that is a poor way to get into Heaven *post mortem*. Such duckers and skulkers, you may be sure, will have extremely unpleasant sessions with St. Peter when they reach the Gates, and Peter will be well justified in razzing them. Either the Christian religion involves a belief in disembodied powers, good and evil, or it doesn't. If it doesn't, then its Sacred Scriptures are a mass of nonsense, and even its Founder was grossly misinformed. If it does, then everyone adhering to it ought to confess the fact frankly, and without ignominious equivocation. This is what Dr. Summers does. In detail, his colleagues in theology may sometimes seasonably challenge him, as when, for example, he lays down the doctrine that the heaving of tables at spiritualist séances is performed by demons from Hell. But his fundamental postulates stand beyond refutation. If he is wrong, then the whole science of theology is an imposture—something which no right-thinking, law-abiding, home-loving American, I am sure, will want to allege. I rejoice to find a holy man so forthright and courageous, and so irresistibly convincing. He has rescued demonology from its long neglect, and restored it to its old high place among the sacred sciences. What a knock-out he would be on an American lecture tour! I offer him $1,000 in advance for his Jackson, Miss., house, with an offer of the fattest pastorate in the town thrown in.

[*American Mercury,* May 1927]

SCIENCE AND THEOLOGY

THE RELIGION OF SCIENTISTS, edited by C. L. Drawbridge. $1.25.
160 pp. New York: *The Macmillan Company.*

The Rev. Mr. Drawbridge (whose ecclesiastical character is nowhere mentioned in the present book) is the secretary of the Christian Evidence Society (London), and the author of many volumes of Christian apologetics, *e.g., Popular Attacks on Christianity, Common Objections to Christianity, The War and Christian Ideals* and *Anti-Christian Socialism.* It occurred to him some time ago that it would be a good idea to poll the fellows of the British Royal Society, and find out how their minds were running on the subject of religion. He had heard, it appeared, that a good many scientific men, shaken by the revolutionary notions of Professors Planck and Einstein, were throwing off the innocent agnosticism that Thomas Henry Huxley had spread in their fraternity, and coming back to the faith of their grandfathers. So he got up a questionnaire, and sent it to all the fellows of the Society, including the fifty foreign fellows, but excluding the Royal Princes. Two hundred of them sent in replies, and 122 authorized him to use their names.

These replies gave great comfort to the Rev. Mr. Drawbridge, and he here passes them on to a candid world. Of the 180 learned men who answered his inquiry about the freedom of the will, 173 said that they thought it was more or less free, and only 7 that they thought it was not. A hundred and forty-three out of 149 told him that they saw no conflict between a belief in evolution and a belief in a Creator. On the question of a personal God, 26 said nay, but 103 were either for the affirmative or on the fence. Finally, coming to survival after death, the crown and corner-stone of Christian theology, 47 said that they did not believe in it, 41 that they did, and 112 "either did not state what their belief is, or said they were uncertain upon the point." All of which convinced Mr. Drawbridge that "men of science are at least as religious as other men," and this belief he sets forth in the last chapter of his little book. To it he adds the somewhat irrelevant corollary that "they are not frivolous and pleasure-loving," but "sympathize most with those who take life seriously and live unselfishly."

The rev. gentleman's conclusions will no doubt be soothing to many persons of his own general cast of mind, but I find myself in considerable doubt that they really prove anything. For one thing, he failed to squeeze answers from *all* the fellows of the Royal Society, and there are two good reasons for believing that those who *did* answer were selected out by the test of piety, and represented, on the whole, the more devout wing. The first of these reasons is that every man he addressed knew that he was a clergryman actively engaged in Christian propaganda—and the pious would obviously be more likely than the infidels to be polite to him. The second is that the pious would have definite beliefs and be eager to expound and justify them, whereas many, and perhaps most of the infidels would have too little interest in the subject to want to put their ideas into words. Mr. Drawbridge's own evidence bears out both of these surmises. On the one hand, his list sh ... a marked representation of notoriously devout scientists, *e.g.,* Professor J. S. Haldane and Sir Oliver Lodge, and a suspicious sprinkling of "scientists" who are such only by courtesy, *e.g.,* the Bishop of Birmingham; and on the other hand it shows that not a few of the skeptics viewed the whole inquiry as vain and foolish, and said so plainly, sometimes in very tart words. Thus the returns were heavily loaded before they came in, and about all they prove is that among scientists and quasi-scientists who lean somewhat toward religion there is something of a leaning toward religion.

But even more important is the fact that the rev. gentleman's questions, at least in large part, scarcely put the matter clearly and fairly. The first of them, for example, was Do you credit the existence of a spiritual domain?

Some of the brethren answered simply (and quite accurately) that the question was vague and meaningless, but others showed by their replies that they confused the domain of mere consciousness with the domain of what the theologians call spirit. The two things are wholly unlike, and yet many who answered yes to consciousness are counted as answering yes to spirit, whatever that may be. For example, Professor Frederick Soddy, the Oxford chemist, who says "I suppose 'I' am the 'spiritual domain'," and an unnamed "fellow of the Institute of Physics," who says, "It is the only thing I do credit, for thought and feeling—both spiritual—are all I know of directly." No wonder 121 of the fellows "answered in the affirmative"! The only ones who answered in the negative, in fact, seem to be those who, despite their unfamiliarity with theology, saw at once the difference between "a spiritual domain" and simple consciousness.

I do not accuse the Rev. Mr. Drawbridge of attempting to bamboozle his laboratory animals: the truth is that he seems to be confused in his own mind. When he comes to free will he is confused even more sadly, for at once he seems to mistake it for free thought. "If men possess no freedom of initiative," he says gravely, "there is no such thing as freedom of thought." But this is nonsense, and Henry Sidgwick disposed of it many years ago—in fact, in 1874, when Mr. Drawbridge was only six years old. I may plan a course of action freely and desire fervently to carry it out, but my resolution may be completely insufficient for the business. If that were not true, there would be no regret and remorse in this world, and little dread. For it is the sad experience of every man that the noble actions he is dissuaded from by the pressure of his environment are as naught compared to the noble actions he is dissuaded from by his own weakness and lack of will. Most of Mr. Drawbridge's scientists, I suspect, had freedom of thought in mind when they voted for freedom of the will, and so their answers are of little significance. A few of them, seeing the dichotomy in the question, dismissed the problem of the will as insoluble, as indeed it probably is. It belongs properly to metaphysics, not to science.

It is curious to note how the fellows divided according to their *Fächer*. The number heard from was too small, of course, to justify any serious generalizations, but certainly it can't be without significance that the five physiologists who replied unequivocally to the question about survival after death were all against it, whereas eight of the nine physicists favored it. Why physicists, as a class, should be more religiously inclined than other men of science is hard to make out, but the fact seems to be undeniable. Whenever one of the recurrent campaigns is under way to reconcile religion and science, physicists are always in the forefront of the fray. I need point only to Sir Oliver Lodge in England and to Dr. Robett A. Millikan in the United States. One never hears of a physiologist or a pathologist mounting a Methodist pulpit and assuring the customers that there is nothing in *The Descent of Man* to shatter their hope of becoming angels when they die, but physicists often do it, at the same time emitting loud hosannahs. I once attempted to account for this phenomenon on the ground that they deal habitually with things either too small to be seen or too large to be grasped, and that they are thus seduced into some sort of acceptance of St. Paul's definition of faith. But the explanation is plainly somewhat defective. The physiologists and pathologists also deal, at least in large part, with invisible things, and yet they show a hearty skepticism, and do not commonly frequent the communion table. The whole biological faculty, indeed, is inclined toward infidelity. Its members are probably far too familiar with man the mammal to cherish any belief that he has an immortal soul, and will sit upon the right hand of God *post mortem*. When one hears of a graduate of the dissecting-room who credits such wonders it always turns out that he is not a laboratory man, but a practising physician or surgeon, which is to say, much less a scientist than an artist.

The Rev. Mr. Drawbridge's book, as I have said, proves little if anything that was not known before; nevertheless, it serves the useful purpose of recalling that common knowledge to the common attention. For one, I find it instructive and exhilarating to observe that no less than forty-seven fellows of the Royal Society still believe innocently that they have immortal souls, and will be transported to some fairer realm when they die. Forty-one reject the miracle as incredible, and a hundred and twelve are in doubt, but forty-seven profess to be sure—fifty years after Darwin and thirty-seven after Huxley! This belief, to me at least, is one of the most fantastic ever cherished by presumably civilized men. I see no difficulty in believing in a personal God—not, of course, the brummagem police sergeant of the Christian proletariat, but a hard-working, honest and not too intelligent Overseer of our miserable rat-hole in the cosmos, beset heavily day and night by the arbitrary and ill-natured mandates of gods still higher. Nor am I repelled by the concept of a moral order of the world—that is, so long as I am permitted to criticize it as inequitable and irrational. As for the freedom of the human will, with its implication of human responsibility, I find that I must admit it as a metaphysical necessity, though it cannot be demonstrated as a scientific fact. But when it comes to the immortality of the soul, whatever that may mean precisely, I can only say that it seems to me to be wholly incredible and preposterous. There is not only no plausible evidence for it: there is a huge mass of irrefutable evidence against it, and that evidence increases in weight and cogency every time a theologian opens his mouth.

All of the common arguments for survival after death may be reduced to four. The first is logical and is to the effect that it would be impossible to imagine God creating so noble a beast as man, and then letting him die after a few unpleasant years on earth. The answer is simple: I can imagine it, and so can many other men. Moreover, there is no reason to believe that God regards man as noble: on the contrary, all the available theological testimony runs the other way. The second argument is that a belief in immortality is universal in mankind, and that its very universality is ample proof of its truth. The answer is (a) that many men actually dissent, some of them in a very violent and ribald manner, and (b) that even if all men said aye it would prove nothing, for all men once said aye to the existence of witches. The third argument is that the dead, speaking through the mouths of gifted mediums, frequently communicate with the living, and must thus be alive themselves. Unfortunately, the evidence for this is so dubious that it takes a special kind of mind to credit it, and that kind of mind is far from persuasive. The fourth and final argument is based frankly on revelation: the soul is immortal because God hath said it is.

I confess that this last argument seems to me to be rather more respectable than any of the others: it at least makes no silly attempt to lug in the methods of science to prove a proposition in theology. But all the same there are plenty of obvious holes in it. Its proponents get into serious difficulties when they undertake to say when and how the soul gets into the body, and where it comes from. Must it be specially created in each instance, or is it the offspring of the two parent souls? In either case, when does it appear, at the moment of conception or somewhat later? If the former, then what happens to the soul of a zygote cast out, say, an hour after fertilization? If the death of that soul ensues, then the soul is not immortal in all cases, which means that its immortality can be certain in none; and if, on the contrary, it goes to Heaven or Hell or some vague realm between, then we are asked to believe that the bishops and arch-bishops who swarm beyond the grave are forced to associate, and on terms of equality, with shapes that can neither think nor speak, and resemble tad-poles far more than they resemble Christians. And if it be answered that all souls, after death, develop to the same point and shed all the characters of the flesh, then every imaginable scheme of *post-mortem* jurisprudence becomes ridiculous.

The assumption that the soul enters the body at some time after con-ception opens difficulties quite as serious, but I shall not annoy you with them in this hot weather. Suffice it to say that it forces one to believe either that there is a time when a human embryo, though it is alive, is not really a human being, or that a human being can exist without a soul. Both notions revolt me—the first as a student of biology, and the second as a dutiful subject of a great Christian state. The answers of the professional theologians are all inadequate. The Catholics try to get rid of the problem by consigning the souls of the unbaptized to a Limbus Infantium which is neither Heaven nor Hell, but that is only a begging of the question. As for the Protestants, they commonly refuse to discuss it at all. Their position seems to be that everyone ought to believe in the immortality of the soul as a matter of common decency, and that, when one has got that far, the details are irrelevant. But my appetite for details continues to plague me. I am naturally full of curiosity about a doctrine which, if it can be shown to be true, is of the utmost personal importance to me. Failing light, I go on believing dismally that when the bells ring and the cannon are fired, and people go rushing about frantic with grief, and my mortal clay is stuffed for the National Museum at Washington, it will be the veritable end of the noble and lovely creature once answering to the name of Henry.

[*American Mercury*, September 1932]

VIII

RELIGION AND POLITICS

ON RELIGION IN POLITICS

I

The Ku Klux Klan being in decay in New Jersey, its enemies now propose to finish it by passing a law making it a misdemeanor to discuss the religion of a candidate in a political campaign. The scheme obviously collides with the First Amendment to the Constitution, but that, of course, is no impediment to it. The First Amendment was blown up during the late war and is now only a wreck, just as the Fourth, Fifth and Sixth Amendments have been blown up by the Volstead act. No one now expects the courts, and especially the Federal courts, to pay any attention to the Bill of Rights. When they mention it at all, it is usually only to argue that it doesn't mean what it plainly says. Judicial cabalism has reduced it to merely historical interest, and any defendant who pleads it confesses thereby that he is extremely romantic, perhaps to the verge of the pathological.

Thus the constitutional objection to the proposed statute need not detain us. The great jurisconsults who adorn the bench of New Jersey may be trusted to dispose of it without difficulty, and if they fail their brethren of the Federal rite will come to their aid. There remains the more formidable objection that such a law could no more be enforced than the Volstead act, and that every effort to enforce it would only magnify the ill-feelings it is designed to abate—that the business of hunting Catholics, now pursued by the Klan and its allies as a mere luxury, would be converted instantly into a matter of right. That right would lie, not in frail Bills of Rights, but in fundamental and immovable common sense. The law of nature would come to the rescue of the busted *lex scripta,* and every man of decent self-respect would be converted into a Klansman.

II

I see no escape from this notion. When a man offers himself as a candidate for public office, I am either free, as a citizen appealed to for my vote, to say plainly what I think of him, or I am not free. If I am free, then every other citizen is free, and it is possible for the citizenry in general, by taking counsel together, to determine the candidate's virtues and so either elect him or reject him. If I am not free, then no such determination is possible, and the whole democratic process is reduced to vanity and futility. As everyone knows, the theory of my freedom is deeply imbedded in American law. Even lawyers, who are, as a class, bitter enemies of every human right, grant it as axiomatic. Even judges, who are simply lawyers turned loose upon the community, with a franchise to inflict their professional prejudices and superstitions upon all the rest of us—even judges, in their construction of the law of libel, have almost unanimously held that I have a clear right to say my say about any man who asks me publicly for my vote, and that my freedom is immensely wider than if he were a private man.

Well, if I have that right and it is fundamental and inalienable, why shouldn't it play upon a candidate's religion as freely as it plays, say, upon his economic ideas or his patriotism? His religion, in fact, may be the most important element in his composition. It may color all his thought, ghostly and secular. I say it may; in more than one concrete instance I know positively that it does. And not infrequently I know that the fact is of capital significance. In the present situation of the Prohibition combat, with the Methodist Church irrevocably committed to alliance with the blacklegs and blackmailers of "enforcement," I'd certainly be an idiot to vote for a candidate for Congress who was a good Methodist. And if birth control were an active issue in politics, I'd be an equal idiot to vote for a candidate who was a good Catholic.

This is surely not religious prejudice, in any rational sense. I have nothing against Methodist theology or Catholic theology as such, save what may be stated in polite and purely logical terms. But I have a bitter and implacable prejudice against any and every effort to write either theology into the law of the land, and so make it binding upon men who disbelieve in it. It is my right as a citizen to oppose such efforts, and my equally clear right to say plainly why I am against them.

III

The common doctrine that religious ideas have a sacrosanct character and are not to be discussed freely and realistically, even when they take the form of schemes to oppress and intimidate those who reject them—in this doctrine I can see nothing save a hollow bombast. Whenever it is entertained human progress is immensely retarded. Nor is there any appreciable gain for religion itself. It becomes the common enemy of all enlightened men, and soon or late, watching their chance, they rise against it and try to destroy it utterly. History is full of examples—and there is not a single compensatory example, at least in civilization, of a theocracy that has endured.

To swathe religion in immunities, either by law or by custom, is simply to prepare the way for its corruption and destruction. Its agents, so protected, invariably lose their heads and make themselves nuisances. However discreetly they may begin, the lack of challenge eventually makes them bold, and in the end they have to be overthrown by force, and their religion commonly goes with them. Observe, for instance, the present state of the Methodist Church in the United States. Is it in higher or in lower repute than it was before its elders began wielding the club of Prohibition? Is it safer or less safe? I think the answer must be plain, even to a Methodist bishop.

The Methodists would be better off today if there had been no conventional immunity to shield them in the first days of their ill-advised jehad. Open criticism, though it might not have fetched the fanatics among them, would at least have fetched the moderate men, and so the church would have been saved from its present scandalous estate. But there was a rule against attacking a religious organization as such, and the Methodist Church went headlong into lamentable excesses. Now, in sheer self-defense, fair men have had to suspend that rule. The result is that there is a rising wave of bitterness, and that the church, in the long run, is bound to be badly punished. This punishment will injure what is good in it quite as certainly as what is bad. The Methodist who is a sincere Christian, with no hatred in his heart for his fellow-men, will be mauled along with the Wayne Wheelers, Andersons, Crabbes, Upshaws and other such mountebanks.

IV

The remedy against the extravagances of the Ku Klux Klan is not to attempt to deprive its members of their plain rights, but to bring home to them, and to their ecclesiastical backers, a just retribution. Let them be hoist with their own petard. They pretend to be alarmed by the doings of the Catholic Church, and perhaps, here and there, they have some reason to be. But what about the doings of the evangelical churches? It seems to me that they are far worse than anything ever brought home to the Catholic Church in this country, and quite as bad as some of the crimes falsely laid to it.

The evangelical churches, in fact, are rapidly becoming public nuisances. Neglecting almost altogether their old concern about individual salvation, they have converted themselves into vast engines for harassing and oppressing persons who dissent from their naïve and often preposterous theology. No one hears of them saving souls any more; they seem to devote their whole energies to getting bodies into jail. To achieve this grossly un-Christian and anti-social end they have made corrupt alliances with dishonest and degraded politicians, and even more sinister alliances with blackmailers, perjurers and gunmen. One contemplates with a shock the spectacle of a Christian church, through its highest officers, consorting with every sort of criminal and actually advocating murder.

Nor is this all. Not content with setting spies and ruffians upon all who reject their pretension to infallibility in ethics, the Ku Klux klergy now set themselves up as popes in philosophy, and in a dozen States they strive to proscribe the scientific knowledge that is the chief glory of the modern world. Because bucolic Baptist pastors cannot understand it, the hypothesis of evolution is to be put down by law. What if they succeed? Then it will become a crime in America to know more than a Baptist pastor knows, as it is already a crime to practise the social amenities that he is incapable of. Then all Americans will be divided into two classes: slaves in the Methodist-Baptist pen, and fugitives from justice.

Plainly, it is nonsense, in the face of such enterprises, to argue that religion shall not be made a political issue. It is already a political issue, and it will remain so until those whose maniacal frenzy made it so are reduced to impotence and silence. Until that time comes it is the right and duty of every citizen to scrutinize carefully the religious ideas and affiliations of every candidate for office, and I believe that it is also his right and duty to denounce them when they seem to him to be dangerous.

[*Baltimore Evening Sun,* December 7, 1925]

DEMOCRACY AND THEOCRACY

Congress shall make no law respecting an establishment of religion, or prohibiting . . . But you know the rest of the First Amendment—that is, if you are not a Methodist bishop or a Federal judge—quite as well as I do. The purport, though not the letter, of its first two strophes is that every free-born Americano shall stand clear of ecclesiastical domination, and be at liberty to serve, dodge or bamboozle Omnipotence by whatever devices appeal to his taste, or his lack of it. As the common phrase has it, church and state are separate in the Federal Union, with the province of each plainly marked out, and each forbidden to invade the province of the other. But in the common phrase, as usual, there is only wind.

The fact is that the United States, save for a short while in its infancy, while the primal infidels survived, has always diluted democracy with theocracy. Practically all our political campaigns have resolved themselves into witch-hunts by the consecrated, and all our wars have been fought to hymn tunes. It remains so to this day, despite the murrain of jazz and gin. The event of November 6[1] will be determined, not on political grounds, nor even on economic grounds, but mainly if not solely on theological grounds. The chief figures in the combat, for all the roaring of politicians in the foreground, are bishops and presbyters, and they have at their opponents with all the traditional ferocity of ambassadors of Christ. The thing to be decided by the plebiscite, as the typical American voter is taught to see it, is whether one gang of these holy men shall continue to run the country, or whether they shall be unhorsed and another gang put in their place.

All this, it appears, is deplored by the judicious. There are many demands that the chief sacerdotal whoopers lie down and be still. Even in the Hookworm Belt, where skeptics are as rare as monogamists on Long

Island, the Baptist pastors are being urged to abate their fury, and consider the nigger question and the Beatitudes. And on the other side, unless circumstantial evidence is worthless, there is a powerful effort to hold hot-blooded young priests in check, and so prevent them making a bad situation worse. But why should it be considered bad? What is the objection to religious men taking religion seriously? I can find none in the books. Why should they not prefer, when a free choice is before them, to be governed by men holding to their own peculiar comforts and certainties, and doomed to sweat with them forever in the same Hell?

Is it a trivial matter? An irrelevant matter? Surely not to true believers. Surely not to earnest Christians. Myself completely neutral in theology, and long ago resigned to damnation, I can afford to treat it with easy philosophy. I'd as lief vote for a Catholic as for a Presbyterian; I'd as lief vote for a Quaker as for an Episcopalian—though Quakers, I confess, are almost too much for me: it takes nine Jews, six Armenians or two Greeks to undo one. I'd call it a red-letter day if the chance ever offered to vote for a Moslem, a Holy Roller, a Spiritualist or a worm-feed, caterpiller-tread, chigger-proof, poppet-valved Lutheran of the Missouri Synod. Even my objection to Baptists is not theological. They have John the Baptist on their side when they duck their customers: the thing I object to is their doctrine that what is good enough to purge the soul is good enough to drink. (What a sect they would be if they abandoned creeks and cow-ponds and set up vats of Pilsner!) But though I am thus happily neutral and lost, it seems to me to be quite clear that the average American remains a partisan. The theological inclinations of his forebears linger in him, though they may be buried in his unconscious. He distrusts all revelations save one. Even when, debauched by reading Tom Paine, Ingersoll and Haldeman-Julius, he comes out boldly for evolution and boasts that his grandfather was a chimpanzee, it is with reservations. Hating all the warring sects, he always hates one of them more than the rest. And to the extent of that superior hatred he remains a faithful and orthodox Christian.

Four Americans out of every five fall under this heading—perhaps even nine out of ten. The proof of it lies in the fact that every American community, large or small, continues to have its local *shaman*, admired, deferred to and revered. His pronunciamentoes are heard with grave respect. The town newspapers treat him politely. He is to the fore in all public orgies. His moral ideas, though they may be challenged, prevail. In the South he is the Baptist parson; in the Middle West he is the Methodist or some other. Coming to big towns, he is commonly a bishop, and hence able to bind and loose. Nowhere in this great land is he missing. Do I forget such Babylons as New York? Specifically, I include New York. Where else (save maybe in Boston) do all the high dignitaries of the local government drop to their knees to kiss an archepiscopal ring?

II

Thus it must be plain that the United States remains a realm of faith, and that religious questions belong properly to its public life. If they are discussed hotly, then it is only proof that Americans hold them to be important. If they smother and shut off the discussion of other questions, then it only shows that no other question is so well worth discussing.

I can see no possible objection to estimating a man by his religion, or by his lack of it. We all do it every day, and experience supports the soundness of the test. There is in all Jews, despite a great play of variation, a common quality, universally recognized. There is a like common quality in all Catholics, in all Presbyterians, in all Methodists and Baptists, in all Lutherans and in all skeptics. Relying upon its existence, we are seldom disappointed. It would be as shocking for a Catholic to react like a Methodist as it would be for a Jew to react like a Holy Roller. When, as happens rarely, God sends the marvel, it always draws a full house. I point to the case of my old friend, Col. Patrick H. Callahan, of Louisville, Ky., a Catholic Prohibitionist, *i.e.*, a Catholic with a Methodist liver. More than once, encountering him in palaver with his fellow drys, I have observed their uneasiness. They welcome his support, and that of his 234 followers, but they feel that there is something unnatural, and hence something a bit sinister about it. They half expect him to produce a bowie knife and begin slitting their throats in the name of the Pope. If, suddenly turning Methodist altogether, he were to loose a hallelujah, nine-tenths of them would run.

The religious label, in truth, tells more about a given man than any other label, and what it tells is more apposite and momentous. All the other classifications that the art of politics attempts are artificial and unsound. The difference between honest politicians and those who have been caught is no more than a difference in bookkeping. Plutocrats and proletarians are brothers, pursuing with equal frenzy the same dollar. Even the gap separating city men from yokels is easily bridged, at least in one direction: half the bootleggers of New York, like half the bank presidents, were born on farms. But it takes a tremendous rubbing to get the theological label off, and even then its mark remains. Convert a High Church Episcopalian to baptism by total immersion, and he still revolts queasily against going into the tank with his fellow Baptists. Turn a Jew into an Episcopalian, and he becomes five times as Jewish as he was before. Make a Catholic of a Methodist, and he has a dreadful time keeping quiet at mass.

These differences ought to be acknowledged, taken account of, and even encouraged, not denied and concealed. They help to make life various and amusing. If Al and Lord Hoover were both sound Presbyterians, the present campaign would be as dull and witless as a love affair between a deaf girl and a blind man. It is their irreconcilable differentiation that now makes the Republic roar, and entertains a candid world. For religious disparities and enmities, being real, cannot be disposed of by weasel words. They crash through the thickest ramparts of politeness, and set off lovely sky-rockets. They have caused all the bloodiest wars of the past, and, properly encouraged in America, they will make for bigger and better campaigns. I protest formally against every effort to dispose of them.

III

Even those idealists who conscientiousiy deplore them—and for such opponents I have all due respect, as I have for psychic researchers, theosophists and believers in international peace—even sincere lamenters of the current fuming and fury must admit that the combat between the Ku Klux clergy and Holy Church may well achieve some salubrious effects. Each side indulges in arguments that have a pleasing persuasiveness to neutrals. On the one hand the Baptist and Methodist brethren seek to prove that a church pretending to secular authority is dangerous to free government; on the other hand the spokesmen of Holy Church argue that intolerance is a villainous pox, and discreditable to civilized man.

I can only say that I hope both sides prevail, up to and including the hilt. If they convince everybody, then there will be an uprising the next time a Catholic archbishop orders the police to put down birth-controllers, and another and greater uprising the next time a Methodist bishop attempts to blackjack a State Legislature. The antagonists argue well, and especially the Ku Kluxers. Their proofs that it would be impolitic to let the College of Cardinals run the United States are logically unanswerable. But the more they prove their case against the College of Cardinals, the more they raise up doubts about the Anti-Saloon League, the Methodist Board of Temperance, Prohibition and Public Morals, and all the other bands of prehensile theologians who now impose their superstitions upon the rest of us.

Thus good may flow out of what is deplored as evil. I insist, however, that it is really good. In a country so hag-ridden by fraud and bombast as this one, *any*thing is good that makes for an honest and unfettered exchange of opinion. Men are surely not at their worst when they say what they actually think, even when it is shocking to their neighbors. Our basic trouble in the United States is that nearly all our public discussion is carried on in terms of humbug, and by professional hypocrites. The typical American statesman for a decade past has been a Prohibitionist with a red nose. Certainly it can do no harm to go behind that obscene imposture to the fundamental realities, and trot them out for an airing. So I rejoice to see men deciding against Al on the frank ground that he is a Catholic, and I rejoice even more to see other men preparing to vote for him on the frank ground that they are tired of being ruled by a rabble of Baptist and Methodist witch burners.

[*American Mercury,* October 1928]

OVERTURE TO A MELODRAMA

I

No one, I take it, was surprised when news came from Washington, a week or so ago, that Monsignor James Cannon, Jr., D.D., had landed there with blood in his episcopal eye, and was preparing to raise what, for want of a prettier name, is called hell. This ferocious ambassador of Christ will have a front seat in Washington hereafter, and it will be his by right, and by favor. For the great moral victory last November was his quite as much as it was Dr. Hoover's—quite as much, and perhaps a shade more. He was the master theologian of the campaign, and carried out his complex and ghostly duties with great skill. He will remain head of the theological department during his colleague's four years as President.

This theological department is now an integral and important part of the American governmental structure. Whether for good or for evil, the old sharp separation of church and state has been definitely abandoned. The Eighteenth Amendment was fastened upon the Constitution, not as a political measure and by political devices, nor even as a moral measure and by moral devices, but as an almost purely theological measure and by devices borrowed from the camp-meeting. Its adoption was advocated and obtained, not by lawyers or sociologists or professors of political science, but by the embattled Christians of the more bucolic sects, functioning as such. And it is suppoorted to-day by the same naïve sectarians, not on logical grounds, but on strictly dogmatic grounds—in other words, as an article of faith.

This fact, of course, is often obscured by the controversy which now rages. When the amendment is attacked on logical grounds, its advocates try to defend it on the same grounds. But they always fail, for logic is not their oyster. Failing, they shift quickly to theology, which is. The typical Prohibitionist is not in favor of Prohibition because he thinks it works secular benefits; he doesn't care whether it does or doesn't. He is in favor of it simply because his pastor has convinced him that it is ordained of God— that going against it is a mortal sin. The Eighteenth Amendment, as he sees it, is not something that can be changed, as Article 1, Section 3, of the original Constitution was changed.[2] It is something complete, perfect, sacrosanct and immutable. All who oppose it, however politely, are damned and will go to Hell.

II

It is important to remember all this, for its obvious meaning is that there is now a state church in the United States, and that every public job-holder, including especially the President, is a sort of minor ecclesiastic. As such he is naturally subject to his spiritual superiors, and at the moment the most eminent and puissant of them is the Monsignor Cannon aforesaid. His powers, as yet, lack statutory definition, but in all essentials they are plain enough. He is, in all matters affecting the Eighteenth Amendment, whether directly or indirectly, the final and absolute authority. When he speaks *ex cathedra* his authority is precisely that of the Pope. And whenever he speaks, he speaks *ex cathedra*.

His puissance, in truth, really runs far ahead of the Pope's. The Pope is supreme and infallible in the realms of faith and morals, but outside he is only an ordinary man. If he essayed to order the Catholics of the United States to vote for this or that candidate for office, they would be under no obligation to obey him. They might even, with perfect legality, tell him to mind his transcendental business. But Monsignor Cannon can venture into such fields with perfect impunity. It is his chief function, indeed, to venture into them, and it was by doing so in the interest of Dr. Hoover that he attained to his present lofty position as primate of the established church.

True enough, he still lacks the means of enforcing all his mandates, but that will follow soon enough. Congress will give him practically anything he wants, and if Congress fails him the Supreme Court will help him out. Already he preaches the bold doctrine that anyone who flouts the Eighteenth Amendment—which is to say, anyone who flouts his own authority—is a bad American, and perhaps even no American at all. It necessarily follows from what has gone before. And from it in turn flows the doctrine that the only real Americans are those who accept his orders, willingly and abjectly—to wit, baptized and faithful members of the new state church. The rest of us are simply subjects of the United States.

III

Our position, in fact, is not quite that of subjects; rather we are in the situation of enemy aliens in time of war. That is to say, we have no definite rights at all. Any outrage against us, however extravagant, may be supported by some provision of the Volstead act or some decision of the Supreme Court. The minor ecclesiastics that I have mentioned are free to deprive us, at their will and inclination, of all the guarantees of the Bill of Rights. They may raid us, chase us, invade us, assault us, lock us up. If we resist, or they think we plan to resist, they may shoot us forthwith. And if our heirs, being heretics, demand justice, they will get it in the nearest United States court, with a judge passed by the Anti-Saloon League on the bench and the district attorney, at the public expense, defending the murderer!

The plain man, contemplating all this and much more like it, is amazed and disquieted. He feels that there is something wrong, perhaps even something immoral. It is simply because he is not trained in the science of theology. To a theologian nothing can be wrong or immoral that defends the true faith, and no measure against a heretic who menaces it can go too far. If he happens to be a humane man, he may regret having to hurt the fellow, but it is not often that he is humane. Mostly he is in favor of war *à outrance,* for what he beholds before him is not a mere heretic, but all the horrible hosts of Hell.

If we would understand the faithful who accept Monsignor Cannon as the American Pontifex Maximus, we must remember this. They see us, not as the victims of an unfortunate habit that will cause us to beat our wives, butcher our children and end on the gallows, but as something far worse. They see us as scoundrelly scoffers at the holy Word of God, revealed by His inspired prophets and confidants. Every time we blow off the foam they shrink as from a hideous blasphemy. Every time we knock off a cocktail they flee as from Beelzebub. No wonder they reach for their fowling-pieces when we talk of our rights! Has any man a right to defy the Holy Ghost?

IV

The *Evening Sunpaper,* of late, has been marvelling at some of the doings of Monsignor Crabbe, bishop of Maryland *in partibus infidelium.* He has, it appears, indulged in various violations of the local *mores.* Worse, he has brought in a shyster politician from Indiana, a corrupt and degraded State, to defend them. The *Evening Sunpaper* has likewise marvelled at the proceedings of ecclesiastics of the establishment elsewhere, notably in Michigan, where they have performed a barbarous war-dance over a poor woman sent to prison for life for harboring a pint of gin.

But I see nothing in such phenomena to lift the eyebrow. They are the veriest commonplaces of theology. What ails the *Evening Sunpaper* is its curious ignorance of that grand science. It should know that to a theologian a deliberate flouting of any of the dogmas he subscribes to is a crime of an especially virulent and heinous variety, and not at all comparable to ordinary crimes. He is willing to condone almost anything else in order to get rid of it. And most of the things he is willing to condone he is also willing to commit. If he is not, then he is no theologian.

Dr. Crabbe, Dr. Cannon and the rest of the hierarchy belong authentically to the faculty; they have true vocations. It would be as idiotic to protest against their ferocity as it would be to protest against the ferocity of soldiers in time of war. They got to their present high dignities by exer-

cising it, to the comfort and consolation of the faithful; they are professionally ferocious. Nor would it be sensible to try to argue them out of the
dogmas which inspire it. They do not subscribe to those dogmas evidentially; they cherish them as matters of faith.

I look forward with great joy to Dr. Hoover's transactions with these
consecrated brethren. If he turns them loose, there will be a dreadul car-
nage, with the Bill of Rights buried beneath a pyramid of arms, legs, ears,
noses and eyes. And if he tries to curb them, there will be the gaudiest
uproar ever heard in a Christian land. In either case it will be a good show.

[*Baltimore Evening Sun,* January 28, 1929]

THE PASTOR AS STATESMAN

One hears on all sides that it is a sort of treason for gentlemen in holy orders
to engage in politics. The Catholics and Liberals—strange bed-fellows!—
damn Monsignor Cannon and his friends for arousing the Confederate
anthropoidæ against Al Smith, and the Methodists and Baptists whoop
against the Catholic brethren for admiring him, praying for him and turning
out the very nuns in their convents to vote for him. It all has a virtuous and
plausible smack, but it is probably mainly nonsense at bottom. There is, in
fact, no sound reason why a professional agent of God, confronting a political question with a moral flavor, should not have his say about it. He is
admittedly an expert in morals: even those who oppose his entrance into
politics do so on the ground that he should stick to his last. Well, if he is an
expert, then why shouldn't he be heard when a moral question is before the
voters? Would it be considered improper, if an engineering question engaged
them, for engineers to offer them advice? Or for medical men to counsel
them on a health question? If not, then it is plainly competent for the rev.
clergy to urge and admonish them when it comes to a question of morals.

The real objection, of course, does not lie here; it lies in the fact that
clergymen, whenever their expertness in morals is put to a concrete test,
turn out to be dreadful duffers. It was certainly so during the last campaign.
Consider calmly what Dr. Cannon and his colleagues taught their customers. In brief, it was that   .g a glass of wine with dinner or a pony
of whiskey before retiring was a gross and intolerable crime, not only
against the Republic but also against God—but that luring another man

into committing it and then turning him over to be punished savagely was an act of Christian merit; nay, that it was virtuous, in procuring his punishment, to spy cravenly upon him, to raid and wreck his house, to do him grievous bodily injury, and even to take his life. The worst sort of scoundrel, by this curious system of morals, became a Christian hero, and the most decent and well-disposed man or woman became a criminal, and what is more, a criminal without any of the ordinary rights that attach to that character. Such was the ethical masterpiece of the Methodist and Baptist experts. To state it plainly, I believe, is sufficient to give most rational persons very grave doubts of their expertness.

But the doctors of the Latin rite are scarcely better. When one hears from them on the subject of morals it is usually to the effect that any woman who, having achieved ten rachitic children, takes steps to avoid having an eleventh is a wicked and abandoned creature, and will surely go to Hell—not for the ten, mind you, but for the evaded eleventh. Or one hears that some bombastic monsignor in New York, having sent an agent to see a play by Aristophanes, is greatly outraged by its immorality, and proposes to set up a committee to police all the theaters, and to see that no drama with any Attic salt in it is ever performed. Or one hears that a cardinal-archbishop from South Boston has become convinced that the Einstein theory is immoral, and is warning all the truck-drivers, servant girls, policemen and bootleggers of his flock to have no traffic with it. These are sample masterpieces of the Roman experts. But if anyone has ever heard one of them denounce the abominable political fraud and corruption that go on in every large American city, with Catholics in the thick of it and the church getting its tithe of their dirty gains—if anyone has ever heard these experts speak *ex cathedra* on that matter, then I can only say that I am not that person. Thus we come to some of the fundamental principles of Roman ethics: Einstein, Aristophanes and the birth-controllers are immoral, but Tammany and the Boston gang are not. It is a sin worthy of public condemnation to believe in relativity, to go to see *Lysistrata* or to lift some poor and suffering woman out of her misery, but it is not such a sin to steal the taxpayers' money, to debauch and degrade the police and to buy and sell public offices, including the judicial.

I am no expert in morals myself, but it seems to me that I could easily do better than that. I could beat Monsignor Cannon after getting down two quarts of Scotch, and Cardinal O'Connell with my hands tied behind me. All that these consecrated experts prove, when they undertake to advise the lawmakers of the land, is that their moral schemes are puerile and idiotic. Perhaps that is why God inspires them to perform. It may be that He is as sick of theology as the rest of us, and yearns to reduce it to an absurdity. If so, He is far more successful than He was when He undertook to create a human race without sin. His pastors play into His hands magnificently. A few more Ku Klux campaigns, and a few more raids on Einstein and Aristophanes, and only half-wits will take their moral virtuosity seriously. Meanwhile, as one who views all moral experts dubiously, I welcome their participation in politics, and hope they keep on with it. It is accomplishing something valuable—but not what they intend.

[*American Mercury,* December 1930]

ON SUNDAY LAWS

I

Twice during the past week or so we have been entertained by amusing and instructive spectacles in the field of moral endeavor. First a small but impudent band of professional wowsers here in Baltimore, doing business under the name of the Lord's Day Alliance, spent three solid days in court trying to prevent the people of the town from deciding what sort of Sunday laws they want. And then a larger and even more impudent band of professional wowsers in Washington, doing business under the name of the Anti-Saloon League, put up a furious battle in Congress to prevent the people of the United States from deciding whether we shall go on with the Prohibition obscenity or return to common sense and common decency.

The conclusion that flows irresistibly from both cases is one to which I have often called attention in this place. It is, in brief, that wowsers care absolutely nothing for the rights of their opponents, and are implacable foes of every sort of free and orderly government. Believing, as they do, that they know vastly more about moral science than the rest of us and are immensely more virtuous personally, they are willing to go to any length to enforce their ideas and practises upon the whole body of the people. If a law is passed that seems to stand in the way, then damn that law and those who made it. If it is the Bill of Rights, then to hell with the Bill of Rights.

In other words, God has appointed them to run us, no matter how loudly we may yell. They alone know what is right and what is wrong. They are superior to the Legislature, to the courts and to the people. The so-called religion which inspires and inflames them, though it may seem only rubbish to the majority of intelligent persons, is the only true kind, and anyone who ventures to flout the least of its mandates is a criminal, and ought to be in jail. Thus the members of the Legislature were criminals for passing the Sunday enabling act, the members of the City Council were criminals for submitting the ordinance to the people, O'Dunne, J., though he is a baptized man and a practising Christian, was a kind of criminal for deciding that these transactions were lawful and proper, and the rest of us will be criminals doubly damned when we go to the polls in May and vote to restore the common liberties of the free citizens of Maryland.

II

The wowsers of the Lord's Day Alliance, of course, are fond of denying that it is theological passion which animates them. Their wiskinski, the chemically pure Dr. W. W. Davis, has often given out interviews saying that they long only to preserve the poor workingman's weekly day of rest, and have no desire to drag him to the mourner's bench. But that assurance is too thin to deceive anyone, and the wowsers themselves always forget it when they come to close quarters. The moment Dr. Davis and his brethren got into court, they began arguing, through their learned counsel, that "Christianity" was part of the Common Law of Maryland, and at once it became as plain as day that this "Christianity" they talked of was their own brand and no other, and that what they were trying to do was to ram it down the throats of the rest of us, Christian and heathen alike.

Judge O'Dunne disposed of this effort without much ceremony. He denied categorically that Christianity, whether their kind or any other, was a part of the Common Law. And he pointed out very sensibly that making it so would put an outrageous and intolerable power into the hands of any sect which managed, whether by persuasion or by intimidation, to get control of the Legislature. The instant such control became effective the successful sect would constitute, to all intents and purposes, a State church, and the religious liberty guaranteed to every citizen by both the State and Federal Constitutions would become a hollow mockery, signifying nothing.

The truth is that the Sunday laws, under the American scheme of things, are simple police statutes, and have nothing to do, legally speaking, with religion as such. They may properly protect a religious man in the practise of whatever devotions he thinks seemly, but that is as far as they may go. Fundamentally, their nature is to be determined by considerations of expediency, decorum and the public welfare, and by none other. It is as outrageous to employ them to force an unwilling man to engage in purely devotional practises, even by mere avoidance, as it would be to use them to force some other man to suspend the practises which he believes to be proper.

III

No opponent of the present preposterous Sunday law, so far as I am aware, denies that a weekly day of rest is necessary, or proposes to do away with it. Such anarchists exist only in the florid imaginations of Dr. Davis and his customers. Even the Bolshevists of Russia, though they profess to hate religion, yet make provision for such a day; indeed, they have it every five days instead of only once a week. Nor is any libertarian of my acquaintance—and I must know thousands of them, including all the worst—against choosing Sunday for the purpose. Sunday is obviously more convenient than any other day, if only on the ground of immemorial habit. Moreover, at least nine-tenths of all the Americans who are religious at all prefer it for their principal devotions.

Such persons plainly have a right to carry on those devotions without unneccessary interference. No one would argue, I suppose, that fire-engines ought to be locked up on Sunday, on the ground that their gongs and whistles disturb worship, but by the same token no one would argue that auctioneers should be allowed to carry on their business on Sunday in front of churches, with congregations within. Here we are in the field of common sense, common decorum, common decency. No one has any right to disturb the lawful acts of another, and his lack of any such right is doubly plain when those acts are of an intimate, solemn and (to the performer) sacred character. It is as crassly indecorous and uncivilized to disturb a service in church as it is to disturb a trial in court, and both offenses are severely and properly punished in all enlightened countries.

But that is as far as the matter goes—so far, and no farther. The man outside the church has rights as well as the man within. He, also, deserves to be protected in his lawful occasions. If what he wants to do is innocent in itself, and invades no other man's rights, and has no baleful effect upon the general welfare, and is supported by a preponderance of public opinion, then any law which prohibits it is a tyrannical and evil law, and ought to be repealed. And if the animus behind that law, as in the present case, is purely theological—if its actual purpose is not the general good, but simply the furthering of some fantastic and oppressive religious idea, cherished only by an obscure and anti-social sect—then it becomes utterly and intolerably abominable, and should be got rid of as soon as possible.

IV

What right have Dr. Davis and his angels to complain if a crowd of boys go out to one of the parks on Sunday afternoon, and play a game of ball— a mile, perhaps, from the nearest church, and maybe even from the nearest wowser? What right have they to send for the police if a crowd of men and woman go to a concert on Sunday night? Or if a poor man, having gone to church on Sunday morning (or even to a speakeasy, if that be his choice), devotes the afternoon to painting his bathroom or papering his parlor? Or if his wife, surprised by unexpected visitors, slips out to the delicatessen on the corner for a can of sardines and a loaf of bread?

They have, in these fields, no right whatsoever. Let them so much as complain, and they become disorderly characters, and enemies of the common peace. For when they horn into such matters they are not protecting their indubitable right to carry on the rituals and austerities of what they believe (on very questionable grounds) to be Christianity; they are invading and destroying the right of every other man to interpret the duties of a Christian in some other way, or even to deny them altogether. The instant the police undertake to carry out the mandates of such wowsers, that instant the police became the bashi-bazooks of an insufferable ecclesiastical despotism, and it is no wonder that they go about the business with blushes.

The new Sunday ordinance is attacked on several grounds, most of them purely legal. I am not learned in the law, and do not pretend to understand these caveats. They will be dealt with by the Court of Appeals, according to the Constitution, and in the frank, thorough and courageous manner characteristic of that able tribunal. It may be that the ordinance as it stands is defective; I do not know. But meanwhile it seems to me that Judge O'Dunne deserves public thanks for so beautifully exposing and disposing of the theological blather of the wowsers. His decision (printed in full in the eminent *Daily Record* of March 15) bared their animus to the light of day. No one, after this, can be in any doubt about it. They care nothing whatever for public opinion, public order or the public welfare. What arouses them to their frenzy is simply a hot desire to bang their tin-pot theology into the rest of us with policemen's clubs.

[*Baltimore Evening Sun,* March 21, 1932]

IX

RELIGION AND SOCIETY

VENTURE INTO THERAPEUTICS

It is not in my nature to believe in remedies for the great moral, social and politico-economic ills that afflict the human race, and so I seldom waste my time trying to devise one, but on this fair day in Spring, with the bulbuls burling under my palace windows and a couple of cases of 8 per cent Pennsylvania malt liquor sweating in the ice-box, it occurs to me that it might be a good idea to proceed against the Ku Klux Klan, the Freemasons, the American Legion, the Rotary Club and other such bands of bellicose morons by attempting a counter-offensive. I do not, of course, propose the thing already proposed and rejected, to wit, a *super*-Klan of the relatively civilized, clad in black chemises instead of white, and armed with rifles instead of clubs and torches. In the South, where the Klan itself chiefly functions, the relatively civilized form too small a minority to make an effective army of liberation; moreover, most of the judges, sheriffs, district attorneys, chiefs of police, militia colonels and other such servants of the secular arm down there are earnest Klansmen, and so the super-Klan would have to face, not only the Klan itself, but the full military and naval strength of all the states south of the Potomac. The scheme thus reduces itself to futility and banality.

My scheme is simpler and, I believe, more charming and romantic. I first proposed it to another end, years ago—in fact, long before the Klan got into motion. I now propose it again, with a few slight changes. In brief, it is this: that the enemies and victims of the Klan get together, make up a war fund of $1,000,000 cash, and then employ it to import Mohammedan missionaries from Turkey and turn them loose among the Aframericans of the South. In six months half the dark brethren would be converted to the Islamic revelation; in nine months the remaining half would be bagged; in a year the whole body would be organized into a compact and formidable army, armed with scimitars and making ready to burn Atlanta and put the Legislature of Georgia to the sword. And then, as we say in Amerikanisch, good-night!

That the Moors of the late Confederacy would quickly succumb to Moslem theology I don't doubt for an instant. In Africa, where Moslem and Christian missionaries have been in conflict for a generation past, the blood brothers of our Southern Ethiops have gone over to the crescent almost unanimously; there are now, indeed, millions of square miles in Africa wherein Christian missionaries are quite as much *ferae naturae,* to be taken freely by anyone's trap, as Prohibition enforcement officers in Michigan. Let a newcomer halt in the plaza of a jungle village, take off his hat and begin to sing "Onward, Christian Soldiers," and at once his head is chopped off, and he is thrown to the hyenas. The reason is not far to seek. Islam promises a paradise that any darkey, however defective his education, can instantly understand and appreciate; Christianity offers a paradise that can charm him only when he is hysterical or drunk. The former is peopled with gaudy houris, and, its days are given over to lucullan feasts; the latter offers only an endless and meaningless playing of harps—a form of music that the dark races have never taken to spontaneously. I say that an Ethiop must be hysterical or drunk in order to believe in the latter. I mean it literally. The Methodist revival embodies a deliberate effort to get him into the former condition. The pastor who would make him genuinely eager for grace must first harrow him so vastly that he begins to foam at the mouth, emit inarticulate yells and roll on the floor—symptoms so characteristic of hysteria that even a chiropractor, an Iowa midwife or a fashionable New York physician would recognize them at once.

The truth is that the darker citizens of the South have been swinging away from Christianity for a number of years past—that is, from the barbarous, hellfire variety of Christianity now chiefly prevailing down there. In slavery days Methodism met their spiritual needs very aptly, and so they embraced it in great numbers, but as they have gradually taken on enlight-enment they have found it increasingly unsatisfactory. Its decay among them, while it remains, in some form or other, endemic among the whites, is due to the fact that the blacks, in recent decades, have been going ahead much faster than the whites. A great many of the more advanced blacks have gone over boldly to the so-called Protestant Episcopal Church, to Christian Science or even to the Church of Rome; a few extraordinarily daring spirits have become rationalists, despite the fact that rationalism is prohibited by law in most of the Southern states.

This movement, of course, is not open and public; its dangers, in a region where even governors and United States senators are Methodists, or even Baptists, enforce secrecy; the emerging Aframericans, like the Chris-tians of the first centuries, have to seek security in catacombs. But this minority, of course, would not succumb to Islam. The recruits would come from the great majority, still faithful to Methodism outwardly but greatly discontented with its lack of sense and dignity, and now much alarmed by its undisguised alliance with the Ku Klux Klan. Christianity, as these infe-rior blacks see it, is little more than a scheme for perpetuating, *post mortem*, the superiorities and immunities of the white trash in this vale. Let a col-ored preacher promise from his pulpit that such a man as Dr. Booker T. Washington will be the full equal of the Hon. Cole Blease in Heaven, and he will be lucky if he escapes slow roasting at the stake. Islam makes no such illogical distinctions. All coons looked alike to Mohammed—which is to say, all appeared to be of the same pure and resplendent white. In his paradise the blackest field hand is the exact equal of Brünnhilde, Jack Dempsey and the Hon. John Sharp Williams.

Christianity, as everyone knows, is based upon counsels of humility. Even Methodism, which preaches a holy war against Catholics, Dar-winians, Jews, Irishmen, Germans, Frenchmen, Italians, Russians, Socialists, bootleggers, dancers, theatrical managers, monarchists, card-players and, in the South, Republicans and negroes, and does not hesitate to incite its communicants to dispatch them in God's name and so get them quickly into hell—even Methodism teaches the colored folk to show an humble mien and accept their persecutions with docility. But Mohammedanism teaches them to rise and resist—more, to take the offensive against their enemies. This teaching, it must be obvious, would not only spread a very grateful ointment upon the abraded egos of the Southern black folk; it would also direct them to the only practicable way out of their present woes. If they wait for their oppressors to let them up voluntarily, they will wait until Gabriel blows his horn. In order to get out at all, they must hack their way out. Islam offers them the counsel and the technique; the same missionaries who teach them the Koran will also teach them how to exercise with the curved sabre. Thus they will leap instantly from the mourners' bench to the trench, and blood will begin to flow before their instructors have come to the collection.

The objections to the plan, of course, are many and obvious. It would cost, I daresay, a great many lives. But the persons likely to be sacrificed by its execution would die, soon or late, anyhow, and not many of them are of much value to the world. As for the black Moslems who would fall in the war, no one, even in the South, argues that they would be greatly missed, save perhaps by the local witch-doctors, collectors for lodges and sellers of decoctions for straightening kinky hair. As for the whites, they already testify, by their membership in the Ku Klux Klan, that they are advocates of murder, and probably a good many of them are experienced practitioners of it. To be dispatched by a neat stroke of steel is certainly more comfortable than to be burned at the stake, or even than to die of malaria, wood alcohol poisoning, tick bites or hookworm—the probable fate of most of these persons by God's inscrutable plan. A grand battle in Georgia, with 100,000 killed, would of course cause some excitement throughout the United States, but that excitement would be purely national. In Europe the news would be received as calmly as intelligence of a disastrous flood on the Ho-ang-ho. In brief, no one of any importance would be killed, save perhaps a few luckless strangers, temporarily deposited on the scene by train-wrecks. The South is extremely fecund. It could replace its losses in one year.

That a rising of the blacks under the banner of Islam would be illegal I presume to doubt. The American courts have decided more than once that a crime committed by a large body of persons, acting deliberately in concert, is not punishable under our laws—that the *posse comitatus* is, in a very real sense, itself a law-making body. In case their acts amount to rebellion, the Federal power, of course, may be called in to oppose them, but such a rising of Moslems as I have pictured would not amount to a rebellion. In the analogous case of public massacres of the blacks the Federal government, in fact, has always refused to interfere. What is sauce for the goose should surely be sauce for the gander. If, under pressure of the theological frenzy, the dark Mohammedans should undertake to put down the Ku Klux Klan by the sword, then they would be quite as clearly within their rights as the Ku Klux Klan is today when it undertakes to put down Catholicism, Judaism and the hypothesis of the evolution of species with the torch, bastinado and tar-pot. The new situation, in truth, would favor the Klan, for its members would be free to resist by force, whereas now their victims are forbidden to resist. . . .

But here, of course, I indulge in speculation. The whole question remains theoretical and academic. It will not take on practical importance until someone sends for the Moslem missionaries.

[*Smart Set,* July 1923]

VOX POPULI, VOX DEI

The voice of the Lord God Almighty, maker of heaven and earth, as reflected by the people of the United States and their self-imposed laws and regulations, severally by municipalities and states (including Kansas) or collectively by the union:

1. God is against cigarettes.
2. God is against playing cards.
3. God is against advertisements of Scotch whiskey.
4. God is against Scotch whiskey.
5. God is against playing billiards.
6. God is against playing pool.
7. God is against moving pictures showing a man kissing a woman for longer than ten seconds.
8. God is against "September Morn."[1]
9. God is against "The Girl with the Whooping Cough."[2]
10. God is against Eugene V. Debs.
11. God is against Little Egypt.
12. God is against playing baseball on Sunday.
13. God is against carrying a pocket flask.
14. God is against dancing after eleven P.M.
15. God is against dancing after twelve P.M.

16. God is against dancing after one A.M.
17. God is against dancing at all.
18. God is against secret societies.
19. God is against German opera.
20. God is against public speaking by a member of the I.W.W.
21. God is against Boccaccio, Balzac, Fielding and Anatole France.
22. God is against bare knees.
23. God is against allowing children to appear on the stage.
24. God is against the female leg.
25. God is against congregating on street corners.
26. God is against letting poor men sleep on the benches in public parks.
27. God is against birth control.
28. God is against speaking in public on birth control.
29. God is against sending birth control literature through the mails.
30. God and the late Hon. Jim Nann are *Corpsbrüder.*
31. God is against the minority at all times.
32. God is against all illiterates save those who are American born.
33. God is against a trade alliance of proficient business men against their inferiors.
34. God believes that a Mississippi nigger bootblack is the equal of John Singer Sargent.
35. God is against one-piece bathing suits.
36. God believes that Sholem Asch's play, *The God of Vengeance,* is very immoral stuff and that the actors who play it should be arrested, tried by a jury, convicted of a criminal offense, and either be fined or locked up in the hoosegow.
37. God believes that if the United States didn't look after South America, South America would go to the dogs.
38. God is against Socialists, but loves all Republicans and Democrats.
39. God is against hoochie-coochie dancing.
40. God is against walking on the grass in public parks.
41. God believes that all bathing beaches should be lighted up with acetylene lamps at night and that policemen should arrest any couple discovered holding hands or kissing.
42. God believes that a teamster whose horse is lazy and won't work and who taps the nag emphatically across the rear in order to make him work should be promptly arrested.

43. God is against prize-fighting.

44. God doesn't believe in betting on the races.

45. God is against masked ball merrymakers wearing their masks on the street on the way to the party, and believes that they should be arrested if they do so.

46. God is opposed to American women wearing aigrettes.

47. God is against anyone bringing banana seed into the United States.

48. God believes that the Japanese are inferior to the Armenians.

49. God believes that it is wrong to shoot and kill rabbits in Rhode Island between January 1st and November 1st, but quite jolly to do so from November 1st to January 1st. He also believes that it is wrong to pot deer in New Hampshire from December 16th to the following December 1st, but good sport to do so from the 1st to the 15th. However, He is against persons living in Colorado, Indiana, Iowa and Kansas shooting deer at any time.

50. God believes that lake trout of $14\frac{1}{2}$ inches should be thrown back into the water but that trout half an inch longer, as served, for example, at the Ritz, make a very desirable and tasty dish.

51. God believes that it was necessary to pass a law making it moral to sell automobile tires on Sunday in New York State.

52. God is against pink lemonade.

53. God believes that Rodin is a very dirty fellow.

54. God believes that it is wrong for anyone to work in any mercantile or commercial house in Utah after six o'clock, except for the six days preceding His birthday, Christmas, which may be appropriately celebrated by working until midnight.

55. God believes that separate washrooms should be supplied for negro laborers in Missouri.

56. God holds that no chiropodist in Connecticut shall call himself a Doctor, but that it is all right in any other state.

57. God believes that the bed sheets in hotels and lodging houses in Indiana should be of a certain exact size, regulated by law.

58. God is of the belief that if a man shines shoes or sells flowers on Sunday in Alliance, Ohio, he should be fined, and that if he does it a second time he should be sent to jail for thirty days.

59. God is against the delivery of ice on Sunday in Omaha, Neb.

60. God believes that if a man or woman writes a poem (for paid publication in a magazine) on Sunday in Utah, he or she should be arrested.

61. God believes that it is wrong to drive an automobile on Sunday in Ocean Grove, New Jersey.

62. God believes that music should not be played on Sunday in Berkeley, Cal.

63. God believes that it is all wrong to sell a bottle of ketchup on Sunday in the Bronx.

64. God believes that all persons in Tangier, Va., who do not go to church should be compelled by ordinance to stay indoors during the period of church services and under no circumstances be permitted to go out.

65. God is against buying, selling or smoking a cigarette in Kansas.

66. God believes that no Nebraska girl should be permitted to wear a short skirt.

67. God believes it is wrong to tip a servant in Iowa.

68. God holds it illegal to teach the doctrine of evolution in Texas.

69. God is against anyone playing pool or billiards in South Carolina.

70. God believes that children should not be allowed to attend private schools in Oregon.

71. God says that one must not whistle on Sunday in Massachusetts.

72. God doesn't believing in shaving on Sunday in Arizona.

[*Smart Set,* August, September, October, and December 1923]

WHAT'S THE MATTER
WITH THE CHURCHES?

If there is a bishop (ἐπίσκοπος) in this great Christian land who has not, at some time or other, composed and uttered an article or diatribe entitled "What Is the Matter with the Churches?" then the present subscriber is prepared to pay $10 cash for his name and address, or, if he has been translated to G. H. Q., for a hair of his episcopal head. And if there is a great organ of refined opinion, ecclesiastical or profane, that has not, within the meagre years of the present century, printed at least six such articles or diatribes, either by ἐπίσκοποι or by lesser fauna, then the subscriber offers the same sum for news of it. Many public journals of high tone, in fact, have made themselves specialists in the matter, as the NewYork tabloids are specialists in fiends—notably the *New Republic* and the *Forum*. And all the rest have dwelt upon it incessantly, and with more or less libido.

Well, to what end? What have the *episkopoi* and the lesser ruminants to say about the malaises now alleged to afflict the Christian church among us, and the Christian faith with it? How do they account for the apparent decay of both, at least in the great towns? In the main, they account for it by saying that church and faith have been corrupted and made impotent by human agencies, working under the orders, or at least with the connivance, of Satan, that scoundrel—that the way of deliverance for both lies through a return to the austere simplicities of the Founder. His teachings, it appears, are the only true teachings, and in them is to be found the only perfect way of life, satisfactory to God and salubrious to man. We must get rid of dogma and go back to faith, hope and charity. We must get rid of priestcraft and go back to love.

Christ, we are told, preached no complicated mysteries and demanded no pedantic allegiance. He knew nothing of transubstantiation, or of reserved sacraments, or of the adoration of the saints, or of the vestments controversy; He was even somewhat vague about original sin. Alive today, could He qualify as a bishop? He could not. Even the Salvation Army would put Him on probation, at least until He had mastered the cornet. Even the Christian Scientists would bar him from their auction-block, at least until He had got a morning coat and paid cash for a copy of *Science and Health*. What would the Congregatio Sancti Officii say of His theology? What would the Methodist Board of Temperance, Prohibition and Public Morals say of His ethics? What would Monsignor Manning say of His patriotism, or of His economic views, or of His probable opinion of the great spiritual filling-station on Morningside Heights? What these high authorities would say, I venture, would be a plenty.

Nevertheless, the bishops join the lay pathologists in arguing that the only salvation for the church is to go back to His teaching. It has taken on crusts, excrescences, an unhealthy and forbidding patina. It is covered with boils, and racked interiorly by grinding pains. The world has debauched it, and it shines with a baleful light. Its deliverance lies in the fifth chapter of Matthew, among the glorious asseverations known as the Sermon on the Mount. Let it throw off its gaudy trappings and its lust for pomp and power, and teach once more that the poor in spirit are the really blessed, and that theirs is the kingdom of Heaven. Let its ordained pastors abandon their bloodthirsty wowserism and delirious money-chasing, and give ocular proof that the meek shall inherit the earth. Let its customers cease their attempts to dispose of one another by the sword, and so restore the old savor to the salt. Thus advise the bishops, who would not be bishops if they were not grave and judicious men. And to the same effect speak the lay pathologists, many of them eminent in good works and some of them, unlike the bishops, actual Christians.

II

All this is grateful to my gills, for as a lazy man I love peace and deplore the uproars now going on. It seems to me to be a pretty safe guess that Christ, coming back to earth, would be against them, as He was against the shouting of the theologians while He lived. I think it evident enough that a Methodist pastor, damning Al Smith and the Pope from the sacred desk and bawling for capital punishment for bootleggers, would please Him very little, and that He would take no interest in such enterprises as Monsignor Manning's effort to knock out Mr. Woolworth, or Monsignor Hayes' smiting of the birth-controllers with the secular arm, or Monsignor O'Connell's mad, sad endeavor to close the Boston bookshops, or the vast striving of the Ku Klux klergy to make us all Baptists by force. He would counsel milder measures, and a good deal less clubbing and noise. If He sought friends among His current agents among us, they would not be the bull-roarers and high-steppers. I'd expect him to be very amiable to the sisters in the hospitals, and perhaps even to some of the rectors of poor parishes, but it would surprise me greatly to hear of Him snooping along Broadway in search of hot stuff or taking to the stump for the Anti-Saloon League.

So far my personal prejudices, which only echo the warnings of the seers I have mentioned. Cherishing them, I long for their satisfaction, and even go to the length of opening negotiations to that end. That is to say, I offer formally to cease denouncing the rev. bishops and their gun-men as public nuisances if they will only agree to cease their cracking of heads and whooping of whoops. What could be fairer: I engage to abandon my holy war for theirs? But I regret to have to add at once that I cherish no hope that they will accept. More, I find myself impelled to say that I believe they are too intelligent to accept. For bishops, whatever their liking for hollow and lascivious utterance, are surely not ignorant men. Their magical trade makes them privy to the secrets of the human heart. They understand mankind, even though they often act as if they did not. And at no time do they give better proof of their understanding than when they forget their own soft murmurs, and give their customers rough and bloody shows. It is, indeed, the rough stuff that maintains them in their levantine luxury; it is hatred that they feed upon, as lawyers feed upon folly. The minute they really went back to the Beatitudes, that minute the business to which they have consecrated their lives would blow up, and the name of Christ would disappear from His Churches, and follow that of Mithras into learned and unreadable books.

The plain fact is that the Sermon on the Mount is today quite as unworkable as it was the day it was uttered. It lies wholly outside the ordinary bounds of human desire and experience. That it represents a sweet dream must be admitted, even by bishops, but that dream remains only a dream: it has no more reality than a young man's hallucination of the damsel who has snared him. There is no record that even the earliest Christians tried to mold their lives according to its counsels. If, for a space, they were humble, then it was with the humility, not of excessive goodness, but simply of sound caution. The minute they escaped from the catacombs, they began the eternal business of driving other folks into them. The history of those days, having been recorded by Christian hands, is discreetly evasive upon the subject. But those schooled in such matters know very well that the Holy Office was in full blast at least a thousand years before its official establishment, and that the throats of heretics were being slit as early as the Fourth Century.

III

Did the early Christians, remembering Matthew 5:3–11, protest against this bloodshed?[3] They did not. On the contrary, they were hot for it, as the Methodists and Baptists are hot for flogging and poisoning to this day. If they protested at all, it was against too much mercy. It was the growing softness of the decaying Roman Empire, in the Seventh Century, that opened the way for Mohammedanism, a frankly sanguinary and hence charmingly satisfying religion, just as it was the fat ease and careless tolerance of Holy Church, in the Sixteenth Century, that opened the way for Luther, and the pervasive skepticism of England in the Eighteenth Century that brought in Wesley and his terrible swift sword. The truly religious man can never be really tolerant and humble. Either he must retreat to the snobbish shades of mysticism, or he must arm himself with an ax. The Beatitudes are as incomprehensible to him as the epigrams of La Rochefoucauld. He cannot imagine a heretic headed for anything save the fires of Hell. Always his demand is for pastors who carry side-arms and are ready to take the field. He is happiest when crusades are on, and saddest when the police forbid them.

To argue that Ku Kluxry has damaged the evangelical sects in the South and Middle West is to argue the most palpable nonsense. It has really revived them and put them on their legs, as every pastor of the Bible Belt well knows. So long as he confined himself to dunning his customers in the interest of the heathen he dunned deaf and flapping ears. But the moment he leaped into his night-shirt and began chasing Jews, Unitarians, Aframericans, fancy women, bootleggers and the Pope, they followed him as ecstatically as the peasants of the Eleventh Century Rhineland followed Peter the Hermit. His takings over the altar-rail doubled overnight, and presently he had the job of Grand Cyclops or Grand Kleagle and was riding around town in a new Buick, chewing the most expensive tobacco made in Richmond. The Klan Krusade, in truth, has produced a vast revival of religion throughout the malaria country. It is almost comparable to the Great Awakening of 1740–42. The faithful are on the march everywhere, radiating a pious and almost cannibalistic zeal. The Old Time Religion, *i.e.,* the Religion With Teeth In It and hair on those teeth, is triumphant again, and there is not a politician south of the Potomac or west of the Susquehanna who has not felt its supernatural pull within him. The Holy Spirit walks the land, armed with a pitchfork and carrying a bucket of tar.

The difficulty is that it probably won't last. Soon or late the Bible Belt ecclesiastics, debauched by the gabble of idealists who remember the Beatitudes, will lose their holy fire. They will compromise with the Pope, maybe even with the Darwinians, just as Dr. Hayes will compromise with the birth-controllers and Dr. O'Connell will compromise with the literati. And then Christianity will go into eclipse again, and doubt will stalk the land. And there will be atheism everywhere until some new Peter the Hermit (or Imperial Wizard Evans, or William Jennings Bryan) gets out the old blunderbuss, and starts another hunt.

[*American Mercury,* May 1928]

WHAT IS TO BE DONE ABOUT DIVORCE?

I see no chance of dealing with the divorce question rationally until the discussion is purged of religious consideration. Certainly the world should have learned by this time that theologians make a mess of everything they touch, including even religion. Yet in the United States they are still allowed, against all reason and experience, to have their say in a great variety of important matters, and everywhere they go they leave their sempiternal trail of folly and confusion.

Why those of the Christian species should be consulted about marriage and divorce is more than I can make out. It would be only a little less absurd to consult members of the W. C. T. U.[4] about the mixing of drinks, for orthodox Christianity, as everyone knows, views even the most decorous kind of marriage with lubricious suspicion and countenances it only as a means of escape from something else. In the whole New Testament there is but one message that speaks of it as an honorable estate, and that one is in the most dubious of the Epistles. Elsewhere it is always assumed to be something intrinsically and incurably vile. The really virtuous man avoids it as a plague—his ideal is complete chastity. If, tempted by Satan, he finds that chastity unbearable, he may take a wife to escape something worse, but that is only a poor compromise with his baser nature.[5]

Modern theologians on divorce do not put the thing as coarsely as Paul did—but they still subscribe to his basic idea, however mellifluous and disarming their statement of it. A wife is primarily a sexual instrument and as such must not flinch her lowly duty. If she tries to avoid having children, then she is doomed to hell. If she finds her husband growing unpleasant and turns from him to another, then she is doomed to hell again. As for him, he is bound in the same way and under the same penalties. Both would be better off if they were chaste, but as long as that is impossible they must be unchaste only with each other, and accept with resignation all the more painful consequences, whether biological or theological.

Such notions, plainly stated, must needs seem barbaric to every civilized man; nevertheless, they continue to color the legislation of nearly all so-called Christian States. In New York, for example, the only general ground for divorce is adultery. The man may beat his wife all he pleases, but she cannot divorce him for it. In her turn she may waste his money, insult him in public and chase his friends out of the house and he cannot get rid of her. So long as neither turns from the venal unchastity of marriage to the mortal unchastity outside they are indissolubly bound together, though their common life be intolerable to themselves and a scandal to everyone else.

Obviously, it will be impossible to come to any sensible rearrangement of the relation between man and woman so long as such ancient imbecilities corrupt all thinking on the subject. The first thing necessary, then, is to get rid of the theologians. Let them be turned out politely but firmly; let us pay no further heed to their archaic nonsense. They will, to be sure, resist going, perhaps very stoutly, but their time has come and they must be on their way. If any lingering superstition about their heavenly authority tends to reprieve them, then let us recall how gaudily they have made fools of themselves of late in another grave and delicate matter—that of drink.

What is needed is a purely realistic view of the whole question, uncontaminated by false assumptions and antediluvian traditions. That review must begin not with remedies but with causes. Why, as a matter of actual practise, do men and women marry? And what are the factors that hold them together when marriage turns out to be endurable? Here there is a great gap in the assembled facts. The sociologists, like their brethren of medicine, have devoted themselves so ardently to the pathological that they have forgotten to study the normal. But no inquiry into the marriage that breaks up can be worth anything unless it is based upon a sound understanding of the marriage that lasts.

The fact explains the shallowness of many of the remedies currently whooped up—for example, that of my romantic friend, Judge Ben B. Lindsey. To propose, as Ben does, that marriage be abandoned and half-marriage be substituted is like advising a man with a sty to get a glass eye. He doesn't want a glass eye; he wants his own natural and perfect eye, with the sty plucked out. All such reformers forget that the real essence of marriage is not the nature of the relation but the permanence of that relation. It is a device for time-binding, like every other basic human institution. Its one indomitable purpose is to endure.

Plainly enough, divorce ought to be easy when the destruction of a marriage is an accomplished fact, but it would be folly to set up conditions tending to make that destruction more likely. Too much, indeed, has been done in that direction already. The way out for people who are incapable of the concessions and compromises that go with every contract is not to fill the contract with snakes but to avoid it altogether. There are, indeed, many men and women to whom marriage is a sheer psychic impossibility. But to the majority it is surely not. They find it quite bearable: they like it; they want it to endure. What they need is help in making it endurable.

My own program I withhold, and for a sound reason—I have none. The problem is not going to be solved by prescribing a swift swallow out of this or that jug. It is going to be solved, if it is ever solved at all, by sitting down calmly and examining all the relevant facts, and by following out all their necessary and inevitable implications. In other words, it is going to be solved scientifically, not romantically or theologically. What marriage needs above all is hard, patient, impartial study. Before we may hope to cure even the slightest of its ills we must first find out precisely what it is, and how and why it works when it works at all.

[*New York World Magazine,* January 26, 1930]

TREASON IN THE TABERNACLE

One of the cheering signs of the times is the appearance of an anti-clerical movement among Americans of dark complexion. It was a long time coming, but here it is at last. Ever since the days of their earliest sojourn on these Christian shores the colored people have been under the hooves of ecclesiastical racketeers, most of them densely ignorant and many of them dishonest. These racketeers were turned loose by the slave-owners, and with malice prepense. It was considered to be prudent to purge the slaves of their savage theology, and to implant in them instead the gentler ideas of Christianity, especially its resignationism. But the planters of tidewater did not want to see mobs of blacks crowding into their own very tidy and charming Episcopal churches, so they hired Baptist and Methodist evangelists to operate in the quarters. Such evangelists were as plentiful in the balmy South in those days as they are in these, and as ready to work hard for their pork-chops. As a result of their wizardries practically all of the slaves were converted to some sort of Calvinism, and their descendants remain a generally pious and Hell-fearing people to this day. There are many American Negroes who seldom if ever go to church, but downright atheists are rare among them. ʾnd even the worst of them, coming to the gallows, commonly ask for spiritual consolation. I have seen many Negroes hanged, but I can't recall one who was not attended by a pastor, whether Methodist or Baptist.

Unfortunately, the theology of these black clerics has kept to a generally low level, and one sees in it little sign of that liberalization to which so many white theologians of the evangelical sects have begun to succumb, even in the South. Not long ago a colored Baptist pastor was boasting that there was not a single Modernist among his people—perhaps a somewhat over-wide boast, but nevertheless one with a certain plausibility in it. The dark brethren have never staged any such combat between Modernists and Fundamentalists as that which lately shook the white Presbyterians. When they believe at all, they believe in the old Hell of the Bible, with sinners frying like chicken-wings in a pan. Their Christianity is thus vastly more honest than that of their white colleagues in the faith, and when they happen to be really soaked in it they show qualities that are almost apostolic. Nothing could be more naïve and charming than the confidence of a devout old colored woman that she will be snatched up to Heaven when she dies, converted into a rich, beautiful and excessively blonde angel, outfitted with a trousseau of pink and blue satin frocks, and put to live rent-free in an alabaster house with a solid gold cookstove in the kitchen.

But it is human experience that believing such things runs into money, and the dark brethren have not escaped the operation of that rule. Their piety costs them more than anything else they pay for in cash—probably more, even, than rent or taxes. Their churches represent an investment greater than their outlay on land; worse, their equity remains small, and so they stagger under a dreadful burden of debt. Even in Harlem there is scarcely a tabernacle without a mortgage, and some of them run to such huge amounts that paying them off will probably be forever impossible. What the upkeep of the pastors comes to I don't know, but it must be a staggering sum, for they are much more numerous, relatively speaking, than white agents of the Word, and on the whole they seem to be better kept. I am informed, indeed, by Aframerican statisticians that they make better incomes than any other class of colored professional men, and that not a few of them become so adept at cadging money that they grow really rich. At worst, they are very well fed by the sistren, and it is uncommon to encounter one who is not fat and radiant. The cadaverous and choleric type of cleric, so numerous among the whites of the hookworm country, is rare among them.

So far, so good. No one could object reasonably to shepherds being well nourished. What the colored intellectuals complain of is the nature of the doctrine they preach. Theologically, it is simply cracker evangelism—the preposterous merchanted with whoops, snortings and rollings of the eyes. And sociologically it is an abject and debilitating resignationism—highly satisfactory to the white crackers, North or South, but of dubious value to Americans of color. The typical black pastor, like the typical white labor leader, is only too willing to trade the dignity and security of his people for his own advantage. Whenever election day rolls 'round he is ready to be seen, and not infrequently his palm is crossed with something far more caressing than silver. This venality, of course, is also common among the lower orders of white evangelical clerics, but among the dark brethren it seems to extend to higher levels, and some of the most gaudy pastors (and even bishops) are very active politicians, and notoriously eager for political jobs. To satisfy that itch they have to deliver their customers on election day, and the safest and easiest way to deliver them is to keep them ignorant.

Against this enterprise the iconoclasts aforesaid now fling themselves—so far, it must be confessed, without much success, but nevertheless with a great deal of hope. They are helped by the intellectual ferment which shows itself among the colored people of the country, on low levels as well as on high. The old simple trust in the eventual justice and benevolence of the whites is passing out, and in place of it there is arising a conviction that the American Negroes, if they are ever to be delivered from their burdens, must manage the deliverance themselves. One hears less and less talk about coöperation with white philanthropists and more and more about coöperation between black and black. It is a good sign, and as a sincere friend of the colored people I view it with great satisfaction. In many obvious ways they are superior to the whites against whom they are commonly pitted. They are not only enormously decenter; they are also considerably shrewder. Thus it would be pleasant to discover that Jahveh had chosen them to lead that revolt against the hog-wallow theology which, in the long run, is bound to come in the South. The whites seem too timorous to make the break; they sweat under their prehensile pastors, but hesitate to do anything about it. I look for the day when Aframerican philosophers will circulate among the Nordic lint-heads and tenant-farmers, offering them blest assurance that their pastors are all wrong, and that there really ain't no Hell. It would be a generous and glorious requital for long years of stupid and barbaric injustice.

[*American Mercury*, June 1931]

A GLOSS UPON CHRISTIAN MORALITY

SIN AND SEX, by Robert Briffault. $3. 253 pp. New York: *The Macaulay Company.*

If the whole of this book were as well done as the opening chapters it would be a masterpiece. Unfortunately, Dr. Briffault starts off at a pace that he is unable to maintain—that very few men, indeed, could maintain—and so there is a palpable let-down toward the middle, and what began as a masterpiece closes as no more than a very thoughtful and informing work. Well, let us thank God from Whom all blessings flow, even when they are not perfect. If there is any better exposition anywhere of the essential conflict between revealed religion and intellectual freedom than Dr. Briffault's opening chapter, then it is certainly unknown to the deponent. And if the Puritan psyche has ever been turned inside out more brilliantly than in his third chapter, then the deponent must confess again to a brutish and lamentable ignorance.

Dr. Briffault raises two objections to the Christian moral system, both of them sound. The first is that it lays far too much stress upon mere physical chastity, and hence tends to overlook the fact that sex is quite as much a matter of mind as of body. The second is that this stress mainly flows, not from any rational purpose to make life more tolerable and the world better, but from a barbaric fidelity to ancient taboos. That sex ought to be regulated in some way or other is plain to everyone, and as a matter of fact attempts have been made to regulate it since time immemorial, and on all the levels of civilization. But it is one thing to regulate it in a logical and prudent manner, and quite another thing to try to dispose of it on the authority of dubious and irrational revelation. The early Christian Fathers did not borrow their concrete view of it from the Jews, for the Jews were not as sex-ridden as they were, but they at least borrowed the Jewish device of putting all of the mandates they concocted into the mouth of Jahveh. These mandates still afflict the Western world, and getting rid of them is an immensely difficult matter, for every attack upon them is instantly translated into an assault upon the divine omniscience.

The first effort of the early Christians was not to regulate sex at all, in any ordinary sense, but to destroy it altogether. They had, for some obscure reason, a tremendous fear of it, and were quite willing to exterminate the human race in order to get rid of it. When that turned out to be too large an order, they proceeded to make it as disreputable as possible, and in some of the more archaic taboos of the Jews, abandoned by most Jews of any enlightenment and categorically denounced by Jesus, they found a convenient authority for that enterprise. The result is visible in Christendom to-day. The true Christian can never think of sex in a clean and realistic manner. He fears it as a savage fears ghosts. An idiotic and inviolable taboo surrounds it. It is dealt with in his theology and his legislation, not in terms of the lives that civilized men and women must now live in the world, but in terms of a series of imaginary colloquys between Jahveh and Moses three thousand years ago. The matter simply cannot be argued. No facts are wanted. One must either conform or be damned.

Dr. Briffault lays this imbecile way of thinking to the Jews—not that they invented it, but that they piped it into Europe from the great theological reservoir of Asia. The Greeks, who were true Europeans, approached the matter from a totally different standpoint. They grounded their moral ideas, not upon the fiats of the gods, but upon a concept of common decency. What they asked of any proposed canon of conduct was not whether it had a divine mandate behind it, but whether it would really promote the security and happiness of human beings on this earth. Thus they produced an ethical theory that was highly intelligent, and it remains worth studying to this day. But Christian moralists do not bother to study it. They are content with their outfit of barbaric taboos, and anyone who presumes to examine those taboos scientifically is sure to taste their venom. Like all other theologians, they brook no criticism, however honest. Hell yawns for anyone who questions them.

In the department of sex the thing works in a vicious circle. The early Christian effort to put down sex altogether has been abandoned, but in the largest and most influential branch of the church the strictest celibacy is still enforced upon the clergy. Thus the members of this order, most of whom are normal and healthy men, suffer chronically from a cruel suppression of their most powerful instinct, and their sufferings naturally cause them to view that instinct with fear and loathing. In consequence, they are ardent supporters of the old taboo, and not infrequently read new rigors into it, as, for example, in the current matter of birth control. Sex seems extraordinarily vile to them because they must avoid it completely. They eat and drink like the rest of us, and they are free, at the cost of moderate penalties, to yield to their instincts in other ways, but sex they must eschew altogether. No Freud was needed to demonstrate that such necessities breed violent aversions. Prohibition is not the invention of men who drink moderately and decently; it is the invention of peasants who fear to drink at all, lest they get drunk, maul their wives and cattle, and lose their souls; their one refuge is complete teetotalism. All of us, alas, are tarred with the same stick. My own chief enthusiasm, it happens, is neither for celibacy or for sobriety; it is for what I choose to regard as justice. But I am not unaware of the fact that, when my natural impulses get the upper hand of my reason, which is not seldom, I am one of the most unjust fellows ever heard of. So I hate injustice with a renewed ferocity, and spend a large part of my time damning and defaming men guilty of it.

But here I run off the track of Dr. Briffault's book. It is the work of a very learned man of science—he is one of the best anthropologists now in practise—and of a thoughtful and realistic publicist. The theologians, I suppose, will presently be trying to make him out a libertine, but as a matter of fact his position is quite decorous, and he does not advocate sexual anarchy. He believes that "the arrangement that two persons, a man and a woman, who are deeply attached to each other should live together and make common cause in their interests is the most reasonable and satisfactory arrangement that can be devised"—at all events, in the present state of civilization. "I can think," he says, "of no improvement upon it." Nor does he seek, like the more romantic of the current iconoclasts, to depict sex as a grand and lofty matter, of overwhelming importance; it is, to him, simply a biological fact, and no more thrilling than any other. What he argues against is simply the vain attempt to deal with this biological fact in terms of an outworn and barbaric theology, by fear out of ignorance. All he asks is that the current reliance upon taboos be quietly shelved, and a calm examination of the whole sex problem substituted for it. He believes that being civilized means living a life of reason, and is thus opposed to listening to moral utopians, the foes of reason at all times and everywhere.

[*American Mercury,* June 1931]

THE CHURCHES AND THE DEPRESSION

One of the curious, and perhaps I should add incredible, phenomena of the Hoover *Katzenjammer* is the silence of the theologians. I am aware, of course, that Cardinal Dougherty has gone on the stand for the bedeviled Philadelphia bankers to testify that *all* of their banks are not ready to bust, and I am no less aware that such transcendental wiseacres as Dr. S. Parkes Cadman and Rabbi Stephen S. Wise are still heard from regularly and at undiminished length. What I presume to note is simply the fact that these great masters of the sacred sciences, in their public outpourings, seldom if ever speak professionally and *ex cathedra*. What Cadman has to say might be said just as well by Arthur Brisbane (as, in fact, it is), and what Wise says today is hardly more than what the Scripps-Howard editorial writers were saying week before last. As for Cardinal Dougherty, he addressed his Philadelphia faithful, not as their shepherd in two worlds, but simply as a fellow depositor in the local banks. In brief, these eminent divines, and their colleagues with them, are heard from only in their purely secular characters as big-wigs, and not in their special capacity as experts in the principles and policies of Yahweh.

This is surely to be regretted, for theologians are full of a kind of knowledge that ordinary men have no access to, and, as Dr. Robert A. Millikan is fond of admitting on the stump, they can often throw light upon problems that baffle even astrophysicists. Moreover, they are usually quite willing to go to the bat whenever they are needed. Everyone will recall, for example, their magnificent effort during the late World War. From the stroke of 1 P.M. on Good Friday, 1917, they disgorged revelations in a constant stream, and the result was that a war which began very dubiously, as a scheme by Wall Street to collect some bad debts, came to its end as a holy crusade of the first calibre, with an archangel leading it in person and Antichrist as its goat.

So in other fields. It is seldom, indeed, that the American people have to face a great calamity without theological support. When, back in 1928 or thereabout, the waters of the deep arose and engulfed a large part of Arkansas and Mississippi, and Mr. Hoover, then Secretary of Commerce, was sent down by Mr. Coolidge to push them back, he was accompanied by a staff of holy men, and their incantations had at least as much to do with returning the waters to the rivers as any device proposed by engineers. Again, it was theologians who broke the drought of a year or so ago, when the Arkansans, having got dried at last, began to bake, and the Federal Reserve Board confessed itself stumped. What ailed Arkansas, they announced, was sin. Inflamed by moonshine, it had forgotten Holy Writ.

The only cure was prayer in the grand manner, so they prayed stupendously, and the rains fell. Again, in 1928, as everyone knows, these same theologians saved the Republic from the Roman Harlot. But now, with an evil far worse than harlotry menacing all of us, they are strangely silent.

I note one exception, and come to my point. The Seventh Day Adventist brethren, alone among the divines of the country, have something to say officially about the depression, and what they have to say is singularly clear and simple. They laugh at all the current diagnoses as so much hooey, and reject every projected cure as vain and preposterous. It is not Hoover who must be blamed, they say, nor is it the tariff war now going on everywhere in the world, nor is it the French or the Japanese, nor is it overproduction, nor is it the foreign bond swindle, nor is it the war debts, nor is it sun-spots or witchcraft or marital and spiritual infidelity or any of the other things that have been accused. It is simply the fact that the world is coming to an end. It is the fact that all of the signs and portents listed in Luke 21:25–27 are now visible, and that on some near to-morrow, maybe next Tuesday, possibly even Monday, the heavens will split wide open, there will be a roaring of mighty winds, a shock troop of angels will come fluttering down to earth, the righteous will be snatched up to bliss, and the wicked will be thrust into Hell.

The argument I spare you, but hasten to add, having read it, that it is excessively persuasive—in truth, completely unanswerable. All of the premonitory symptoms, as set forth not only in Luke but also in countless other passages of Infallible Scripture, are now clearly visible—"the distress of nations, with perplexity," "men's hearts failing them for fear," millions turned "lovers of their own selves, covetous, boastful, proud, blasphemers, disobedient to parents, unthankful, unholy, without natural affection, truce-breakers, false accusers, incontinent, fierce, despisers of those that are good, traitors, heady, high-minded, lovers of pleasures more than lovers of God." I quote the Apostle James:

> Go to now, ye rich men, weep and howl, for your miseries shall come upon you. Your riches are corrupted, and your garments are motheaten. Your gold and silver is cankered; and the rust of them shall be a witness against you, and shall eat your flesh as it were fire. . . . Be patient therefore, brethren, unto the coming of the Lord . . . Establish your hearts, for the coming of the Lord draweth nigh.[6]

I refrain from further quotation. The texts are all too depressing to be set forth at length. If you thirst for misery, then apply at the nearest Seventh Day Adventist basilica, and the pastor will supply you with a complete list, neatly printed. All I desire to point out here is that the New Testament offers precise and elaborate specifications of the events preceding the inevitable end of the world, and that a fair reading of them must lead any rational man to conclude that those events are now upon us. If the Bible is really the Word of God, as we are assured not only by the Council of Trent but also by all the principal Protestant authorities and even by the Supreme Court of the United States, then it is as plain as day that the human race is on its last legs.

Not long ago, writing in this place, I set forth the vast advantages of the so-called Fundamentalists in their combat with the so-called Modernists. The latter, logically speaking, simply haven't a leg to stand on. If the Bible is inspired, then they have no right to change the least jot or tittle of it, and if they can't change it then they must swallow everything that the Fundamentalists find in it, which is surely a plenty. What I'd like to know today is how either faction, the Fundamentalists or the Modernists, contrive to get around the implacable and irrefutable proofs of the Adventists. How can they profess to believe in Holy Writ, and yet stand silent before its plain and indubitable wa......ngs? How can Cardinal Dougherty parley with money-changers (glance back at James) while the predestined signs stare him in the face? How can Dr. Cadman continue his radio talks on necking when the heavens may crack at any moment, and he may find himself confronting a "woman set upon a scarlet-colored beast, full of names of blasphemy, having seven heads and ten horns"?[7]

As for me, I counsel caution. I am naturally of a skeptical and even ribald turn of mind; nevertheless, I take certain measures, as a prudent householder locks up for the night. I have cleared my library of bawdy books. I have taken down the portraits of Ibsen, Nietzsche and Darwin. If I cling to a few jugs, it is only because the flesh is eternally weak. There are four plain descriptions of Hoover in the Book of Revelation alone, and half a dozen of Andy Mellon. If any reader of these lines can think of a sufficient answer to the Seventh Day Adventist proofs I'll be glad to print it in this place. But how could it be put together without rejecting the whole canon of Holy Writ? How could it be squared with the infallibility of Luke, James, John and Paul? I suspect that the theologians are on a hot spot. And I suspect that they will be on an even hotter spot if the Seventh Day Adventists turn out to be right. No wonder they are so unprecedentedly mum!

[*American Mercury,* April 1932]

EPILOGUE

MEMORIAL SERVICE

Where is the grave-yard of dead gods? What lingering mourner waters their mounds? There was a day when Jupiter was the king of the gods, and any man who doubted his puissance was *ipso facto* a barbarian and an ignoramus. But where in all the world is there a man who worships Jupiter to-day? And what of Huitzilopochtli? In one year—and it is no more than five hundred years ago—fifty thousand youths and maidens were slain in sacrifice to him. To-day, if he is remembered at all, it is only by some vagrant savage in the depths of the Mexican forest. Huitzilopochtli, like many other gods, had no human father; his mother was a virtuous widow; he was born of an apparently innocent flirtation that she carried on with the sun. When he frowned, his father, the sun, stood still. When he roared with rage, earthquakes engulfed whole cities. When he thirsted he was watered with ten thousand gallons of human blood. But to-day Huitzilopochtli is as magnificently forgotten as Allen G. Thurman. Once the peer of Allah, Buddha and Wotan, he is now the peer of General Coxey, Richmond P. Hobson, Nan Patterson, Alton B. Parker, Adelina Patti, General Weyler and Tom Sharkey.

Speaking of Huitzilopochtli recalls his brother, Tezcatilpoca. Tezcatilpoca was almost as powerful: he consumed twenty-five thousand virgins a year. Lead me to his tomb: I would weep, and hang a *couronne des perles*. But who knows where it is? Or where the grave of Quitzalcoatl is? Or Tialoc? Or Chalchihuitlicue? Or Xiehtecutli? Or Centeotl, that sweet one? Or Tlazolteotl, the goddess of love? Or Mictlan? Or Ixtlilton? Or Omacatl? Or Yacatecutli? Or Mixcoatl? Or Xipe? Or all the host of Tzitzimitles? Where are their bones? Where is the willow on which they hung their harps? In what forlorn and unheard-of hell do they await the resurrection morn? Who enjoys their residuary estates? Or that of Dis, whom Cæsar found to be the chief god of the Celts? Or that of Tarves, the bull? Or that of Moccos, the pig? Or that of Epona, the mare? Or that of Mullo, the celestial jack-ass? There was a time when the Irish revered all these gods as violently as they now hate the English. But to-day even the drunkest Irishman laughs at them.

But they have company in oblivion: the hell of dead gods is as crowded as the Presbyterian hell for babies. Damona is there, and Esus, and Drunemeton, and Silvana, and Dervones, and Adsalluta, and Deva, and Belisama, and Axona, and Vintios, and Taranuous, and Sulis, and Cocidius, and Adsmerius, and Dumiatis, and Caletos, and Moccus, and Ollovidius, and Albiorix, and Leucitius, and Vitucadrus, and Ogmios, and Uxellimus, and Borvo, and Grannos, and Mogons. All mighty gods in their day, wor-shiped by millions, full of demands and impositions, able to bind and loose—all gods of the first class, not dilettanti. Men labored for generations to build vast temples to them—temples with stones as large as hay-wagons. The business of interpreting their whims occupied thousands of priests, wizards, archdeacons, evangelists, haruspices, bishops, archbishops. To doubt them was to die, usually at the stake. Armies took to the field to defend them against infidels: villages were burned, women and children were butchered, cattle were driven off. Yet in the end they all withered and died, and to-day there is none so poor to do them reverence. Worse, the very tombs in which they lie are lost, and so even a respectful stranger is debarred from paying them the slightest and politest homage.

What has become of Sutekh, once the high god of the whole Nile valley? What has become of:

Resheph	Baal
Anath	Astarte
Ashtoreth	Hadad
El	Addu
Nergal	Shalem
Nebo	Dagon

Ninib	Sharrab
Melek	Yau
Ahijah	Amon-Re
Isis	Osiris
Ptah	Sebek
Anubis	Molech?

All these were once gods of the highest eminence. Many of them are mentioned with fear and trembling in the Old Testament. They ranked, five or six thousand years ago, with Jahveh himself; the worst of them stood far higher than Thor. Yet they have all gone down the chute, and with them the following:

Bilé	Gwydion
Lêr	Manawyddan
Arianrod	Nuada Argetlam
Morrigu	Tagd
Govannon	Goibniu
Gunfled	Odin
Sokk-mimi	Llaw Gyffes
Memetona	Lleu
Dagda	Ogma
Kerridwen	Mider
Pwyll	Rigantona
Ogyrvan	Marzin
Dea Dia	Mars
Ceros	Jupiter
Vaticanus	Cunina
Edulia	Potina
Adeona	Statilinus
Iuno Lucina	Diana of Ephesus
Saturn	Robigus
Furrina	Pluto
Vediovis	Ops
Consus	Meditrina
Cronos	Vesta
Enki	Tilmun

Engurra	Zer-panitu
Belus	Merodach
Dimmer	U-ki
Mu-ul-lil	Dauke
Ubargisi	Gasan-abzu
Ubilulu	Elum
Gasan-lil	U-Tin-dir ki
U-dimmer-an-kia	Marduk
Enurestu	Nin-lil-la
U-sab-sib	Nin
U-Mersi	Persephone
Tammuz	Istar
Venus	Lagas
Bau	U-urugal
Mulu-hursang	Sirtumu
Anu	Ea
Beltis	Nirig
Nusku	Nebo
Ni-zu	Samas
Sahi	Ma-banba-anna
Aa	En-Mersi
Allatu	Amurru
Sin	Assur
AbilAddu	Aku
Apsu	Beltu
Dagan	Dumu-zi-abzu
Elali	Kuski-banda
Isum	Kaawanu
Mami	Nin-azu
Nin-man	Lugal-Amarada
Zaraqu	Qarradu
Suqamunu	Ura-gala
Zagaga	Ueras

You may think I spoof. That I invent the names. I do not. Ask the rector to lend you any good treatise on comparative religion: you will find them all listed. They were gods of the highest standing and dignity—gods of civilized peoples—worshiped and believed in by millions. All were theoretically omnipotent, omniscient and immortal. And all are dead.

[*Smart Set,* March 1922; rev. in *Prejudices: Third Series* (1922)]

NOTES

INTRODUCTION

1. "The Monthly Feuilleton," *Smart Set* 69, No. 4 (December 1922): 140.

2. Bertrand Russell, "Free Thought and Official Propaganda" (1922), in *Sceptical Essays* (1935; reprint, London: Unwin Paperbacks, 1977), p. 116.

3. The best account of the day-to-day events of the trial remains L. Sprague de Camp's *The Great Monkey Trial* (1968). Edward J. Larson's *Summer for the Gods: The Scopes Trial and America's Continuing Debate over Science and Religion* (1997), although it won the Pulitzer Prize, seems to me unduly sympathetic to Bryan and the Fundamentalists and insufficiently aware of the threat they posed to intellectual advance. See also Ray Giner, *Six Days or Forever: Tennessee vs. John Thomas Scopes* (1958); Jerry R. Tompkins, *D-Days at Dayton: Reflections on the Scopes Trial* (1965); Paul Keith Conklin, *When All the Gods Trembled: Darwinism, Scopes, and American Intellectuals* (1998). A complete transcript of the proceedings of the Scopes trial can be found in the anonymous compilation, *The World's Most Famous Court Trial: Tennessee Evolution Case* (1925).

4. L. Sprague de Camp, *The Great Monkey Trial* (Garden City, N.Y.: Doubleday, 1968), p. 441.

5. Herbert Asbury, *The Great Illusion: An Informal History of Prohibition* (Garden City, N.Y.: Doubleday, 1950), pp. 94, 98–99.

6. Kenneth T. Jackson, *The Ku Klux Klan in the City 1915–1930* (New York: Oxford University Press, 1967), p. 18.

I. THE BELIEFS OF AN ICONOCLAST

1. "Malicious animal magnetism" (M.A.M.) is a famously absurd idea propounded by Mary Baker Eddy, founder of Christian Science, apparently referring to evil thoughts or emanations that cause illness. As a recent biographer has noted: "M. A. M. . . . was widespread throughout the physical world, a colorless, odorless, insidious influence affecting Mrs. Eddy's health, her food and clothing, the air she breathed, and the weather outside her home; it also preyed on her students and aides. It made lost objects impossible to find and ruined the printing of her books. It required constant vigilance." Caroline Fraser, *God's Perfect Child: Living and Dying in the Christian Science Church* (New York: Metropolitan Books/Henry Holt, 1999), p. 107.

2. HLM repeatedly confused the celebrated tale of the whale swallowing Jonah ("And Jonah was in the belly of the fish three days and three nights": Jonah 1:17), assuming that it was Jonah who swallowed the whale. The biblical version is, indeed, scarcely less preposterous than HLM's.

3. The Industrial Workers of the World, a radical labor organization founded in 1905.

4. Modernism was a movement within the Roman Catholic church in the later nineteenth and early twentieth centuries that sought to bring Catholic doctrines in line with modern discoveries in science, philosophy, and other areas of knowledge; it included such principles as the acceptance of biblical criticism in regard to the authorship of the Bible and a downplaying of the role of scholasticism in defense of doctrine. It was formally condemned as a heresy in 1907 by Pope Pius X. See further "The Impregnable Rock" (p. 135).

5. From the German: Is dark ale (*Dunkles*) better than pale ale (*Helles*)?

6. HLM quotes from the King James version (Hebrews 11:1) of this celebrated utterance, whose exact translation from Greek has been much debated. The Revised English Bible (1989) now translates it as follows: "Faith gives substance to our hopes and convinces us of realities we do not see."

7. HLM refers to two notorious political bosses in the Tammany organization in New York City during the later nineteenth and early twentieth centuries, Richard Croker (1841–1922) and Charles Francis Murphy (1858–1924).

8. The Pope at this time was Pius XI (1922–39).

9. *Pollyanna* (1913) by Eleanor H. Porter was a best-selling novel about a young woman who, in spite of numerous misfortunes, retained a resolutely optimistic view of life.

10. HLM refers to *The Dissenting Opinions of Mr. Justice Holmes,* arranged by Alfred Lief (1930), which he reviewed in the *American Mercury* (May 1930).

II. SOME OVERVIEWS

1. Morris ("Mawruss") Perlmutter is a Jewish-American character invented by Montague Glass in short stories collected in such volumes as *Potash and Perlmutter* (1910), *Abe and Mawruss* (1911), and others. HLM was particularly fond of these stories.

2. The first complete edition in English of Nietzsche's works was published in eighteen volumes by the Edinburgh publisher T. N. Foulis in 1909–13.

3. Haeckel's biogenetic law is now regarded with skepticism by evolutionary biologists.

4. Lotario di Segui (1160–1216) became Pope Innocent III in 1198; during his tenure the papacy reached the zenith of its power. He presided over the Fourth Crusade and the suppression of the Albigensian heresy.

5. On September 10, 1924, Nathan Leopold and Richard Loeb were sentenced to life imprisonment for the kidnapping and murder of Bobby Franks. An impassioned defense by Clarence Darrow saved them from the death penalty. The judge in the case was John R. Caverly.

6. W. C. P. Breckinridge (1837–1904), a Kentucky congressman, and Madeleine Pollard were involved in a much-publicized breach of promise suit in 1894. The suit spelled the end of Breckinridge's political career. The reference to "Hannah and her amazing glands" is unclear.

7. The *Freethinker,* founded in 1881 by the British journalist George William Foote, is England's oldest atheist periodical; it is still being published. It emphasized ridicule and satire of religion.

8. HLM refers to the story of the prophet Elisha cursing some children who had made fun of his baldness, with the result that two bears came out of the forest and killed the children.

9. HLM refers to some of the leading American poets of his day: Vachel Lindsay (1879–1931), Robert Frost (1874–1963), George Sterling (1869–1926), Edwin Arlington Robinson (1869–1935), Carl Sandburg (1878–1967), and Edgar Lee Masters (1868–1950). For Sterling, see *From Baltimore to Bohemia: The Letters of H. L. Mencken and George Sterling,* ed. S. T. Joshi (Rutherford, N.J.: Fairleigh Dickinson University Press, 2001). Edgar A. Guest (1881–1959) was a voluminous American poetaster whose work enjoyed a great vogue among the uncultured.

10. HLM refers to three celebrated poetical works by Algernon Charles Swinburne: the poems "Ave atque Vale" and *Tristram of Lyonesse* (1882) and the verse tragedy *Atalanta in Calydon* (1865).

11. *The History of Christianity in the Light of Modern Knowledge: A Collective Work* (London: Blackie & Son, 1929; New York: Harcourt, Brace, 1929). One of

the contributors was William Temple (1881–1944), archbishop of York (1929–42) and archbishop of Canterbury (1942–44).

12. Matthew 1:1–16 relates the "generation of Jesus Christ" from Abraham to Joseph.

13. In the presidential campaign of 1928, anti-Catholic propaganda was widely broadcast when the Catholic Al Smith received the Democratic nomination. He lost to Herbert Hoover.

14. In the year 1054 the eastern and western branches of the Christian church irrevocably split, leading to the formation of the Greek Orthodox Church.

15. New Thought was a mystical popular philosophy that enjoyed a great vogue at the turn of the twentieth century.

III. PROTESTANTS AND CATHOLICS

1. The Clean Books Bill was a very broad censorship measure sponsored chiefly by the New York Society for the Suppression of Vice. It was introduced into the New York State Lesiglature in 1923 and sought to ban literary material thought to be obscene. The bill was not passed, but a revised version was reintroduced into the Legislature in 1924; it was again defeated.

2. The date when Constantinople was captured by the Turks, who renamed it Istanbul and made it the capital of the Ottoman Empire.

3. Sumner coined the term "the Forgotten Man" in a lecture of 1883, referring to self-supporting persons who must endure the incompetence and quackery of politicians.

4. Ignatius Loyola (1491?–1556) was the founder of the Jesuit order, which was formally established in 1540. He wrote the *Spiritual Exercises* (1541) and drew up the Jesuit constitutions to serve as the foundation of the order.

5. *War Cry* was a British Salvation Army paper established in 1879. An American edition began publication in 1882.

6. The *Chandala* are the so-called Untouchables, the lowest caste of Indian society. HLM frequently used the term figuratively to denote the ignorant masses.

IV. FUNDAMENTALISTS AND EVANGELICALS

1. HLM refers to such popular novelists of the day as George Barr McCutcheon (1866–1928), Harold MacGrath (1871–1932), Robert W. Chambers

(1865–1933), and Elinor Glyn (1864–1943), and such best-selling novels as *Pollyanna* (1913) by Eleanor H. Porter (see Section I, n. 9), *Trilby* (1897) by George du Maurier, *Eben Holden* (1900) by Irving Bacheller, and *Dora Thorne* (1883) by Bertha M. Clay (pseudonym of Charlotte M. Brame).

2. HLM refers to a hysteria around the turn of the twentieth century among politicians and vice crusaders who believed that large numbers of young white women were being forcibly kidnapped and forced into prostitution. The result was the passage in 1910 of the Mann Act, which prohibited the interstate transportation of women for "immoral" purposes.

3. *Feuersnot* (1900–01) is a comic opera by Richard Strauss.

4. *Elektra* is an opera (1909) by Richard Strauss.

5. "Drink no longer water, but use a little wine for thy stomach's sake and thine often infirmities" (1 Timothy 5:23).

6. In the course of a civil war in China, anti-foreign riots broke out in late 1926 and early 1927, directed in part against Christian missionaries of various denominations. On March 23, 1927, the army of the Nationalist (KMT) party captured Nanking; 145 Americans, including many missionaries, had to be evacuated onto U.S. destroyers stationed offshore.

7. George Creel (1876–1953) was a progressive politician whom President Woodrow Wilson named chairman of the Committee on Public Information in April 1917 to drum up support for the war.

8. HLM's title is probably taken from William Ewart Gladstone's *The Impregnable Rock of Holy Scripture* (1890), a defense of the veracity of the creation story in Genesis. See further Section VII, n. 1.

9. All the passages in question refer to the drinking of wine (see also n. 5 above).

V. SPIRITUALISM, THEOSOPHY, AND CHRISTIAN SCIENCE

1. See Craig F. Thompson, "Christian Science Censorship," *New Republic* (December 11, 1929): 59–62; (February 26, 1930): 44–46.

2. H. A. L. Fisher, *Our New Religion* (1929), a study of Christian Science.

3. Georgine Milmine, *The Life of Mary Baker G. Eddy and the History of Christian Science* (1909).

4. Adam Dickey, *Memoirs of Mary Baker Eddy* (1927).

VI. THE SCOPES TRIAL

1. No periodical of this title has been verified.

2. "Andy Gump" is a cartoon character created in 1917 by the cartoonist Robert Sidney Smith (1877–1935).

3. Westminster is the seat of Carroll County in Maryland, about twenty-five miles northwest of Baltimore. According to the 1940 WPA guide to Baltimore, it is a "prosperous, conservative community of neat homes where neither affluence nor poverty are apparent." Its population in 1940 was 4,518. Bel Air is the seat of Harford County in Maryland, about twenty miles northeast of Baltimore. Its population in 1940 was 1,650.

4. Joseph Weber (1867–1942) and Lew Fields (1867–1941) were a hugely popular vaudeville team from 1877 to 1904.

5. Herrin, a town in southern Illinois, was the site of the "Herrin Massacre" on June 22, 1922, when twenty-one nonunion coal miners were killed by striking union miners. Because local public sentiment was on the side of the strikers, all the miners brought to trial for murder were acquitted. Homestead, a town in southwestern Pennsylvania, was the site of a celebrated steel strike in 1892 against the Carnegie Steel Company. Violence broke out when private detectives hired by Carnegie killed ten strikers on July 16, 1892, in an attempt to break picket lines.

6. In the presidential election of 1896, the Republican William McKinley defeated the Democrat William Jennings Bryan by an electoral vote of 271 to 176, and by a popular vote of 7,113,734 to 6,516,722. It is not clear why HLM believed Bryan to have been the true winner of this election.

7. HLM alludes to an unsigned editorial, "The Conduct of the Scopes Trial," *New Republic* No. 559 (August 19, 1925): 331–33. The *New York World* article has not been located.

8. The anarchist Leon Czolgosz shot President William McKinley on September 6, 1901. McKinley died eight days later.

VII. RELIGION AND SCIENCE

1. Huxley and former British prime minister William Ewart Gladstone (1809–1898) engaged in a heated exchange over the scientific veracity of Genesis in a succession of articles published in the *Nineteenth Century* in 1885–86, and again in 1890–91, when Gladstone published his treatise, *The Impregnable Rock of Holy Scripture* (1890). Earlier, in 1860, at a meeting of the British Association for the Advancement of Science, Huxley had a celebrated encounter over evolution

with Samuel Wilberforce (1805–1873), successively Bishop of Oxford (1845–69) and Winchester (1869–73).

2. This date was arrived at by Archbishop James Ussher (1581–1656) from his calculations of genealogies in the Old and New Testaments. See Ussher's *Annales Veteris et Novis Testamenti* (1650–54).

VIII. RELIGION AND POLITICS

1. The presidential election of 1928, in which the Republican Herbert Hoover defeated the Democrat Al Smith. The campaign saw an outbreak of prejudice directed against Smith, a Catholic.

2. Article 1, Section 3 of the U.S. Constitution specifies that U.S. senators be elected by state legislatures. Direct election of senators was decreed by the Seventeenth Amendment (1913).

IX. RELIGION AND SOCIETY

1. "September Morn" is a translation of a German song, "Septembermorgen" (1915), by Joseph Marx.

2. Unidentified; possibly fictitious.

3. The reference is to the beginning of the Sermon on the Mount as recorded in Matthew 5:3–11 ("Blessed are the poor in spirit . . ."), including the phrases "Blessed are the meek" (5:5) and "Blessed are the peacemakers" (5:11).

4. The Woman's Christian Temperance Union, founded in 1874.

5. HLM refers to the celebrated passage in 1 Corinthians 7:8–9 in which Paul states: "I say therefore to the unmarried and widows, It is good for them if they abide even as I [i.e., unmarried and celibate]. But if they cannot contain, let them marry: for it is better to marry than to burn."

6. James 5:1–3, 7, 8.

7. Revelation 17:3.

GLOSSARY OF NAMES

All names, save where noted, are Americans.

Anderson, Paul Y. (1893–1938), a reporter for the *St. Louis Post-Dispatch* who won the Pulitzer Prize in 1928. He was born in Knox County, Tennessee.

Anderson, William H. (1874–1959) was long associated with the Anti-Saloon League in Illinois, New York, and Maryland, and was a member of the executive and legislative committee of the Anti-Saloon League of America (1912–24).

Asbury, Francis (1745–1816), first bishop of the Methodist Episcopal church in the U.S. He became a bishop in 1785.

Asch, Sholem (1880–1957), Yiddish novelist and playwright. His play, *The God of Vengeance*, first staged in Berlin in 1910, deals with religious mania. It was performed in New York in 1922 but was closed by the police in 1922, apparently because it dealt with prostitution.

Babbitt, Irving (1865–1933), literary critic and proponent of the New Humanism.

Barrett, E. Boyd (1883–?), Jesuit writer on psychology and author of *The Jesuit Enigma* (1927).

Beecher, Henry Ward (1813–87) was an immensely influential Presbyterian clergyman of his day. His later years were tarnished by accusations of adultery, culminating in the 1870s in one of the most sensational trials of the nineteenth century.

Belloc, Hilaire (1870–1953), British novelist, poet, historian, and essayist. Author of numerous polemical and apologetical works on Roman Catholicism, including *Anti-Catholic History: How It Is Written* (1918), *The Catholic Church and History* (1926), *How the Reformation Happened* (1928), and *Essays of a Catholic Layman in England* (1931).

Blavatsky, Helena P. (1831–91), Russian-born spiritualist who cofounded the Theosophical Society in 1875. Among her many works are *Isis Unveiled* (1877) and *The Secret Doctrine* (1888). "The Stanzas of Dzyan" is a section from *The Secret Doctrine*. Some scholars believe that this is an ancient Tibetan Buddhist text on which *The Secret Doctrine* is an immense commentary; others believe that it was fabricated by Blavatsky herself.

Blease, Coleman (1868–1942), governor (1910–16) and U.S. senator (1924–30) from South Carolina, who defended lynching and denounced African Americans.

Böhme, Jakob (1575–1624), German philosophical mystic whose thought combined philosophy, theology, astrology, and alchemy.

Bok, Edward W. (1863–1930), longtime editor of the *Ladies' Home Journal* (1889–1919).

Booth, William (1829–1912), a British Methodist preacher, founded the Salvation Army in Britain in 1865. The American branch was established in 1880.

Borah, William Edgar (1865–1940), U.S. senator (Republican) from Idaho (1907–40).

Briffault, Robert (1876–1948), British physician, anthropologist, and novelist. Among his anthropological works, several of which provoked controversy, are *The Making of Humanity* (1919), *The Mothers* (1927), *Rational Evolution* (1930), and *Sin and Sex* (1931).

Brisbane, Arthur (1864–1936) was a prolific journalist and editor who worked initially for the *New York Sun* (1883–90), then became managing editor of the *New York World* (1890–97), then worked for the Hearst newspapers.

Broun, Heywood (1888–1939), journalist for the *New York Tribune* (1912–21), the *New York World* (1921–28), and the *New York Telegram* and *World-Telegram* (1928–37). He was the author of *Christians Only* (1931), a study of anti-Semitism.

Brown, Elijah P. (1842–?), writer on religion who also wrote under the pseudonym "Ram's Horn Brown." Among his works are *Blasts from a Ram's Horn* (1892) and *The Real Billy Sunday* (1914).

Bryan, William Jennings (1860–1925), leading Democratic politician of the later ninetenth and early twentieth centuries. He was Democratic candidate for president in 1896, 1900, and 1908, and secretary of state under Woodrow Wilson (1913–15). His role in the prosecution of the Scopes trial is infamous.

Bryan, William Jennings, Jr. (1889–1978), son of William Jennings Bryan who assisted his father in the Scopes trial.

Bushnell, Horace (1802–76), a leading Congregationalist minister, created controversy when he published *Discourses on Christian Nurture* (1847), in which he advocated a gradual nurturing of the young into religious faith without the need for a dramatic conversion.

Butler, Nicholas Murray (1862–1947), longtime president of Columbia University and author of many books on education, politics, and other subjects. Although a Republican, he did not support Prohibition.

Cadman, Samuel Parkes (1864–1936), originally a Methodist clergyman and later pastor of the Central Congregational Church of Brooklyn (1900–1936). He was a popular radio preacher.

Callahan, Patrick H. (1865–1940), businessman and Catholic layman. He established the successful Louisville Varnish Company in 1915. He advocated the repudiation of religious bigotry, but supported Prohibition and William Jennings Bryan's Fundamentalism at the Scopes trial.

Cannon, James (1864–1944), perhaps the leading Methodist clergyman of his time, was elected bishop in 1918. He was a vigorous proponent of temperance, being the leading lobbyist for the Anti-Saloon League both before and after the passage of the Eighteenth Amendment.

Carranza, Venustiano (1859–1920), a leader in the Mexican Civil War. From 1915 to 1917 he was provisional president of Mexico; from 1917 until his death he was the first constitutional president of the Mexican Republic.

Chesterton, G. K. (1874–1936), prolific British novelist and essayist who wrote numerous works defending religion (specifically Roman Catholicism) against the attacks of scientists and secularists, including *Heretics* (1905), *Orthodoxy* (1908), and *The Everlasting Man* (1925).

Clark, James Beauchamp ("Champ") (1850–1921), U.S. representative (Democrat) from Missouri (1893–95, 1897–1921) and Speaker of the House (1911–19).

Comstock, Anthony (1844–1915), founder of the New York Society for the Suppression of Vice who frequently waged campaigns to ban books he found "obscene."

Conklin, Edwin G. (1863–1952), professor of biology at the University of Pennsylvania (1896–1908) and Princeton (1908–33) and author of numerous scholarly works, including *Heredity and Environment in the Development of Men* (1915), *The Direction of Human Evolution* (1921), and *Man, Real and Ideal* (1943).

Coxey, Jacob Sechler (1854–1951), businessman who formed "Coxey's army" in the 1890s, leading a march from Ohio to Washington, D.C., to protest the government's neglect of the unemployed.

Crabbe, George William (1875–1951), attorney for the Anti-Saloon League in Ohio, West Virginia, Maryland, and Delaware.

Crane, Frank (1861–1928) was a clergyman and journalist and one of the most widely read columnists of his day. HLM regarded his work as trite and naively optimistic.

Curtis, Charles (1860–1936), U.S. representative (1892–1907) and senator (1907–29) from Kansas (Republican) and vice president under Herbert Hoover (1929–33).

Dakin, Edwin F. (1898–1976), author and businessman who worked chiefly at the Institute of Aerodynamic Research. He wrote *Mrs. Eddy: The Biography of a Virginal Mind* (1929).

Daniels, Josephus (1862–1948), North Carolina politician who began his career as a journalist. He later became deeply involved with the Democratic party, serving on the Democratic National Committee from 1896 onward and ardently supporting William Jennings Bryan, Woodrow Wilson, and Prohibition. He was secretary of the navy under Wilson (1913–21).

Darrow, Clarence (1857–1938), lawyer whose defense of unpopular defendants (*e.g.*, the Socialist leader Eugene V. Debs in 1895, and the murderers Leopold and Loeb in 1924) gained him celebrity and notoriety, as did his defense in the Scopes trial of 1925. He wrote prolifically on law, crime, society, and religion, including the anthology *An Agnostic's Anthology* (1929; with Wallace Rice). See also his autobiography, *The Story of My Life* (1932), and *Why I Am an Agnostic and Other Essays* (Prometheus Books, 1995).

Davis, John W. (1873–1955), diplomat and Democratic candidate for president in 1924; he lost badly to Calvin Coolidge.

Davis, William Whiting (1859–?), Protestant clergyman and vicar of St. Mary's church in Chappaqua, New York (1911f.).

Debs, Eugene V. (1855–1926), Socialist advocate and labor leader who proved a thorn in the side of several Republican presidents in the late nineteenth century. He ran as Socialist candidate for president in 1900, 1904, 1908, 1912, and 1920. He was imprisoned for sedition in 1919–21.

de Valera, Eamon (1882–1975) was an Irish politician and, from 1913 onward, one of the leaders of Ireland's attempts to secure independence from England. He was president of Sinn Fein (1918–24) and later prime minister of Ireland.

Dougherty, Dennis Joseph (1865–1951), cardinal of the Philippines (1903–15), archbishop of Buffalo (1915–18), and archbishop of Philadelphia (1918–51).

Dowie, John Alexander (1847–1907), Scottish-born American theologian who founded the Christian Catholic Apostolic Church in Zion. He was a predecessor of Billy Sunday in his use of emotive preaching, faith healing, and abstention from tobacco and alcohol.

Drawbridge, C. L. (1868–1937), British theologian and author of *Popular Attacks on Christianity* (1913), *The War and Religious Ideals* (1915), *Anti-Christian*

Socialism (1915), *Common Objections to Christianity* (1924), and *The Religion of Scientists* (1932).

Dunaley, Henry S. (1849–1928), Baltimore businessman and philanthropist; trustee of Moody Bible Institute and director of the Maryland Society to Protect Children from Cruelty and Immorality.

Eddington, Arthur S. (1882–1944), British mathematician and astrophycist. His leading works are *Stellar Movements and the Structure of the Universe* (1914) and *The Mathematical Theory of Relativity* (1923); he wrote many works of popular science, including *The Nature of the Physical World* (1928). He dealt delicately with the issue of religion and science in *Science and the Unseen World* (1929) and the pamphlet *Science and Religion* (1931).

Eddy, Mary Baker (1821–1910), founder of Christian Science and author of the Christian Science Bible, *Science and Health* (1875).

Edmonds, Richard H. (1857–1930), founder in 1882 of the *Manufacturers' Record* and a trustee of the Southern Baptist Theological Seminary (Louisville, Kentucky).

Ellis, William T. (1873–?), author of the biography *"Billy" Sunday: The Man and His Message* (1914). Ellis wrote numerous other works on religion, including *Men and Missions* (1909) and *Bible Lands To-day* (1927).

Evans, Hiram W. (1881–?), Imperial Wizard of the Ku Klux Klan (1922–39) during the mid-1920s, when the Klan reached its apogee of strength and influence.

Fiske, Minnie Maddern (1865–1932), American stage actress.

Fleming, Sandford (1888–?), author of *Children and Puritanism* (1933), *Where Jesus Walked* (1953), and other books on religion.

Frietchie, Barbara (1766–1862) was purportedly shot at when, in her nineties, she hung a Union flag out her window in Frederick, Maryland, while the Confederate army occupied the town in 1861. The veracity of the anecdote is now in doubt. John Greenleaf Whittier wrote a ballad about her, "Barbara Frietchie" (1863).

Gaynor, William J. (1849–1913), jurist who, as member of the appellate division of the New York State Supreme Court (1905–9), vigorously supported individual rights against misuse of power by the government, especially the police. He continued his reforms as mayor of New York City (1909–13).

Gibbons, James, Cardinal (1834–1921), archbishop of Baltimore and later a cardinal (1886). He was one of the leading Catholic theologians of his day and author of the popular volume *The Faith of Our Fathers* (1876).

Gompers, Samuel (1850–1924), labor leader who founded the American Federation of Labor in 1886.

Grundy, Joseph Ridgway (1863–1961), founder and president of the Pennsylvania Manufacturers' Association (1909–47) and U.S. senator (Republican) from Pennsylvania (1929–30).

Guthrie, William N. (1868–1944), Protestant clergyman and rector of St. Mark's in the Bouwerie in New York (1911–37). Author of numerous works on religion, literature, and social questions.

Haeckel, Ernst (1834–1919), German zoologist and enthusiastic proponent of Darwin's theory of evolution, today best known for a widely influential popular treatise on biology and physics, *Die Weltrathsel* (1899), translated into English as *The Riddle of the Universe* (1900).

Haldane, J. S. (1860–1936), British physiologist and philosopher who, in such works as *Mechanism, Life and Personality* (1913), *Materialism* (1932), and *The Philosophy of a Biologist* (1935), put forth a generally mechanistic view of life but nonetheless asserted that the universe is spiritual.

Haldeman-Julius, Emanuel (1889–1951), author and publisher who established the Haldeman-Julius Company in Girard, Kansas, for the purpose of issuing inexpensive books for the masses, many of them on secularism, atheism, and free thought.

Halsted, William Stewart (1852–1922), professor of surgery at Johns Hopkins Hospital (1890–1922) and a pioneer in anaesthesiology.

Hanna, Mark (1837–1904) was a leading Republican politician of the later nineteenth century. He vigorously supported William McKinley for president and was U.S. senator from Ohio (1897–1904). Although an ally of big business, he advocated the right of labor to organize as a means of efficiently dealing with disputes between labor and capital.

Harris, Julian La Rose (1874–1963), son of the author Joel Chandler Harris, worked for the *New York Herald* and then was owner of the Columbus (Georgia) *Enquirer-Sun* (1920–29), using it to attack the Ku Klux Klan. The paper won the Pulitzer Prize in 1926. Harris later worked for other newspapers, including the *New York Times* (1942–45).

Harvey, George (1864–1928), American journalist who, as editor of *Harper's Weekly* (1901–13), ardently supported the political ambitions of Woodrow Wilson.

Hayes, Patrick Joseph (1867–1928), Roman Catholic theologian and first bishop of the U.S. armed forces (1917). He became archbishop of New York in 1919 and a cardinal in 1924.

Hays, Arthur Garfield (1881–1954), attorney for the ACLU and Clarence Darrow's assistant in the Scopes trial. He later helped HLM in the "Hatrack" case in 1926 (when the Watch and Ward Society of Boston sought to ban an issue of the *American Mercury*) and was an attorney in the Scottsboro case in 1932.

Henty, G. A. (1832–1902), British author of dozens of popular historical novels for boys, published from 1867 to 1906.

Hobson, Richmond P. (1870–1937), naval officer who distinguished himself in the

Spanish-American War in 1898 but who resigned from the navy in 1903. He was later U.S. representative from Alabama (1907–15).

Holmes, Oliver Wendell, Jr. (1841–1935), son of the author Oliver Wendell Holmes, Sr., and justice of the U.S. Supreme Court (1902–32).

Huxley, Thomas Henry (1825–95), British naturalist and vigorous opponent of religious orthodoxy. HLM thought his essays a model of English prose. He engaged in celebrated debates with William Wilberforce and William Ewart Gladstone over the issue of science and religion. See *Agnosticism and Christianity and Other Essays* (Prometheus Books, 1992).

Ingersoll, Robert G. (1833–99), voluminous American author and one of the most popular lecturers of the later nineteenth century. His pungent attacks on religion and his espousal of agnosticism were embodied in numerous volumes, including *Some Mistakes of Moses* (1879) and *The Christian Religion* (1882). See *On the Gods and Other Essays* (Prometheus Books, 1990) and *Reason, Tolerance, and Christianity: The Ingersoll Debates* (Prometheus Books, 1993).

Jones, Sam (1847–1906), itinerant Methodist evangelist.

Kaufman, Herbert (1878–1947), American journalist who established the Kaufman Newspaper Syndicate and for many years was a widely syndicated editorial writer for several leading newspapers and magazines.

Kelly, Howard A. (1858–1943), gynecologist and surgeon who taught at Johns Hopkins Hospital (1889–1919) and Johns Hopkins Medical School (1893–1919). Aside from many works on medicine, he wrote *A Scientific Man and the Bible* (1925).

Kilmer, Joyce (1886–1918), American poet and Roman Catholic.

Köhler, Wolfgang (1887–1967), director of the Psychological Institute of the University of Berlin (1922–25) and later professor of psychology at Swarthmore; one of the founders of Gestalt psychology. Among his publications are *The Mentality of Apes* (1925; a translation of *Intelligenz Prüfungen an Anthropoiden,* 1917) and *Gestalt Psychology* (1929).

Krishnamurti, Jiddu (1895–1986), author of *At the Feet of the Master* (1911) and numerous other theosophical works. His teaching later attracted such authors as Aldous Huxley, George Bernard Shaw, and Henry Miller. In late October 1931 he made headlines by initiating a two-month lecture tour in the United States.

Krutch, Joseph Wood (1874–1937), author, journalist, and associate editor of the *Nation* (1924–37). He was the author of *The Modern Temper* (1929) and other works on literature and society. He was born in Knoxville, Tennessee.

Lee, Gerald Stanley (1862–1944) was the author of *The Shadow Christ* (1896), *Crowds* (1913), and other works on religion, social problems, and popular psychology.

Lindsey, Ben B. (1869–1943), a Colorado judge, gained notoriety by cowriting (with Wainwright Evans) the treatise *The Companionate Marriage* (1927), advocating divorce by mutual consent and birth control to delay parenthood until a marriage was firmly established.

Lodge, Oliver (1851–1940), British physicist and a pioneer in the development of wireless telegraphy. Late in life he became a credulous believer in psychic phenomena.

Mabie, Hamilton Wright (1845–1916), editor and critic whose work HLM always regarded as prototypical of conventional, moralizing, unimaginative criticism.

Machen, J. Gresham (1881–1937), an instructor at the Princeton Theological Seminary (1906–36) and also a Presbyterian minister. He did sound philological work on the Gospels (*The Virgin Birth of Christ*, 1930) and on the teachings of Paul (*The Origin of Paul's Religion*, 1921). His hostility to Protestant liberalism was expressed in *Christianity and Liberalism* (1923) and other works; these views led him to be expelled from the Presbyterian church in 1936, whereupon he formed the Presbyterian Church of America (later the Orthodox Presbyterian Church).

Malone, Dudley Field (1882–1950), Clarence Darrow's chief assistant in the Scopes trial.

Manning, William Thomas (1866–1949), Episcopal clergyman, most prominently associated with Trinity Parish in New York City. He was consecrated bishop of the Diocese of New York in 1921.

Martin, T. T., Baptist minister and field secretary of the Anti-Evolution League of America.

McElwee, F. B., lawyer (a former student of John R. Neal), and assistant for the defense in the Scopes trial.

McKenzie, Ben G., former assistant attorney general in Tennessee and assistant to the prosecution in the Scopes trial.

McPherson, Aimée Semple (1890–1944), American Pentecostal evangelist. In 1926 she disappeared for five weeks; upon her return she claimed to have been kidnapped. The Los Angeles district attorney accused her of spending time with a married man, Kenneth G. Ormiston, and indicted her on charges of obstruction of justice and subornation of perjury. Although the charges were eventually dropped, McPherson's reputation suffered serious damage.

Mellon, Andrew (1855–1937), industrialist and financier.

Metcalf, Maynard M. (1868–1940), professor of zoology at the Women's College, Baltimore (1893–1906), Oberlin (1906–14), and Johns Hopkins University (1925–40) who testified for the defense in the Scopes trial.

Miller, William (1782–1849), farmer and leader of the Adventists or "Millerites." He believed that Christ's second coming would occur in 1843 or 1844.

Millikan, Robert Andrews (1868–1953), son of a Congregational preacher, became one of the leading physicists of his day, known chiefly for his work on cosmic rays. He won the Nobel Prize in 1923. In the 1920s he devoted his efforts to reconciling science and religion in such works as *Science and Life* (1924) and *Evolution in Science and Religion* (1927).

Moody, Dwight L. (1837–99) was a leading fundamentalist evangelist of his day, emphasizing a literalist interpretation of the Bible and looking forward to an imminent Second Coming. See HLM's review of William Revell Moody's *D. L. Moody* (*American Mercury*, September 1930).

More, Paul Elmer (1864–1937) was a prominent literary critic who achieved critical esteem with his eleven-volume series, *Shelburne Essays* (1904–21). HLM considered him a proponent of an attenuated and timorous classicism.

Nann, James P. (1889–1936), soldier who won the Distinguished Service Cross while a sergeant with the 308th Infantry, Seventy-Seventh Division, in France in World War I.

Neal, John Randoph (1876–1959), dean of the University of Tennessee Law School, founder of the John R. Neal School of Law, and Clarence Darrow's assistant in the Scopes trial.

Newman, John Henry (1801–90), British theologian who helped to found the Oxford Movement and then converted to Roman Catholicism in 1845, becoming a cardinal in 1879. He wrote *The Idea of a University* (1873), *Apologia pro Vita Sua* (1864), and other works.

O'Connell, William Henry (1859–1944), Roman Catholic clergyman who was made archbishop of Boston (1907) and subsequently a cardinal (1911). He aggressively exercised both religious and political influence during much of his tenure.

Osborn, Henry Fairfield (1857–1935), paleontologist and longtime president of the American Museum of Natural History in New York (1908–33). He treated the relation of religion and science in such works as the pamphlet *Evolution and Religion* (1923; reprinted in *The Earth Speaks to Bryan*, 1925, a book dedicated to Scopes) and *Evolution and Religion in Education* (1926). He lent scientific advice to Scopes's defense team during the trial.

Parker, Alton B. (1852–1926), jurist and Democratic candidate for president in 1904, losing badly to Theodore Roosevelt.

Parkhurst, Charles H. (1842–1933), Presbyterian minister who vigorously attacked political corruption in New York City. He wrote of his battles in *Our Fight with Tammany* (1895).

Patterson, Nan, an actress who was accused of killing a bookmaker, "Caesar" Young, in a hansom cab in New York on May 4, 1904. Although apparently guilty, she was freed after two separate trials ended in hung juries.

Patti, Adelina (1843–1919), Italian soprano and the most celebrated opera singer of her day.

Peay, Austin (1876–1927), Democratic governor of Tennessee (1923–27) who reluctantly signed the antievolution bill that triggered the Scopes trial.

Phillips, Wendell (1811–84), prominent American abolitionist and social reformer.

Pinkham, Lydia (1819–83) created, in the 1870s, a "Vegetable Compound" from ground herbs and alcohol, claiming that it could cure any "feminine complaint." The patent medicine continued to be sold well into the 1920s.

Rappleyea, George W., local manager for the Cumberland Coal and Iron Company in Dayton, Tennessee, and one of the few supporters of evolution among the local population. Although disagreeing with the state's antievolution law, he initially took on the prosecution of the Scopes case (largely because he thought it would bring favorable publicity to the town), but later withdrew.

Raulston, John Tate (1868–1956), judge in the Eighteenth Judicial Circuit in Tennessee and presiding judge in the Scopes trial.

Roberts, C. E. Bechhofer (1894–1949), British novelist, playwright, and biographer; author of *The Mysterious Madame: A Life of Madame Blavatsky* (1931) and biographies of Lord Birkenhead (1926) and Paul Verlaine (1937).

Scopes, John Thomas (1900–1970), Tennessee teacher of biology who offered to test the state law against the teaching of evolution in 1925. After the sensational case (in which he was found guilty, although the conviction was later overturned on a technicality) he returned to teaching.

Sharkey, Tom, a boxer prominent in the 1890s. Before and during Prohibition he was a saloonkeeper.

Sidgwick, Henry (1838–1900), leading British ethical philosopher who advocated a Utilitarian ethic in the landmark volume *The Methods of Ethics* (1874). He also wrote on politics and economics. In 1882 he helped found the Society for Psychical Research.

Smith, Al (1873–1944), governor (Democrat) of New York (1919–21, 1923–29) who became, in 1928, the first Roman Catholic to be nominated for president. He lost to Herbert Hoover in a landslide.

Smith, Joseph (1805–44), founder of the Mormon church.

Smith, Rodney (1860–1947), American evangelist who wrote under the pseudonym Gipsy Smith. See his autobiography, *Gipsy Smith: His Life and Work* (1901).

Soddy, Frederick (1877–1956), British chemist; lecturer in chemistry at the University of Glasgow (1904–14), Aberdeen University (1914–19), and Oxford (1919–36). He won the Nobel Prize for chemistry in 1921. He wrote voluminously on science, economics, and society.

Sonntag, Charles F. (d. 1925), author of *The Morphology and Evolution of the Apes and Man* (1924).

Stall, Sylvanus (1847–1915), Lutheran clergyman who founded the Vir Publishing Company (Philadelphia) in 1897 for the purpose of issuing elementary sex manuals, mostly for men. Stall wrote several of them himself, including *What a Young Boy Ought to Know* (1897), *What a Young Husband Ought to Know* (1899), and *What a Man of Forty-five Ought to Know* (1901).

Stewart, A. T. (1892–1972), attorney general in the Eighteenth Judicial Circuit of Tennessee and chief attorney for the prosection in the Scopes trial. He was later a U.S. senator from Tennessee (1938–43).

Straton, John Roach (1875–1929), Baptist clergyman and frequent butt of HLM's attacks.

Summers, Montague (1880–1948), British historian, editor, and essayist. He was ordained as an Anglican deacon in 1908 but converted to Roman Catholicism the next year. Aside from many editions of the Restoration playwrights, Summers published *The Geography of Witchcraft* (1927), *The Vampire: His Kith and Kin* (1928), *The Werewolf* (1933), and other works on Gothic literature and legendry.

Sumner, William Graham (1840–1910) was a priest of the Protestant Episcopal church in 1869–72, but then turned his attention to political and social issues, becoming a professor of political science at Yale in 1872.

Sunday, Billy (1862?–1935), itinerant evangelist who became immensely popular in the first two decades of the twentieth century by his histrionic outdoor sermons. Aside from the *Smart Set* column of July 1916, HLM discussed his witnessing of one of Sunday's lecture tours in the *Baltimore Evening Sun* (February 17, March 14 and 27, May 2, 1916).

Thurman, Allen G. (1813–95), U.S. representative (Democrat) from Ohio (1845–47) and U.S. senator (1867–79); vice presidential candidate (with Grover Cleveland) in 1888.

Tyler, Wat (d. 1381), leader of the first popular rebellion in England in 1381, in protest against harsh taxation of the poor.

Upshaw, William David (1866–1952), temperance advocate and politician openly affiliated with the Ku Klux Klan. He was presidential candidate for the Prohibition party in 1932.

van Dyke, Henry (1852–1933) was a clergyman and essayist who achieved tremendous popularity with a succession of volumes on religion, nature, and personal conduct. HLM felt that his work was a byword for unoriginality and superficiality of thought.

Watson, James Eli (1864–1948), U.S. representative (1896–97, 1899–1909) and senator (1916–33) from Indiana (Republican).

Welch, William Henry (1850–1934), pathologist at Johns Hopkins University (1883–1918) and president of the Maryland Board of Health (1898–1922). He was a leader in the development of pathology and bacteriology.

Weyler y Nicolau, Valeriano, marqués de Tenerife (1838–1930), Spanish general whose harsh treatment of rebels in Cuba led to the Spanish-American War of 1898.

Wheeler, Wayne Bidwell (1869–1927), superintendent of the Anti-Saloon League of Ohio (1904–15), general counsel for the Anti-Saloon League of America (1915–27), and vigorous supporter of Prohibition.

Wheless, Joseph (1868–1950), lawyer and freethinker who wrote *Is It God's Word?* (1926), *Forgery of Christianity* (1930), and other works debunking religion.

White, Andrew D. (1832–1918), first president of Cornell University (1868–85) and author of the landmark treatise, *A History of the Warfare of Science with Theology in Christendom* (1895).

Wickham, Harvey (?–?), American novelist and author of works attacking modern science and philosophy, including *The Misbehaviorists* (1928), *The Impuritans* (1929), and *The Unrealists* (1930).

Willard, Jess (1883–1968), American boxer and heavyweight champion of the world from 1915 to 1919, when he was defeated by Jack Dempsey.

Williams, John Sharp (1854–1932), U.S. representative (Democrat) from Mississippi (1893–1909) and U.S. senator (1911–23). He was a strong defender of white supremacy, although in his congressional campaign of 1907 he repudiated his opponent's proposal to repeal the Fifteenth Amendment.

Windle, Sir Bertram C. A. (1858–1929), professor of cosmology and anthropology at St. Michael's College, University of Toronto, and author of numerous works attempting to reconcile science and religion, including *The Church and Science* (1917) and *The Catholic Church and Its Reactions with Science* (1927).

Wise, Stephen S. (1874–1949), probably the most celebrated and accomplished rabbi of his time. He was prominent in social, economic, and political causes, mostly of a liberal nature: he cofounded both the NAACP (1909) and the ACLU (1920).

Wright, Willard Huntington (1888–1939), prolific journalist and novelist and friend of HLM. He worked extensively for the *Los Angeles Times* early in his career and also edited the *Smart Set* in 1913–14. Among many other volumes on literature, art, and philosophy, he wrote *What Nietzsche Taught* (1915). As S. S. Van Dine, he published a dozen popular novels in the 1920s and 1930s featuring the detective Philo Vance.

Yerkes, Robert M. (1876–1956), animal psychologist who taught at Harvard (1902–17) and Yale (1924–44). In the interim he worked in the Office of the

Army Surgeon General and attracted controversy for his views over army test results and immigration restriction. Among his publications are *The Mental Life of Monkeys and Apes* (1916), *Almost Human* (1925), *Chimpanzee Intelligence and Its Vocal Expressions* (1925; with B. W. Learned), and *The Great Apes* (1929; with A. W. Yerkes).

INDEX

socialism, 79, 80, 82, 83, 274
Soddy, Frederick, 244
Solomon, 118
Sonntag, Charles F., 227
soul, 57, 246–47
Spencer, Herbert, 73
Spiritual Exercises (Loyola), 106
spiritualism, 58, 139–41, 254
Stalin, Josef, 40
Stall, Sylvanus, 30–31
"Stand Up! Stand Up for Jesus!," 27
Stanzas of Dzyan, The (Blavatsky), 144
Sterling, George, 80
Stetson, Augusta, 152
Stevens, Ray, 24
Stewart, A. T., 188, 196, 199, 200–201
Stone, Clare, 57
Story of the Devil, The (Graf), 91
Straton, John Roach, 75, 135, 193
Stribling, Pastor, 214
Summers, Montague, 239–42
Sumner, William Graham, 106
Sunday, Billy, 12, 22, 43, 59, 74, 115–20, 130, 135, 203
superstition, 57–61
Sutherland, D. F., 117
Swedenborg, Emanuel, 78
"Sweet Adeline," 26
"Sweet By-and-By, The," 27
Swinburne, Algernon Charles, 82, 301n. 10

Taft, William Howard, 46
Taine, Hippolyte, 93
theosophy, 11, 22, 141–44
"There Is a Fountain Filled with Blood," 27
"There Is a Green Hill Far Away," 27
Thompson, Craig F., 158

"Throw Out the Life-Line," 105
Thurman, Allen G., 293
Tierney, Father, 107
Trattner, Ernest R., 90, 95
Treatise on Right and Wrong (Mencken), 14
Treatise on the Gods (Mencken), 14
Tristan and Isolde (Wagner), 32
Twain, Mark, 92
Tyler, Wat, 190

Unitarian church, 173, 181, 192–93, 205, 240
United Brethren, 128
Universalist church, 240
Up from Methodism (Asbury), 20
Upshaw, William David, 252
Ussher, James, 305n. 2

van Dyke, Henry, 85
Views of Christian Nurture (Bushnell). *See Discourses on Christian Nurture.*
Vidal, Gore, 18
Voltaire (François Marie Arouet), 238

War Cry, 108
Washington, Booker T., 271
Washington, George, 169
Watson, James Eli, 40
Weber, Joseph, 201
Welch, William Henry, 229
Wesley, John, 88, 89, 104, 118, 174, 280
Wesley, Old, 29
"What a Friend We Have in Jesus," 27
What a Young Boy Ought to Know (Stall), 31
What Is There Left to Believe? (Parrish), 90, 91, 95
What Nietzsche Taught (Wright), 12, 52